THE THREE Rs OF SOFTWARE AUTOMATION

A *Carma McClure* BOOK

ALSO BY CARMA McCLURE
and available from Prentice Hall

- CASE Is Software Automation

with James Martin
- Action Diagrams: Clearly Structured Specifications, Programs, and Procedures, Second Edition
- Diagramming Techniques for Analysts and Programmers
- Software Maintenance: The Problem and Its Solutions
- Structured Techniques: The Basis for CASE, Revised Edition

THE THREE Rs OF SOFTWARE AUTOMATION

Re-engineering
Repository
Reusability

CARMA McCLURE

PRENTICE HALL
Englewood Cliffs, New Jersey 07632

Library of Congress Cataloging-in-Publication Data
MCCLURE, CARMA L.
   The three Rs of software automation : re-engineering, repository,
   reusability / Carma McClure.
      p.   cm.
   "A Carma McClure book."
   Includes bibliographical references and index.
   ISBN 0-13-915240-7 :
   1. Computer-aided software engineering.   I. Title.   II. Title 3
Rs of software automation.   91-36831
QA76.758.M34 1992   CIP
005.1—dc20

Editorial/production supervision: *Kathryn Gollin Marshak*
Jacket design: *Lundgren Graphics Ltd.*
Prepress buyer: *Mary Elizabeth McCartney*
Manufacturing buyer: *Susan Brunke*
Acquisitions editor: *Paul W. Becker*

Copyright © 1992 by Carma McClure

 Published by Prentice-Hall, Inc.
A Division of Simon & Schuster
Englewood Cliffs, New Jersey 07632

The publisher offers discounts on this book when ordered
in bulk quantities. For more information, write:
   Special Sales/Professional Marketing
   Prentice-Hall, Inc.
   Professional & Technical Reference Division
   Englewood Cliffs, NJ 07632

All rights reserved. No part of this book may be
reproduced, in any form or by any means,
without permission in writing from the publisher.

Printed in the United States of America

10 9 8 7 6 5 4 3 2 1

ISBN   0-13-915240-7

PRENTICE-HALL INTERNATIONAL (UK) LIMITED, *London*
PRENTICE-HALL OF AUSTRALIA PTY. LIMITED, *Sydney*
PRENTICE-HALL CANADA INC., *Toronto*
PRENTICE-HALL HISPANOAMERICANA, S.A., *Mexico*
PRENTICE-HALL OF INDIA PRIVATE LIMITED, *New Delhi*
PRENTICE-HALL OF JAPAN, INC., *Tokyo*
SIMON & SCHUSTER ASIA PTE. LTD., *Singapore*
EDITORA PRENTICE-HALL DO BRASIL, LTDA., *Rio de Janeiro*

TO JAMES

CONTENTS

PREFACE *xi*

PART I RE-ENGINEERING

1 Software Maintenance Automation 3

*Tip of the Iceberg 3; Size of Software Maintenance 3;
Cause of the Software Crisis 5;
Ways to Reduce Software Maintenance 5; False Hope 6;
Direct Attack 8; References 8*

2 Software Maintenance 11

*Understanding Software Maintenance 11;
Maintenance Definitions 11;
Causes of Software Maintenance 14;
The Change Perspective 14; Nature of Maintenance Work 15;
Factors Affecting Maintenance Effort 16;
What Do Maintainers Do? 17;
Difficult to Understand, Dangerous to Change 19;
Fragile Software 19; Maintenance First 20; References 21*

3 Software Re-engineering 23

*Managing Maintenance 23; Types of Re-engineering 25;
Types of Re-engineering Tools 25;
The Bridge to New Technologies 27;
What to Do with Existing Systems 28; References 31*

4 Program Code Analyzers and Metrics Tools 33

Measuring Maintainability 33; Automating Software Metrics 34; Software Understandability 34; Program Code Analyzers 36; Flow Graphs 37; Mathematically Rigorous Flow Graphs 40; Predictors of Understandability 42; Program Complexity Metrics 42; McCabe Cyclomatic Complexity 44; Knot Count 49; Halstead Software Science 50; Counts and Lists 53; Portfolio Summary Analysis 54; Rulers of Software Maintenance 59; References 59

5 Restructuring 61

Productivity Through Restructuring 61; Reducing the Maintenance Burden 62; Program Logic Restructuring 63; Structured Retrofit 64; Well-Structured Programs 64; When to Restructure 66; Program Logic Restructuring Process 67; Program Logic Restructuring Tools 71; A Known Re-engineering Technique 81; References 81

6 Data Restructuring 83

Road Blocks to Understandability 83; Data Restructuring 84; Data Restructuring Tools 85; Summary 94; Reference 94

7 Reverse Engineering 95

Fact or Fantasy 95; What Is Reverse Engineering? 95; Reverse Engineering Benefits 96; One True Source Code 97; Reverse Engineering and Forward Engineering 99; Future Software Maintenance Automation 100; Reverse Engineering into a Repository 100; Reverse Engineering Tools 101; Data Reverse Engineering 101; Logic Reverse Engineering 111; Logic Reverse Engineering Process 114; Data Versus Logic Reverse Engineering 127; References 128

8 Configuration and Change Management 129

The Fact of Change 129; Configuration Management Functions 130; Library Management 130; Change Control 134; Summary 141; Reference 143

9   Re-engineering Case Studies   145

Re-engineering in Practice 145;
Re-engineering at Shearson Lehman Brothers 145;
Reverse Engineering at Integral 148;
Restructuring at Pacific Bell 151; References 153

PART II   REPOSITORY

10   Repository Concepts   157

Repository-Based 157; Repository 157; Repository Benefits 158;
Repository Contents 159; More than a Dictionary 161;
More than a CASE Repository 162; Enterprise Repository 163;
What Does Tool Integration Mean? 164;
Repository Meta Model 165; Repository Implementation 172;
Repository Information Management 173;
Repository Architectures 178; Examples of Repositories 180;
IBM Repository 186; Repository Services Summary 190;
References 191

11   Repository Standards   193

Era of Standardization 193;
CASE Data Interchange Format (CDIF) 194;
Information Resource Dictionary System (IRDS) 196;
IRDS Functions and Processes 201;
IBM SAA and AD/Cycle 204;
A Tools Integration Standard (ATIS) 208;
Portable Common Tool Environment (PCTE) 208;
Standards for Automation 209; References 210

12   Preparing for Repositories   211

Repository Issues 211; Preparing for a Repository 212;
Repository Implementation Plan 214;
Training and Experience 214; Enterprise Models 215;
A Repository Future 217; References 217

PART III   REUSABILITY

13   Software Reuse   221

A Software Reusability Story 221; A Growing Trend 223;
A New Paradigm 223; An Old Software Idea 224;

Benefits of Reuse 225; Many Forms of Software Reuse 226;
Opportunities for Reuse 226;
Problems with Software Reuse and Solutions 228;
Organization Level Reuse 230; Making Reuse Practical 230;
References 231

14 **Reusable Software Components** 233

What Is a Reusable Software Component? 233;
Higher-Level Reusable Components 238; References 245

15 **Tools and Methods for Reusability** 247

Reusable Components Library 247; Tools for Reusability 249;
Using Reusable Components 252; Methods for Reusability 255;
Object-Oriented Development 256;
Software Reusability: A Development Scenario 258;
Parts Approach Versus Whole Approach 259;
Reusability: A Development and Maintenance Strategy 262;
Summary 252; References 263

PART IV EPILOGUE

16 **The Three Rs** 267

Enabling Technologies of Software Automation 267

Index 271

PREFACE

Whenever we begin something new, such as a new project or a new year, we resolve to do things better and differently. This means making decisions and resolutions about how we will change. When we begin something really big, such as a new decade, the decisions and resolutions are usually on a much grander scale. The software industry is no exception. It began the 1990s with great resolve to make some very big changes—changes that may be the most profound ever for the software industry and that ultimately may have more impact on businesses and industries than the industrial revolution.

We began the 1990s with a resolution to automate the software process, with CASE as the dominant software technology. CASE sits at the center of the IS strategy for a growing number of corporations that believe their ability to survive and compete in the 1990s hinges on successfully automating the software process.

These corporations know that the move to CASE is a long, expensive, and risky road. They must find a way to position themselves to reduce the risk and to move the CASE as quickly as possible. This requires laying the proper foundation for effective use of the most appropriate CASE tools and methods. Re-engineering, repository, and reusability are the technologies that form the foundation on which to build solid software automation strategies. They are the three Rs of software automation and the enabling technologies for ensuring that we can take full advantage of the benefits that CASE offers.

Re-engineering is the counterpart technology to CASE. While CASE is the application of software automation to software development, re-engineering is the application of software automation to software maintenance.

Re-engineering is the application of the newest technologies and tools to software maintenance. Re-engineering technologies include restructuring, reverse engineering, and migration. Re-engineering tools include program analyzers, metrics tools, restructuring tools, reverse engineering tools, translators, and converters. Re-engineering is used to help identify and separate those systems that are worth maintaining from those that should be replaced; to extend the useful life of existing systems; and to perform maintenance more efficiently and correctly.

Although the primary focus of re-engineering is on its use during software maintenance, it is more than maintenance automation. Re-engineering is the bridge to the technologies of the 1990s. For many corporations, re-engineering is not an optional technology. It is an absolute necessity for moving into the future.

The *repository* lies at the very heart of the software automation concept. It is the basis for software tools and life cycle integration, enterprise information management, project management and control, and software reusability. The repository is the mechanism for defining, storing, and managing all information concerning an enterprise and its software systems—logical data and process models, physical definitions and code, and organization models and business rules.

The repository is the link connecting the various software life cycle steps and tools. It is the vehicle by which system work from different developers can be combined, checked, and consolidated into one consistent, complete, and on-going description of a software system. The repository is the life cycle integrator that enables tools used at one phase of the life cycle to pass data easily on to tools used in other phases.

Not only does the repository play a major role in integrating CASE tools but also in integrating re-engineering tools, third-, fourth-, and fifth-generation tools into integrated tools environments. The repository is the single, most important component of an integrated tools environment because it is the basis for tools integration and the major productivity gains that we hope software automation will bring.

Understanding the repository concept and the key repository services are necessary prerequisites for making software automation practical and efficient across the entire software life cycle. Choosing an appropriate repository can help ensure the maximum flexibility in using the best CASE and re-engineering tools and easy migration to new software automation technologies as they become available. Building an integrated, full-function software tools environment must begin with the repository.

Reusability is an approach to software development that is based on creating software systems from reusable components that are stored in automated libraries. Software reusability is a much broader concept than simply reusable code. Possibilities of reusable components include more abstract, higher-level software components such as software design models, data, and project management information. These higher levels of reusability offer greater promise because they have greater potential to increase software productivity.

Software reusability is a technology whose time has come because the tools needed to support it are now available. A repository-based integrated software tools environment provides the basis for supporting software reusability. The repository, along with its meta model, provides the library mechanism and representation formalism needed for reusability. Re-engineering tools help to discover, understand, and modify reusable software components. Thus, the repository and re-engineering tools are the enabling tools for software reusability.

When coupled with software automation, software reusability has the potential to increase greatly software productivity across the entire life cycle and truly to revolutionize the way we build and maintain software systems. Ultimately, software reusability will be the technology that helps corporations leverage their huge investments in software systems and tools to the fullest extent.

ACKNOWLEDGMENTS I would like to thank the vendors that provided the software tools product examples that appear throughout the report. A special thank you to Jeanne Follman for her research and writing efforts, which greatly contributed to the creation of this book. Also, thank you to Stasiann Rikard for a fine job of typing and editing the manuscript. And finally, thank you to Extended Intelligence, Inc.—William B. McClure, President, and staff members Scott Pederson, Susan Levine, and Barbara Triplett—for their work and support in publishing this book.

Carma McClure

THE THREE Rs OF SOFTWARE AUTOMATION

PART I   **RE-ENGINEERING**

1 SOFTWARE MAINTENANCE AUTOMATION

TIP OF THE ICEBERG

Do you ever wonder why over the years software technologies have had little impact on the software crisis—our inability to develop high-quality software systems quickly enough and cheaply enough to meet the demand, which is growing now at a rate of about 12 percent per year?[1] Since the software crisis was first recognized in the mid-1960s, the general consensus has been that the labor-intensive nature of software development, coupled with a shortage of skilled, experienced software professionals, is the cause of the software crisis. Therefore, most solutions proposed for dealing with the crisis have emphasized improving software development methods and tools and have focused on the development phases of the software life cycle.

High-level programming languages were introduced in the 1960s, software engineering and structured methodologies in the 1970s, fourth-generation tools and end user computing in the early 1980s, and CASE (Computer-Aided Software Engineering) in the late 1980s. Unfortunately, these powerful development technologies are great solutions aimed at the wrong problem. A closer look at the cause of the software crisis reveals that software development represents just the tip of the iceberg (see Fig. 1.1). Software maintenance dominates the life cycle of software. Thus, maintenance, not development, is where we spend most of our software resources and most of our software dollars.

SIZE OF SOFTWARE MAINTENANCE

More than $43 billion per year is being spent on software maintenance in the United States.[2] It is estimated that nearly $2.5 trillion has been invested in the creation of more than 100 billion lines of code that support current business application systems worldwide.[3] Business and industry have become so dependent on their computers that they would fold in a

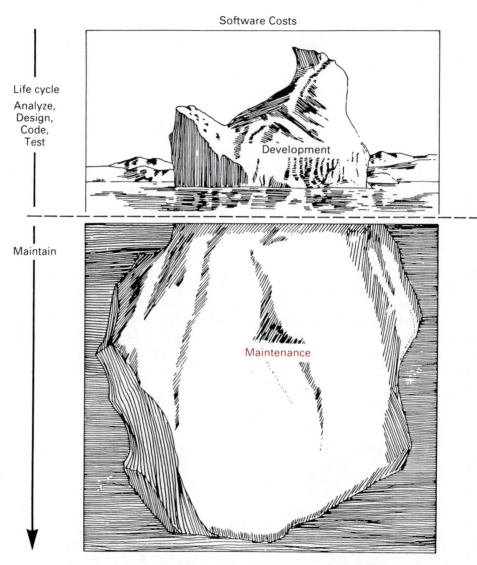

Figure 1.1 Software development represents the tip of the iceberg. The majority of the software budget and the majority of the software professional's time are spent on software maintenance, not software development.

matter of days if their software systems stopped running. A very serious problem facing most organizations is where to find the resources to relieve a mounting software backlog and at the same time support a critical and growing software maintenance function. In a survey of more than 1000 MIS departments in U.S. companies and organizations, software maintenance was cited most frequently as the major cause of software backlogs, which were reported to range between 18 and 46 months.[4]

Software maintenance is also a major concern in the world of realtime/embedded systems. For example, the software development cost for the U.S. Air Force F-16 jet fighter was $85 million, but the estimated lifetime software maintenance cost is $250 million.[5] In total, the air force estimates that it will require 25 percent of the country's entire 18- to 25-year-old population to maintain all its software systems by the year 2000.[6]

A former U.S. Pentagon chief aptly summed up the concern for the software crisis when he said, "If anything kills us before the Russians, it will be our software."[7] However, rephrasing this quotation to reflect more accurately the real cause of the software crisis, we might say, "If anything kills us before our software backlogs, it will be the maintenance of existing systems."

CAUSE OF THE SOFTWARE CRISIS

Past software failures and current software cost trends point to the underlying causes of the software crisis. We have learned from past experience that high-quality software is difficult to develop. Also, we have learned that most software efforts of any magnitude are fraught with problems and failures and that software projects usually take longer to complete and cost more than planned. When we look at the reasons for these failures, we find some important facts that we must recognize in order to solve the software crisis.

Users are dissatisfied with software systems, not because of system bugs and defects, but because of poor documentation, unfriendly interfaces, and fragile software that breaks when it is changed. Furthermore, software projects fail not because of technical problems but because of a lack of management direction and control. Finally, software costs are rising, not simply because of the difficulty of developing software systems, but mostly because of the difficulty of maintaining a growing number of critical, existing systems that must be frequently changed to keep up with new business requirements.

WAYS TO REDUCE SOFTWARE MAINTENANCE

There are several possibilities to consider in trying to reduce the software maintenance burden:

1. Do nothing; just continue the status quo.
2. Add more people to the system development and maintenance staff to reduce the software backlog.
3. Launch an indirect attack on software maintenance by focusing on new development technologies to build new systems that are easier to maintain and gradually will replace existing, aging systems.

4. Adopt a more aggressive plan to rewrite existing systems as soon as possible.
5. Adopt a direct attack on software maintenance by using automated tools to improve the maintainability and technology of existing systems and the efficiency of the maintenance process.

FALSE HOPE The hope has been that software maintenance problems, along with aging software systems, would disappear with the introduction of new software development technologies and the gradual replacement of existing systems. However, history and experience have shown that this is a false hope (see Fig. 1.2).

In 1976, de Rose and Nyman reported that 60 to 70 percent of the DOD software dollar was spent on maintenance,[8] and Mills estimated that 75 percent of MIS personnel time was allocated to maintenance.[9] In 1980, Cashman and Holt reported estimates as high as 80 percent of software resources were devoted to maintenance.[10] In the 1989 Sentry study of 862 MIS departments, software personnel on average spent 63 percent of their time on software maintenance and maintenance-related activities.[11]

Despite the introduction of powerful, new software development technologies, at the start of the 1990s, the majority of the software effort is still on software maintenance. Continuing to rely on software development strategies to solve software maintenance problems is unlikely to reduce the software maintenance burden. The Gartner Group predicts that software maintenance will demand 90 percent of the software resources by 1995.[12] Software development

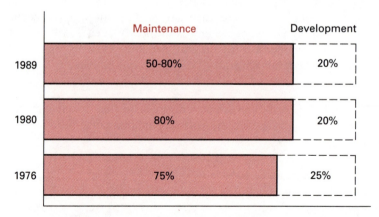

Figure 1.2 History shows that a reliance on software development technologies is unlikely to reduce software maintenance.

technologies at best can have only a limited impact on maintenance. There are two reasons.

First, the cause of software maintenance work is misunderstood. Most maintenance work is caused by a change in system requirements, not by software defects or other deficiencies.[13] Software systems used in industry are modified continually to adopt to new technologies and, most importantly, to meet changing user/organization needs—even a system that is totally reliable, completely meets user requirements, and is well-structured requires maintenance. Unless new technologies such as CASE help us build systems that can be easily changed without jeopardizing quality, software maintenance will continue to be a time-consuming, costly activity. The key to reducing maintenance is to make it easier and safer to change systems.

Second, it is unlikely that existing systems will be replaced in the near term with easier to maintain new systems. Not only was the dollar investment in initially creating these systems very large, but so too is their replacement cost. It is estimated that about 60 billion lines of unstructured COBOL code are currently in use and must be maintained. To rewrite these systems would cost more than $1 trillion.[14] For example, Amoco has estimated the replacement value of its application system portfolio at $500 million.[15]

Also, there is the question of what language to use for rewriting the systems. Most CASE tools used to develop business application systems generate COBOL. Will these new COBOL systems really be substantially easier and cheaper to maintain than their predecessors? Because many of these systems, although not well structured, perform satisfactorily and are not entirely unacceptable to their users, it is not a given fact that they should be replaced, especially if the replacement systems are also written in COBOL. Many companies view their existing systems as a valuable asset that is to be preserved, not thrown away. They want to extend the lives of these systems by improving their structure and documentation and upgrading them to utilize newer technologies.

Another factor blocking any near-term replacement of existing systems is the time it takes to introduce and adopt new technologies. New ideas often are met with resistance because it is human nature to resist change. More time than expected is needed for technological advancements to penetrate fully the computing community. From idea conception to widespread use of a technology tends to require 15 to 20 years.[14] For example, programming productivity aids such as structured techniques, test data generators, and database dictionaries that were introduced in the early 1970s were still not widely used a decade later. It is estimated that at the end of the 1980s only a small percentage of the 750,000 business application system developers in the United States actually used structured methodologies in software development projects. Also, CASE is proving to be more difficult to implement in practice than originally expected. It will be the turn of the century before CASE will become a mature technology and fully implemented in most organizations.

DIRECT ATTACK

Isn't it time, then, that we consider a direct attack on software maintenance? Our strategy should be to attack maintenance problems on multiple fronts by:

- Anticipating and efficiently handling software changes
- Instituting good management practices and controls and planning for maintenance
- Improving the efficiency and quality of software maintenance work
- Improving the future maintainability of existing systems

Re-engineering is a direct attack armed with automated tools on software maintenance. First and foremost, it is a declaration of action—a recognition that a problem exists and our ignoring the problem will not make it go away.

To begin, we must look at existing systems from a new perspective, one in which existing software is seen as an asset that should be properly managed and protected and that can be reused, not necessarily thrown away. For many corporations, it is the 10- to 20-year-old production systems that are the anchor of corporate computing. Another part of this new perspective is to adopt a more comprehensive view of the software life cycle that includes maintenance and unites rather than separates software development and maintenance functions by sharing the same tools and methods in both.

Furthermore, an essential part of any direct attack strategy is the use of automated tools. Use of automated tools to support the software lifecycle process is called **software automation.** CASE is the application of software automation to software development. Re-engineering is the counterpart to CASE for software maintenance. **Re-engineering is software maintenance automation.**

Automated tools can help us build high-quality software systems more quickly and cheaply. Also, automated tools can help us better perform software maintenance tasks. For example, automated tools can aid in identifying and separating those systems that are worth upgrading and continuing to maintain from those that should be replaced, in improving the future maintainability of existing systems, and in more efficiently and correctly changing existing systems.

Just as it is quickly becoming unthinkable to develop new systems without CASE tools, it will soon be considered ridiculous to attempt to maintain systems without re-engineering tools. Both forms of software automation—CASE and re-engineering are needed to solve the software crisis.

REFERENCES

1. "The Software Trap: Automate or Else," *Business Week,* May 9, 1988, pp 142–150.

2. Mary Alice Hanna, "Defining the 'R' Words for Automated Maintenance," *Software Magazine* (May 1990), 41–48.

3. "ViaSoft News Release," December 2, 1986, ViaSoft, Inc., Phoenix, Arizona.

4. *CASE 1987 Survey, Software News,* Sentry Market Research, Westborough, MA (1987).

5. William Suydam, "CASE Makes Strides Towards Automated Software Development," *Computer Design,* January 1, 1987, pp. 49–70.

6. Eric Bush, "A CASE for Existing Systems," *Language Technology White Paper*, Salem, MA (1988), p. 27.

7. "Atherton Technology White Paper," Atherton Technology, Sunnyvale, CA (August 1987).

8. B. de Rose and T. Nyman, "The Software Life Cycle—A Management and Technology Challenge in the Department of Defense," *IEEE Transactions on Software Engineering*, SE-4, no. 4 (July 1978), 309–318.

9. H. D. Mills, "Software Development," *IEEE Transactions on Software Engineering*, 2, SE-2, no. 4 (December 1976), 265–273.

10. P. M. Cashman and A. W. Holt, "A Communication-Oriented Approach to Structuring the Software Maintenance Environment," *Software Engineering Notes,* 5, no. 1 (January 1980), 4–17.

11. *CASE 1988–89,* Sentry Market Research, Westborough, MA, 1989, pp. 13–14.

12. Jeff Moad, "Maintaining the Competitive Edge," *Datamation,* February 15, 1990, pp. 61–66.

13. B. P. Lientz, E. B. Swanson, and G. E. Tompkins, "Characteristics of Application Software Maintenance," *Communications of the ACM,* 21, no. 6 (June 1978), 466–471.

14. R. Glass, "How About Next Year?" *System Development* (October 1988), 4.

15. Jack D. Wilson, "The Challenges and Rewards of Systems Re-engineering—Secondary and Tertiary Recovery for Computer Systems," *Amoco Visions* (Summer 1990), 12–13.

2 SOFTWARE MAINTENANCE

UNDERSTANDING SOFTWARE MAINTENANCE

Any successful attack on software maintenance problems presupposes a thorough understanding of software maintenance. However, in most organizations, relatively little attention has been paid to software maintenance and relatively little is known about it. What is the source of most maintenance work? What are the major difficulties in performing software maintenance? What makes a software system easy or difficult to maintain?

A first step toward getting software maintenance under control is to understand what activities are involved in software maintenance and to identify what factors contribute to the high cost and difficulty of maintaining software systems. With this understanding, more effective techniques and tools can be selected for reducing the maintenance burden.

MAINTENANCE DEFINITIONS

As shown in Fig. 2.1, maintenance is often depicted as the last phase of the software life cycle. Over the years, many definitions have been proposed to describe software maintenance. Box 2.1 lists several representative examples. These definitions identify three fundamental maintenance operations that typically are performed to keep production software operational, technically up to date, and able to serve user needs:

1. Correcting errors
2. Revising original requirements
3. Enhancing function and performance

Strict definitions of maintenance include only the first operation, correcting errors, as a maintenance function. Changes to an existing software system that

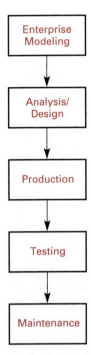

Figure 2.1 This view of the software life cycle is the IBM AD/Cycle Software Life Cycle Process. Like most views of the life cycle, it shows maintenance as the final life cycle phase.

require a modification of the original requirements are not included as maintenance activities but instead are classified as continuing development or redevelopment projects. Arguments in favor of this exclusive interpretation of software maintenance claim that an inclusive definition encompassing all three operations encourages an informal treatment of software enhancements leading to the deterioration of software quality.[10]

Some organizations classify an activity as maintenance or development on the basis of who performs the activity. If it is performed by the development staff, it is a development activity; if it is performed by the maintenance staff, it is a maintenance activity. For example, the rewrite of the inventory control system is considered a development project when assigned to the development staff even though the design and many modules from the original inventory control system are used as building blocks in creating the replacement system. On the other hand, if the maintenance staff replaces the inventory control system with a software package that they customize to fit the organization's particular requirements, it is considered a maintenance effort.

Other organizations classify a task as maintenance or development on the basis of the size or complexity of the task. For example, if the task requires more than three staff-months to complete, it automatically is considered a development task and is assigned to the development staff.

We shall assume the all-inclusive definition of software maintenance, considering all three maintenance operations as fundamental parts of the mainte-

BOX 2.1   Definitions of software maintenance

- Maintenance is the modification of a software product after delivery to correct faults, to improve performance or other attributes, or to adapt the product to a changed environment (ANSI/IEEE Std. 729-1983).[1]
- Maintenance is fixing software bugs.[2]
- Maintenance is the process of modifying existing operational software while leaving its summary function intact.[3]
- Maintenance is the mechanism for combating software deterioration, which over time tends to become unstructured, unreliable, and resistant to change.[4]
- Maintenance refers to modifying a program—updating an existing program's functions to reflect new constraints or additional features.[5]
- Maintenance is performed in response to system failures, to changes in data and processing requirements, to eliminate processing inefficiencies, and to improve maintainability.[6]
- Maintenance includes updating as well as fixing bugs in existing applications.[7]
- Maintenance consists of changes that need to be made to a computer program after the software has been turned over to the customer or goes into production.[8]
- Maintenance is adapting software to meet constantly changing business needs.[9]

nance function. We shall not describe an activity as maintenance or development based on who performs the activity, what type of operation is performed, or the magnitude of the effort. Rather, what we consider software maintenance is determined by the point in the software life cycle at which the activity is undertaken and by the use of the system specification and other documentation from the existing system to guide that activity.

Software maintenance is the process of keeping a production software program (or system of programs) operational or of improving the program.

This definition suggests that maintenance involves a variety of activities some of which are similar to new development projects and some of which are quite unique to the maintenance phase. This variety is the first clue as to why maintenance is such a difficult life cycle phase.

CAUSES OF SOFTWARE MAINTENANCE

A convenient way to understand the basis of application software maintenance is in terms of the causes of maintenance. Swanson divides the causes into three basic categories:[11]

1. Failures
2. Environmental changes
3. User and maintenance personnel requests

Failures are attributed to errors in the software. Abnormal termination of a program, invalid output results, missing data edit checks, performance inefficiencies, and programming standards violations are examples.

Environmental changes are a common occurrence in software systems that are used by an organization over a period of time. Two types of changes are to be expected: changes in the data environment, such as a change in a transaction code or restructuring a database; and changes in the processing environment, such as the installation of new hardware or a new operating system or transferring a program to a new hardware platform.

Users and software maintainers are also causes of maintenance. They may request changes to a software system to improve operating efficiency, to reformat the output produced, to add new features, to change existing functions, or to improve future system maintainability.

Maintenance activities performed in response to these basic causes are defined by Swanson as (see Box 2.2):[12]

1. Corrective maintenance
2. Adaptive maintenance
3. Perfective maintenance

THE CHANGE PERSPECTIVE

Perhaps a better definition for software maintenance that more clearly portrays what maintenance entails is as follows:

Software maintenance is the process of changing software systems.

Software maintenance includes all types of changes made to an existing system, including corrections, enhancements, and extensions. From this perspective, we can see that to improve the software maintenance function we must find tools, methods, and management techniques to support changing systems. And to have systems that are easier to maintain, we must develop systems that are easy to change. Handling change is key to getting on top of software maintenance.

> **BOX 2.2 Types of maintenance activities**
>
> ### Corrective Maintenance
>
> Performed to identify and correct:
>
> **Processing failures:** Abnormal program termination, missing input data validation, incorrect program output
>
> **Performance failures:** Slow response time or inadequate transaction processing rates
>
> **Implementation failures:** Standards, violations or inconsistencies/incompleteness in program design
>
> ### Adaptive Maintenance
>
> Performed to adapt software to changes in the environment of the program:
>
> **Data environment changes:** Changes in data media or converting from flat files to a database management system
>
> **Processing environment changes:** Moving to a new hardware platform or operating system
>
> ### Perfective Maintenance
>
> Performed to enhance performance, change or add new program features, or improve future maintainability of the program

NATURE OF MAINTENANCE WORK

Because software maintenance work often is associated with correcting errors, the common assumption is that corrective maintenance is the number one maintenance activity. However, several studies have shown that this is incorrect. For example, in the early 1980s, a survey by Lientz and Swanson of 487 data processing organizations showed that only 20 percent of the maintenance effort was spent on corrective maintenance.[13] In a more recent study by George DiNardo of 25 organizations with IBM mainframe equipment, corrective maintenance accounted for only 17 percent of the total maintenance effort.[14] As shown in Fig. 2.2, both studies reported that most maintenance effort is spent performing adaptive and perfective maintenance (although the studies have very different views of how effort was split between adaptive and perfective maintenance).

Most maintenance surveys have identified perfective maintenance as the dominant maintenance activity in MIS organizations. In particular, the Royal

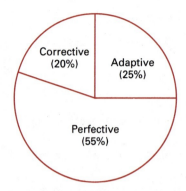

Lientz and Swanson Maintenance Study

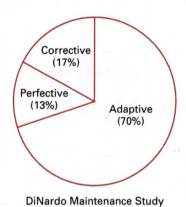

DiNardo Maintenance Study

Figure 2.2 Both the 1980 Lientz/Swanson software maintenance study and the 1988 DiNardo software maintenance study show that correcting software deficiencies is not the major cause of most maintenance work.

Bank of Canada found that the fastest growing part of software maintenance was adding functionality to its existing systems.[15] Furthermore, user enhancements usually dominate the perfective maintenance activity, and for that matter, all maintenance work. As shown in Fig. 2.3, user enhancements account for almost half of all maintenance work.[16] Most user enhancements involve giving the user more information, which may partly explain why systems tend to grow in size and complexity over time.

The top maintenance problems are "user demands for enhancements" and "competing demands for maintenance personnel time," as reported in the 1980 Lientz/Swanson study and again in the 1989 Swanson/Beath study.[17]

FACTORS AFFECTING MAINTENANCE EFFORT

Maintenance studies also have helped to reveal the factors that increase the software maintenance effort. System size, system age, and maintainer's familiarity with the system and software experience level are important factors affecting maintenance effort.

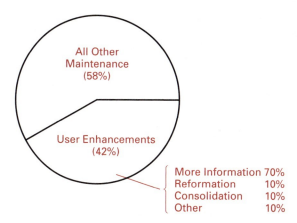

Figure 2.3 Most maintenance work is performed to change or enhance software. Perfective maintenance accounts for over half of all maintenance work, and responding to user enhancements alone accounts for almost half of all maintenance work, according to the 1980 Lientz-Swanson maintenance study.

As expected, larger software systems require more maintenance effort than do smaller systems. There is a greater learning curve associated with larger systems, and larger systems are more complex in terms of the variety of functions they perform. Also, older software systems require more maintenance effort than do newer systems. Software systems tend to grow with age, to become less structured as they are changed, and to become less understandable with staff turnover. A larger portion of maintenance work is devoted to corrective maintenance, especially routine bug fixes, for larger, older systems.[18]

Also, it appears that a larger portion of maintenance work is spent on corrective maintenance as the maintainer's familiarity with the system declines. System maintainers who were not part of the original system development team often spend more time debugging the system because they are not as familiar with the system structure and inner workings as its original authors.

These factors predict an increasing maintenance effort as systems grow older and staff members change. Many systems in the United States have already passed the one-decade age mark. A recent study by Swanson and Beath reported an average system age of 6.6 years, with 26 percent of the systems more than 10 years old.[19] At Amoco, 40 percent of the application portfolio is more than 10 years old.[20]

WHAT DO MAINTAINERS DO?

Many maintenance problems have grown out of a mistaken belief that software maintenance is generally easier to do than software development and therefore can be performed by less experienced software personnel with less tool support and less management. On the contrary, software maintenance is often more challenging than new development. Why? What exactly do software maintainers do?

Simply put, software maintainers change systems. Often this must be accomplished in a very short time without the aid of proper documentation and automated tools. As part of the change process, maintainers typically perform a variety of analysis and programming tasks:

- Studying system specifications and designs
- Interviewing end users
- Examining programs and associated documentation
- Tracking the source of program errors and deficiencies
- Designing a program change
- Modifying a program
- Revalidating a program
- Updating program documentation

Three basic functions are involved in changing software:

1. Understanding the software and the change(s) to be made
2. Modifying the software to incorporate the change(s)
3. Revalidating the software

First and foremost, changing software requires an understanding of the software program(s)—the purpose, internal structure, and operating requirements. If the maintainer does not thoroughly understand the program, he or she runs a great risk of jeopardizing program quality and reliability by unknowingly introducing errors when the program is changed. A series of haphazardly made program changes can quickly destroy program structure and lead to a maintenance mess.

Modifying a program involves creating new or changing existing program data structures and/or process logic and updating the documentation accordingly. The maintainer must make certain that the change does not affect program integrity or increase complexity. Also, he or she must be aware of possible negative side effects that can result from the change. In other words, the maintainer must understand the impact of change on the whole system.

Whenever software is modified, its correctness should be revalidated. The maintainer performs selective retesting to demonstrate that the changes have been made correctly. Assuming that even a small change is so straightforward that it requires no retesting will almost certainly lead to program quality deterioration and reliability problems.

DIFFICULT TO UNDERSTAND, DANGEROUS TO CHANGE

In Fig. 2.4, the IBM study by Fjeldstad and Hamlen shows the primary tasks that software maintainers perform.[21] Figure 2.5 gives the same information in terms of the three basic maintenance functions discussed earlier, clearly pointing out that understanding the software demands the biggest share of the maintenance effort. In Fig. 2.6, Currier gives another perspective of what software maintainers do. Currier's view also shows that most of the maintenance effort is devoted to understanding (i.e., thinking about) a software system.[22]

A major cause of maintenance problems is the difficulty of understanding the intention of programmers who previously worked on the system. Because of poor structure, convoluted logic, meaningless program names, and no standards for data names, definitions, and documentation, software is extremely difficult to understand.

Software that is difficult to understand is also difficult and dangerous to change. For example, in 1983 Weinberg reported that the top ten most expensive programming errors were all maintenance errors.[23] The top three, which involved changing only a single line of code cost their companies $1.6 million, $900 million, and $245 million. Although the cost of these errors is far from typical, the cavalier manner in which the maintenance changes that lead to the errors were handled is definitely typical. Each change was verbally assigned without any written instructions or plan for retesting the software.

FRAGILE SOFTWARE

The rule, not the exception, is that there is a good chance of introducing errors whenever software is changed. The probability of introducing an error

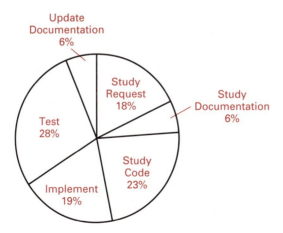

Figure 2.4 The IBM study by Fjeldstad and Hamlen shows the primary tasks that software maintainers perform.

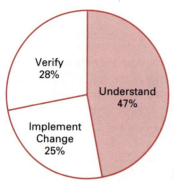

Figure 2.5 Looking at the results of the Fjeldstad and Hamlen study in terms of the three basic maintenance functions shows that understanding the software requires the biggest share of the maintenance effort.

when fewer than 200 lines of code are changed ranges between 35 and 75 percent.[24] The maintenance world is full of **fragile software**—software that is likely to "break" whenever it is changed.

Maintenance is difficult because, on the one hand, there is an abundance of fragile systems that must be maintained, whereas on the other hand, there is an acute lack of powerful maintenance tools. We are in dire need of tools to help maintainers understand, change, and revalidate existing software systems (see Fig. 2.7). Just as we look to tools to improve software productivity and quality during development, we should also use tools to improve software productivity and quality during maintenance. The need is even greater for maintenance because that is where software professionals spend most of their time and also where their productivity is lower. (Software development productivity for third generation language systems averages 10 to 15 lines of code per day, but software maintenance productivity averages only 1 to 2 lines of changed code per day.[25])

MAINTENANCE FIRST

Improving the maintenance support for an organization's application portfolio is as important as, if not more important than, developing new systems. Ac-

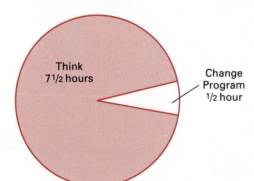

Figure 2.6 Currier's view of what software maintainers do emphasizes the difficulty of understanding the software system and the maintenance changes to be made.

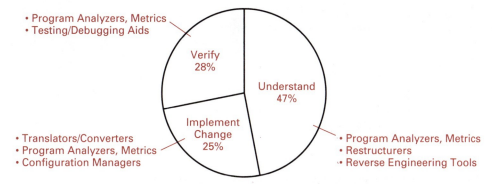

Figure 2.7 Re-engineering tools help software maintainers to understand, change, and revalidate existing software systems.

cording to Swanson and Beath: "The application portfolio is at the heart of the relationship between IS and the organization and it is through this portfolio that we see the long-term kernel of that relationship. It is maintenance."[26]

REFERENCES

1. Elliot Chikofsky and James Cross, "Reverse Engineering and Design Recovery," *IEEE Software,* 7, no. 1 (January 1990), 13–17.

2. John Reutter, "Maintenance Is a Management Problem and a Programmer's Opportunity," *AFIPS Conference Proceedings on 1981 National Computer Conference,* vol. 50 (Chicago, May 4–7, 1981), pp. 343–347.

3. B. Boehm, J. Brown, and M. Lipow, "Quantitative Evaluation of Software Quality," *Second International Conference on Software Engineering Proceedings* (San Francisco, October 13–15, 1976), pp. 592–605.

4. M. J. Lyons, "Salvaging Your Software Asset (Tools-Based Maintenance)," *AFIPS Conference Proceedings on 1981 National Computer Conference,* vol. 50, (Chicago, May 4–7, 1981), pp. 337–342.

5. C. Liu, "A Look at Software Maintenance," *Datamation,* 22, no. 11 (November 1976), 51–55.

6. E. Swanson, "The Dimensions of Maintenance," *Second International Conference on Software Engineering Proceedings* (San Francisco, October 13–15, 1976), pp. 492–497.

7. Jeff Moad, "Maintaining the Competitive Edge," *Datamation,* February 15, 1990, pp. 61–66.

8. Tony Scott and Dennis Farley, "Slashing Software Maintenance Costs," *Business Software Review* (March 1988).

9. Eric Bush, "A CASE for Existing Systems," Language Technology White Paper, Salem, MA (1988), p. 4.

10. B. Lientz and E. Swanson, *Software Maintenance Management* (Reading, MA: Addison-Wesley, 1980), pp. 151–157.

11. E. Swanson, "The Dimensions of Maintenance," pp. 492–497.

12. Ibid.

13. Lientz and Swanson, *Software Maintenance Management*.

14. Roger Philips, "The Neglected Wasteland," *Computer World Extra*, June 20, 1988, pp. 42–43.

15. Moad, "Maintaining the Competitive Edge."

16. Lientz and Swanson, *Software Maintenance Management*.

17. E. Swanson and C. Beath, *Maintaining Information Systems in Organizations*, Information Systems Series (New York: John Wiley, 1989).

18. Lientz and Swanson, *Software Maintenance Management*, pp. 67–96.

19. E. Burton Swanson and Cynthia Beath, *Maintaining Information Systems in Organizations*, Information System Series (New York: John Wiley, 1989).

20. Jack D. Wilson, "The Challenges and Rewards of Systems Re-engineering—Secondary and Tertiary Recovery for Computer Systems," *Amoco Visions* (Summer 1990), 12–13.

21. Fjeldstad and Hamlen, "Application Program Maintenance Study—Report to Our Respondents," IBM Corporation, DP Marketing Group, 1979.

22. Len Horton, "Tools Are an Alternative to Playing Computer," *Software Magazine* (January 1988), 58–67.

23. G. Weinberg, "Kill that Code," *InfoSystems* (August 1983).

24. Ibid.

25. Philips, "The Neglected Wasteland."

26. Swanson and Beath, *Maintaining Information Systems in Organizations*.

3 SOFTWARE RE-ENGINEERING

MANAGING MAINTENANCE Software system maintenance often comes as a surprise to an organization. When the system was planned, little thought was given to the type or amount of maintenance work it would require. Once the system moves into production, the organization reacts to maintenance requests as they arise. However, because maintenance is the most common software activity for most organizations, it should be treated as a well-planned, well-managed life cycle function, not with surprise. Re-engineering helps an organization move away from reactive maintenance to active management of its production system portfolio.

Re-engineering is based upon the following premises:

- Existing systems are a valuable corporate asset on which the corporation depends and therefore the existing system portfolio should be properly managed.
- Software maintenance can be most effectively and efficiently performed when aided by powerful tools.

Re-engineering is automated maintenance. It involves improving the software maintenance process and improving existing systems by applying new technologies and tools to software maintenance. Re-engineering suggests a long-term strategy for maintenance, instead of simply looking at the immediate software maintenance change. It offers a way to get organized and stay that way, to clean up the maintenance mess and to operate from a position of knowledge and control.

Re-engineering is the process of examining an existing software system (program) and/or modifying it with the aid of automated tools to

- **Improve its future maintainability**
- **Upgrade its technology**

- **Extend its life expectancy**
- **Capture its components in a repository where CASE tools can be used to support it**
- **Increase maintenance productivity**

The purpose of re-engineering is both to position existing systems to take advantage of new technologies and to enable new development efforts to take advantage of reusing existing systems. Re-engineering has the potential to improve software productivity and quality across the entire life cycle.

Re-engineering usually involves changing the form (e.g., changing data names and definitions, restructuring process logic) of a program and improving its documentation. In this case, the functionality (behavior) of the program is not changed; only its form is modified. In other cases, the re-engineering process goes beyond form and includes redesign to change the functionality of the program to meet user requirements better. Box 3.1 lists the objectives of re-engineering.

Re-engineering can help us understand existing systems and discover software components (e.g., design architectures, data structures) that are common across systems. These common components then can be reused in the development (or redevelopment) of systems, thereby significantly shortening the time and lessening the risk of developing systems.

BOX 3.1 Objectives of re-engineering

- Better manage portfolio of existing systems
- Provide automated assistance for maintenance
- Reduce maintenance errors and costs
- Increase maintenance staff interchangeability
- Make system easier to understand, change, test
- Enable system conversion and migration
- Enforce adherence to standards
- Improve response to maintenance request
- Improve maintenance staff morale
- Protect and extend system life
- Use CASE to support existing systems
- Reuse existing system components

TYPES OF RE-ENGINEERING

Like CASE, re-engineering is an umbrella technology that incorporates several major technologies. We shall focus on four types of re-engineering that will play an important role in improving software in the 1990s:

1. Analysis
2. Restructuring
3. Reverse engineering
4. Migration

Analysis is the process of examining the existing systems portfolio to understand system components better and how its programs work, to identify top candidates for re-engineering, and to measure system quality.

Restructuring is the process of changing the form of software (e.g., data names and definitions and program source code) without altering its functionality. The primary purpose of restructuring is to make the program easier to understand.

Reverse engineering is the process of analyzing a software system (program) to reconstruct a description of its components and their interrelationships. A higher-level description of the program is recovered from its lower-level, physical form. The purpose of reverse engineering is to redocument the system and discover the design information as an aid in improving program understandability.

Migration is the process of converting a software system (program) from one language to another, moving it from one operating environment to another, or upgrading its technology.

TYPES OF RE-ENGINEERING TOOLS

Tools are an important part of re-engineering. Box 3.2 lists eight basic types of re-engineering tools. Re-engineering tools can substantially increase software maintenance productivity and the quality of maintenance work. They not only help programmers perform maintenance tasks more efficiently but also much more thoroughly than is possible with only manual techniques. Tasks such as determining all the dead code or unused variables in a large, complex software program that were previously impossible can now be easily accomplished with the aid of re-engineering tools.

For example, due to growth, one hospital needed to increase the size of its patient number field in the patient accounting system. However, because finding every occurrence of the patient number field in the system was a horrendous task to do manually, the hospital decided to reuse the number of dead patients rather than attempt the change to its software. This approach will work as long as the number of dead patients exceeds the number of live patients. Would you

BOX 3.2 Types of re-engineering tools

Program Analyzers

- Data/logic tracers
- Cross-references

Metrics

- Program standards monitors
- Program quality analyzers
- Program complexity checkers

Restructurers

- Process logic restructures
- Data names and definition standardizers
- Reformatters/beautifiers

Reverse Engineering

- Data reverse engineering
- Process logic reverse engineering

Testing

- Test data generators
- Test coverage analyzers
- Regression testers
- Debuggers
- Comparers

Translators/Converters

- Language converters

Change/Configuration Management

- Change control managers
- Library managers
- System builders

Redocumentation Tools

- Cross-references
- Pretty printers
- Diagram generators

want to be a patient at this hospital? With the aid of re-engineering tools, the hospital could have quickly and safely increased the size of the patient number field.

Re-engineering tools take the guesswork out of maintenance. They can greatly increase both the confidence level of the maintainers and the quality of the software being maintained. Maintainers no longer have to wonder exactly where to make the change in a program and what the impact of the change will be. Program analyzers can help maintainers better understand a program by automatically tracing program logic paths and data elements and identifying unreachable code and unused variables. For example, the maintainer can know with 100 percent certainty everywhere in the program where a variable is referenced or a procedure is invoked. The result is increased accuracy and efficiency of any program changes that are made.

With the use of testing tools, test data cases that exercise new or changed program code can be automatically created. Because the system can be more thoroughly retested, the probability of introducing errors as a side effect of change is greatly reduced.

Metrics tools such as complexity analyzers offer a quantitative measure of program quality and a way to judge whether a change has jeopardized the quality of the system.

THE BRIDGE TO NEW TECHNOLOGIES

Although the primary focus of re-engineering is on its use during software maintenance, re-engineering is more than simply a software maintenance aid. It is the bridge from outmoded technologies to the new technologies that organizations must use today to be responsive to changing business requirements. For many organizations, re-engineering is not an option. It is an absolute necessity if they are to provide cost-effective software that

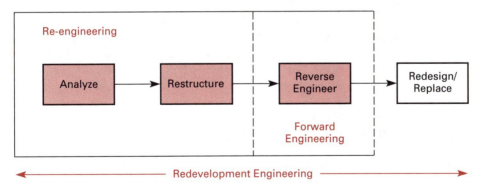

Figure 3.1 Re-engineering is the preparation step for system redesign and replacement during which forward engineering CASE tools can be used.

gives them a competitive edge. For example, PacBell estimated that it would require five to seven years at a cost of $44 million to update its payroll applications manually.[1] Automated re-engineering technologies are an absolute requirement at corporations like PacBell because automation can decrease the time and cost for critical software updates to a reasonable level.

Perhaps the most important benefits of re-engineering concern bringing together the software development and maintenance functions by enabling the same tools and techniques to be applied to both development and maintenance. Information about the system, its components, and their interrelationships that is recovered as a result of the re-engineering process can be stored in a repository where CASE tools can be used to provide future support for these systems. As shown in Fig. 3.1, re-engineering is the preparation and clean-up step for system redesign and replacement during which forward engineering CASE tools can be used. Applying CASE tools and re-engineering tools to the entire software process, not simply isolated phases, will lead to the greatest possible software productivity gains and the greatest leverage for the corporate investment in these technologies.

WHAT TO DO WITH EXISTING SYSTEMS

Often, the first solution that is proposed for reducing the software maintenance burden is to replace existing systems with new systems that better meet user requirements, use advanced software technologies, and are easier to maintain. However, other solutions may be more appropriate, depending on the particular system and the organization. Replacement lies at one extreme of our choices, status quo maintenance support lies at the other extreme, and re-engineering is somewhere in the middle.

Fragile Systems

In most organizations, there is an 80/20 rule operating. Twenty percent of the software systems causes 80 percent of the maintenance problems. Sometimes, it is as little as 5 percent of the code that causes 80 percent of maintenance work. This 5 to 20 percent represents an organization's **fragile systems**—systems that are difficult to change and are error-prone. They exhibit characteristics such as those shown in Box 3.3.[2]

Re-engineering these fragile systems can have a direct impact on greatly reducing the software maintenance effort because re-engineering can change the system form so it will be easier to understand and safer to change. On the other hand, status quo manual maintenance support for fragile systems will probably result in escalating the maintenance effort over time because fragile systems are likely to become more difficult to maintain with each change.

BOX 3.3   Reasons to re-engineer

- Frequent production failures (questionable reliability)
- Performance problems
- Outdated technology
- System integration problems
- Poor quality code
- Difficult (dangerous) to change
- Difficult to test
- Expensive to maintain
- System problems increasing

Re-engineering versus Replacement

Fragile systems that are likely to be top candidates for re-engineering are systems that

- Are of critical importance to the corporation
- Are the target of frequent maintenance work and require a large percentage of maintenance resources
- Are understood and can be safely changed by only one or a very select few members of the software staff
- Contain bugs that no one can find
- Require a major enhancement

Re-engineering such systems is often a viable alternative to replacement because it is cheaper, easier, and safer. The cost of a manual rewrite is $10 to $25 per line of code;[3] the cost of re-engineering lies in the range of $0.02 to $2.00.[4]

Sometimes, though, re-engineering is not enough. When a system is totally unreliable, is implemented using a poor algorithm choice, or provides only a small portion of the needed functionality, then it is necessary to go beyond re-engineering and replace the system through a rewrite or a package. However, even in the case of replacement, re-engineering is done as the first step toward acquiring a better understanding of the existing system and its interfaces with other systems. Box 3.4 summarizes the reasons for re-engineering and those for replacement.

BOX 3.4   Software re-engineering versus replacement

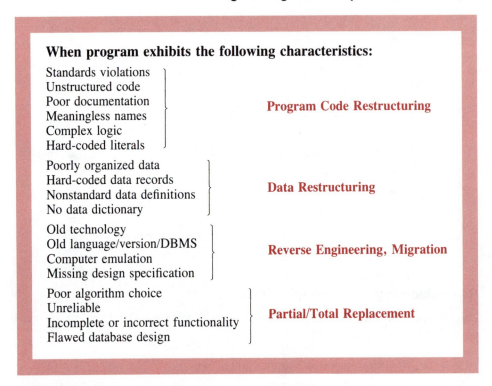

Recognizing Fragile Systems

By concentrating re-engineering efforts on the fragile systems—that 5 to 20 percent of the code that is most troublesome—organizations can quickly and cost-effectively reduce maintenance. Of course, this presumes that we can recognize the fragile systems.

Most organizations keep records about their existing production systems, such as those listed in Box 3.5. The records are used to give management information about the characteristics and production behavior of existing systems relative to one another, and they can be used to suggest candidate systems for re-engineering. However, the records offer only limited guidance because often they are manually prepared and are not always complete, accurate, or up to date. Also, it is not necessarily the oldest, largest, or even the unstructured systems that are the most fragile. Just a few modules, not the whole system, may be the cause of major maintenance problems.

Re-engineering tools along with maintenance records can help pinpoint the fragile systems and those portions of a system that are most complex and error-prone. For example, metrics tools can make quality assessments at the program

BOX 3.5 System maintenance statistics

- Size in lines of code
- Size in function points
- Age
- Language and language versions
- Batch or online
- Operation environment (hardware, O.S., TP monitor, DBMS, emulation)
- Maintenance cost per year
- Abends and production failure rate
- Average error correction time and cost
- Average change correction time and cost
- Number of errors corrected per year
- Number of errors outstanding
- Number of change requests performed per year
- Number of change requests outstanding
- Staffing requirements
- User satisfaction
- Maintainer opinion of maintainability

or module level. Code analyzers can report such program deficiencies as dead code, recursion, runaway logic, poor structure, and language violations.

With re-engineering tools, management can practice active rather than reactive maintenance of the corporation's application portfolio. By identifying those systems that should be replaced and those that should be preserved and improved through the use of re-engineering tools, maintenance work can be planned and managed.

REFERENCES

1. Jeff Moad, "Maintaining the Competitive Edge," *Datamation,* February 15, 1990, pp. 60–61.
2. "Application Re-engineering," MP-1411, *Guide* 72 (May 1989).

3. Steven Pfrenzinger, "Re-engineering with CASE," *ComputerWorld,* April 18, 1988, p. 27.
4. M. J. Lyons, "Salvaging Your Software Asset (Tools-Based Maintenance)," *AFIPS Conference Proceedings on 1981 National Computer Conference,* vol. 50 (Chicago, May 4–7, 1981), pp. 332–342.

4 PROGRAM CODE ANALYZERS AND METRICS TOOLS

MEASURING MAINTAINABILITY

A primary objective of re-engineering is to improve the future maintainability of software systems. **Maintainability** is defined as the ease with which a software system can be corrected when errors or deficiencies are discovered and can be expanded or contracted to satisfy new requirements. Based on the primary software maintenance tasks, we know that a maintainable system must be easy to understand, modify, and test. But how do we know whether or not a system is maintainable in terms of these characteristics? How can we determine the degree to which the characteristics of maintainability are present in a particular software system?

Metrics provide a quantitative measure of maintainability. Several different metrics are being used to measure objectively how maintainable a system (program) is. There are many strong, convincing experiences in industry that support the usefulness of measuring software maintainability. Use of metrics has lead to significant savings in software life cycle costs and improvements in software quality. Long-term benefits include the ability of metrics to predict where errors and difficulties are likely to occur in a software system. For example, metrics can accurately predict the number of errors remaining in a system and can be used to determine when the system has been adequately tested.[1]

Different metrics measure different characteristics of software quality such as understandability or modifiability. Some metrics provide important insights into the limitations of existing software systems; others can help pinpoint potential problems in newly developed systems; and still others such as productivity metrics measure the software process.

AUTOMATING SOFTWARE METRICS

Metrics tools automatically measure software maintainability. They measure various program and system attributes, such as size and complexity, that help maintainers and managers understand, compare, and evaluate programs and systems. Metrics tools are used to identify software requiring re-engineering, to evaluate software packages, and to ensure that software quality does not degrade during maintenance changes. The ability to measure automatically system quality in an objective, quantitative manner is essential for taking control of software maintenance. Remember, you cannot control what you cannot measure.

Most metric tools read program source code to produce

- Complexity metrics
- Size metrics
- Counts and lists
- Existing system portfolio analysis reports

Each metrics tool typically produces its own subset of information in graphic and/or report form. Newer metrics that measure the design specification and help control quality during the early phases of the life cycle are also available.

SOFTWARE UNDERSTANDABILITY

Understandability is a fundamental requirement for a maintainable program. The decision of whether to replace or re-engineer a system is often based on how easily and completely the system can be understood. If a program is not understandable, it is virtually impossible to maintain in any sort of efficient or effective manner. Unfortunately, in industry today countless programs are difficult to understand, and this is a major factor in the high cost of maintenance. Many trainees have been dissuaded from pursuing a programming career after a succession of frustrating and unsuccessful attempts to understand someone else's program.

Understandability is defined as the ease with which we can understand the purpose of a program and how it achieves this purpose by reading the program source code, JCL, database, and file descriptions and its associated documentation. In an understandable program there is adequate information to determine the program objectives, assumptions, constraints, inputs, outputs, components, relationship to other programs, and status. Understandability also implies that we can easily understand the program at varying levels of detail and abstraction.

Factors of Understandability

Several factors influence how easy or difficult it is to understand a particular program. These factors can be categorized into two groups: programmer ability and program form. The programmer's experience and fluency with a particular programming language greatly influences his or her ability to understand a program. Also, a programmer's familiarity with the application domain can influence the ease with which a program is understood.

Understandable programs are typically characterized by certain properties, such as the following:

- Modularity
- Consistency of style
- Avoidance of "trick" or obscure code
- Use of meaningful data and procedure names
- Structuredness

Much of the work in structured programming was aimed at formalizing the notion of good program structure as the key to controlling programming understandability and software costs. Structured programming attempts to improve understandability through a standardization of program form. This standardization imposes restrictions on program control constructs, modularization, and documentation. Automatic structure checkers are available to measure the structuredness of a program.

Although helpful, good structure does not completely ensure all aspects of program understandability. Boehm et al. suggest that in addition to being well structured, an understandable program also must be concise, consistent, and complete.[3]

A **concise** program is one in which no excess pieces are present. For example, in a concise program every program instruction must be reachable. This property is considered important because unreachable or "dead" code means extra maintenance work and may be a source of confusion to the maintainer. Automatic program code analyzers that trace logic and data can be used to detect unreachable code and unused data elements.

A **consistent** program is a program that is written in a consistent coding style and follows a consistent design approach. Consistency of coding style implies that the program contains uniform notation, terminology, and symbology that comply with corporate naming conventions and standards. Consistency of a design is what Brooks calls conceptual integrity.[4] Conceptual integrity is preserved when one basic design architecture is carried through the entire program. In a program that has conceptual integrity, the task of understanding the rationale behind the program architecture is greatly simplified.

A **complete** program is a program all of whose components are present and fully developed. This is an obvious requirement for understandability. If pieces of the source code or the design specification are missing, the maintainer loses confidence in being able to correct and change the program accurately.

Tools of Understandability

As shown in Fig. 4.1, the largest portion of the maintenance effort is spent on understanding the software to be maintained. Re-engineering tools such as program code analyzers and metrics tools can greatly reduce the time and effort needed to understand a program, especially when it was written and modified by other people. Without these tools, it may be impossible, regardless of the amount of effort and time spent, to understand large, complex software systems.

PROGRAM CODE ANALYZERS Program code analyzers, such as logic analyzers and data tracers, provide automated assistance for understanding a program—its procedural and data components and their interrelationships. By automatically tracing program logic forward and backward and tracing data element references, the system maintainer can understand exactly how the program works and what the impact of a maintenance change will be on the program, as well as how to revalidate the software most effectively.

Logic analyzers help maintainers understand the program control structure and the flow of logic through the program and identify program logic problems and other defects. A static view of the program structure can be shown in a graphic form (e.g., tree structure diagram) or by indenting and annotating the source code listing (see Fig. 4.2). A dynamic view of the program structure highlights the source code online to show the calling hierarchy of the program (see Fig. 4.3). Batch **data tracers** can trace data element usage in a program

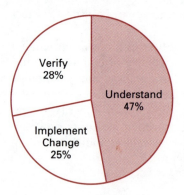

Figure 4.1 What do maintainers do? Software maintenance work entails three types of activities: understanding, modifying, and testing software systems. The largest portion of maintenance effort is spent on understanding the software to be maintained.

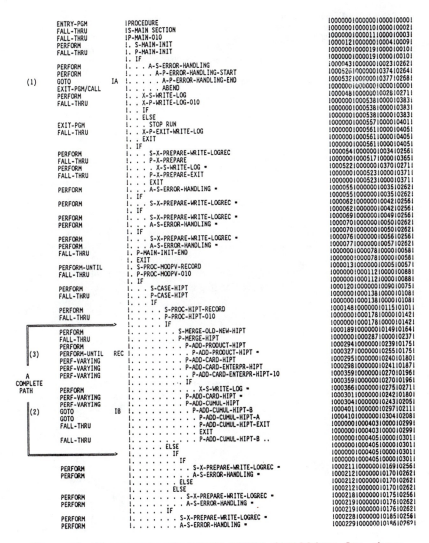

Figure 4.2 The program code analyzer Auditec, from Maintec, Inc., shows the structure of a COBOL program by indenting and annotating the source code listing.

(see Fig. 4.4). Interactive data tracers can highlight the next place in a program along an executing path where a variable will be referenced (see Fig. 4.5).

FLOW GRAPHS

Flow graphs are used to model the control flow logic in a program. Figure 4.6 shows a small program and its associated flow graph. The points represent one or more sequential (i.e.,

```
------------------------- SOURCE VIEW -----------------PROGRAM: PAYROLL
===> DI STRUCTURE                                      SCROLL ===> PAGE
        PROCEDURE DIVISION.
            OPEN INPUT PAYROLL-FILE
                 OUTPUT PRINT-CHECKS.
        - - - - - - - - - - - - - - - - - - - - - -   12 lines not displayed
            PERFORM P010-MAINLINE THRU P010-EXIT.
        - - - - - - - - - - - - - - - - - - - - - -   19 lines not displayed
            PERFORM P900-SHUTDOWN THRU P900-EXIT.              FALLTHRU
        P000-END.
            GOBACK.                                             PGM EXIT
        - - - - - - - - - - - - - - - - - - - - - -    9 lines not displayed
        P010-MAINLINE.
        - - - - - - - - - - - - - - - - - - - - - -    8 lines not displayed
            CALL 'DATEUTIL' USING PAY-DATE.
            PERFORM P015-READ-RECORD.
            PERFORM P120-COMPUTE-TAX THRU P150-EXIT.
        - - - - - - - - - - - - - - - - - - - - - -   16 lines not displayed
        P010-EXIT.
            EXIT.                                                RETURN

        P015-READ-RECORD.
            READ PAYROLL-FILE
        - - - - - - - - - - - - - - - - - - - - - -   11 lines not displayed
```

Figure 4.3 Via/Insight, from ViaSoft, gives a dynamic view of the program structure of a COBOL program by highlighting the source code online.

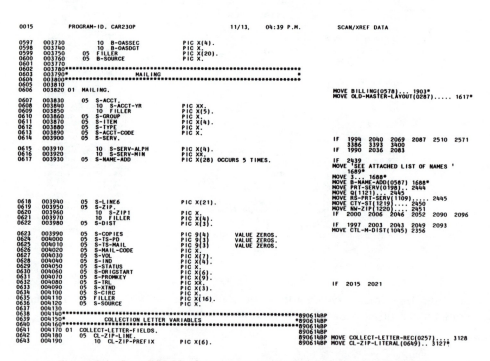

Figure 4.4 Scan/COBOL, from Computer Data Systems, Inc., shows all places a data element is referenced in the program logic of a COBOL program by annotating the source code listing.

```
VIA/Insight ---------------- SOURCE VIEW -----------PROGRAM: VIAP100X  2.2
===>                                                      SCROLL ===> CSR
VIA04431 19 DATA REFS: 6 DEFS, 9 USES, 4 MODS, FOUND FOR PRM-REPORT-LEVEL
****** ************************** TOP OF DATA ********************************
- - - - - - - - - - - - - - - - - - - - - - - 233 LINES NOT DISPLAYED
000234  01  INPUT-PARM.                                          DATA DEF
- - - - - - - - - - - - - - - - - - - - - - -   1 LINE NOT DISPLAYED
000236      05  PROCESSING-PARMS.                                DATA DEF
- - - - - - - - - - - - - - - - - - - - - - -   4 LINES NOT DISPLAYED
000241          10  PRM-3RD-PARM-1.                              DATA DEF
000242              15  PRM-REPORT-LEVEL     PIC X.              DATA DEF
000243          10  PRM-3RD-PARM-2 REDEFINES PRM-3RD-PARM-1.     DATA DEF
000244              15  PRM-PENALTY-FACTOR   PIC 9.              DATA DEF
- - - - - - - - - - - - - - - - - - - - - - -  50 LINES NOT DISPLAYED
000295                      PRM-PENALTY-FACTOR                   DATA USE
- - - - - - - - - - - - - - - - - - - - - - -  47 LINES NOT DISPLAYED
000343              IF PRM-REPORT-LEVEL NOT = SPACES              DATA USE
000344                  MOVE 1 TO PRM-PENALTY-FACTOR              DATA MOD
- - - - - - - - - - - - - - - - - - - - - - -   1 LINE NOT DISPLAYED
000346                  MOVE 2 TO PRM-PENALTY-FACTOR              DATA MOD
- - - - - - - - - - - - - - - - - - - - - - -   1 LINE NOT DISPLAYED
000348              MOVE PRM-REPORT-LEVEL TO WK-REPORT-LEVEL      DATA USE
- - - - - - - - - - - - - - - - - - - - - - -   1 LINE NOT DISPLAYED
000346                  MOVE ZERO TO PRM-PENALTY-FACTOR           DATA MOD
```

Figure 4.5 Via/Insight, from ViaSoft, can identify the next place in a COBOL program along an executing path where a particular variable will be referenced.

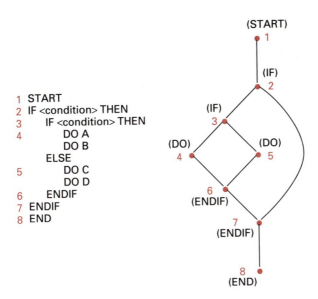

```
1  START
2  IF <condition> THEN
3      IF <condition> THEN
4          DO A
           DO B
       ELSE
5          DO C
           DO D
6      ENDIF
7  ENDIF
8  END
```

Figure 4.6 Sample program and its associated flow graph.

noncontrol) program statements and the lines represent the control flow paths between the statements. The flow graph shows all possible logic paths through the program (three paths in Fig. 4.6). Figure 4.7 shows a flow graph produced automatically by a program code analyzer.

MATHEMATICALLY RIGOROUS FLOW GRAPHS

Flow graphs are a powerful tool to aid in program understanding because they provide a visual way to understand complicated and very convoluted program logic and because they are mathematically rigorous. Flow graphs are an application of graph theory to software programs. Graph theory is a branch of mathematics related to topology whose roots can be traced back to the eighteenth century.

Koenigsberg, a small town in Prussia, is bisected by the Pregel River, which contains an island and a peninsula. In 1736, the town, the island, and the peninsula were connected by seven bridges. A local mathematician named Leonhard Euler tried to determine mathematically if one could cross all seven bridges in sequence without crossing any of them twice. To solve his problem, Euler drew a graph to represent the connections provided by the bridges. The points in the graph represent land and the lines between the points represent the bridges (see Fig. 4.8).

Euler proved that it would be impossible to cross those seven bridges in sequence without crossing one of them twice, and then applied this and other mathematically based rules to graphs in general. Over the years, mathematicians have proved various other theorems defining the rules of how points may or may not be connected by lines. This body of work is known as graph theory. Thus, everything we model with graphs is subject to mathematically provable theorems and mathematical rigor.

Graph theory is the theoretical basics for complexity metrics, logic restructuring tools, and structured programming.

Boehm and Jacopini proved that all possible program logic flows could be expressed using only two control constructs: sequence and selection. A 1966 paper on this subject by Boehm and Jacopini proved that GO TOs are an unnecessary programming construct and thus began the structured revolution.[5]

Testing Aid

In addition to acting as an aid to program understanding, flow graphs can be very useful as a program testing aid. Figure 4.9 shows a segment of source code and its associated test path listing, which indicates all possible paths through the code. The listing was produced automatically from flow graphs created by a re-engineering tool. With the information provided in the test path listing, the maintainer can decide exactly which paths should be retested and the test data needed to follow each of these paths. Because testing consumes a large portion

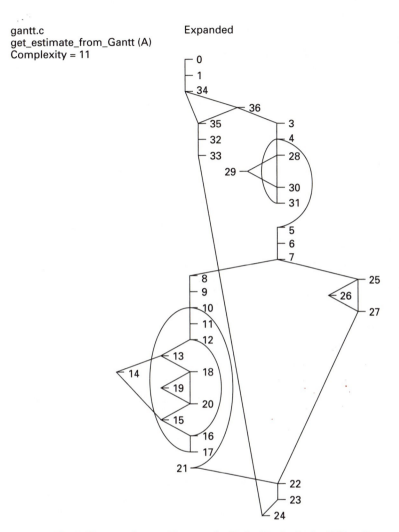

Figure 4.7 A flow graph created automatically by the Analysis of Complexity Tool (ACT), from McCabe and Associates, from the program source code listing.

(20 to 40 percent) of software life cycle effort,[6] as well as a large portion of maintenance effort (28 percent),[7] testing tools offer both a tremendous boost to software productivity and great insurance for software quality. If making existing systems easier to understand is the primary way of reducing software maintenance costs, then surely the second most important way is automation of software testing.

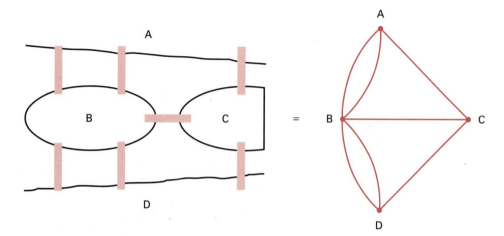

Figure 4.8 On the left is a diagram showing Koenigsberg's seven bridges. On the right is the graph Euler drew to represent the connections provided by the bridges. The points in the graph represent land and the lines between the points represent the bridges.

PREDICTORS OF UNDERSTANDABILITY

Whereas program code analyzers are examples of automated aids for understanding a program, metrics tools are re-engineering tools that measure and predict how easy a program is to understand.

PROGRAM COMPLEXITY METRICS

Program complexity is a measure of program understandability. The more complex a program, the more difficult it is to understand. Program complexity is introduced by the difficulty of the programming problem and the size of the program. It is a function of the number of possible execution paths in a program and the difficulty of tracing paths. As a simple example, a program that has only one execution path (regardless of its input data) has no complexity. Avoiding excessive program complexity will improve program reliability and reduce the effort needed to develop and maintain a program.

Several program complexity metrics have been proposed. Whereas some may be applied to the program design specification, most examine the source code. Some measure the complexity of a module; others measure the complexity of an entire program. Several uses for complexity metrics have been suggested:

1. *A design tool:* To evaluate the quality of a modularization scheme for the program design and to suggest when a module should be subdivided.

```
                              Test Path Listing
Module Name: get_estimate_from_Gantt      File:  gantt.c
Complexity 11                             Date/Time: Wed Aug 17 10:10
Language: CC                              Page 1


Test Path 1 (Baseline):  0 1 34 36 3 4 28 29 30 31 4 5 6 7 25 26 27 22 23 24
        34: ! task => FALSE
        36: ! task [ 0 ] => FALSE
         4: task [ a ] => TRUE
        28: task [ a ] -> min != task [ a ] -> max => TRUE
         4: task [ a ] => FALSE
         7: deviation ( estimate , avg_path ) > 1 => FALSE
        25: deviation ( estimate , avg_path ) < .25 => TRUE

Test Path 2:   0 1 34 35 32 33 24
        34: ! task => TRUE

Test Path 3:   0 1 34 36 35 32 33 24
        34: ! task => FALSE
        36: ! task [ 0 ] => TRUE

Test Path 4:   0 1 34 36 3 4 5 6 7 25 26 27 22 23 24
        34: ! task => FALSE
        36: ! task [ 0 ] => FALSE
         4: task [ a ] => FALSE
         7: deviation ( estimate , avg_path ) > 1
        25: deviation ( estimate , avg_path ) < .2

Test Path 5:   0 1 34 36 3 4 28 30 31 4 5 6 7
        34: ! task => FALSE
        36: ! task [ 0 ] => FALSE
         4: task [ a ] => TRUE
        28: task [ a ] -> min != task [ a ] -> max =
         4: task [ a ] => FALSE
         7: deviation ( estimate , avg_path ) > 1
        25: deviation ( estimate , avg_path ) < .2
```

An annotated source listing relates the nodes on the flow graph with their associated source code.

```
                          Annotated Source Listing
File:  gantt.c                                    Date/Time: Wed Aug 17 10:04
Language: CC              Expanded                Page 2


 1    A0    A1              get_estimate_from_Gantt(task)
 2    A1                      struct tasks **task;
 3    A1                      {
 4    A1                      int min_path=0,max_path=0,avg_path=0,estimate=0;
 5    A1                      int a=0,loop,interval;
 6    A1                      struct tasks *tmp;

 8    A34   A36   A35        if (! task || ! task[0])
 9    A32                       {
10    A32                       printf("No tasks on Gantt diagram.\n");
11    A33                       return(-1);
12    A3                        }
13    A4                        while (task[a])
14    A28                          {
15    A28                          if (task[a]->min != task[a]->max)
16    A29                             {
17    A29                             min_path = min_path+task[a]->min;
18    A29                             max_path = max_path+task[a]->max:
19    A30   A29                       }
20    A31                          avg_path = avg_path + task[a]->expected;
21    A31                          a++;
22    A31   A5                      }
23    A6                         estimate = (3.5*avg_path + min_path+max_path)/5.5;
24    A6                         interval = estimate/a;
25    A6                         printf("Estimated completion time: %d %s\n",
26    A6                                estimate,units);
27    A7                         if (deviation(estimate,avg_path) > 1)
28    A8                            {
29    A8                            printf("Strategic tasks:\n");
30    A9    A10   A17              for (loop=0;  loop < a;  loop++)
31    A11                              {
32    A11                              tmp = task[loop];
33    A12                              if (tmp->max - tmp->min > interval)
34    A13                                 if (tmp->max > interval)
35    A14                                    printf("%s (escalating)\n", tmp->task);
36    A18                                 else if (tmp->min < interval)
37    A16   A20   A15   A19                  printf("%s (diminishing)\n",tmp->task);
38    A21   A16                           }
39    A21                            }
40    A25                         else if (deviation(estimate,avg_path) < .25)
41    A27   A22   A26                 printf("High confidence in estimate.\n");
42    A23                         return (estimate);
43    A24                         }
```

Figure 4.9 This test path listing was produced automatically from the program source code listing by ACT, from McCabe and Associates.

2. *A testing tool:* To identify which modules will be most difficult to test and most error-prone, thus providing criteria for selecting test cases.

3. *A maintenance tool:* To predict which modules and programs will be most difficult and risky to modify.

McCABE CYCLOMATIC COMPLEXITY

The **McCabe Cyclomatic Complexity** metric, named after its creator, is the most widely used complexity metric today. It has been used to measure programs written in FORTRAN, COBOL, PL/1, C, and Pascal. It has been automated by many re-engineering and CASE tools.

Thomas McCabe was the first to use graph theory and flow graphs to measure the complexity of programs.[8] Cyclomatic complexity is a graph theory complexity measure that is based on counting the number of individual logic paths contained in the program. For example, recall the small program in Fig. 4.6. There are three possible logic paths, depending on the IF statement conditions:

Path 1: Statements 1, 2, 3, 4, 6, 7, 8
(If both IFs are true)
Path 2: Statements 1, 2, 3, 5, 6, 7, 8
(If the first IF is true and the second IF is false)
Path 3: Statements 1, 2, 7, 8
(If the first IF is false)

This program has a cyclomatic complexity of 3.

Because it employs flow graphs, the McCabe metric not only measures complexity but also identifies the exact number of logic paths in the program, which in turn indicates the minimum number of test cases required to test the program adequately. (It is the minimum number of test cases because the metric only addresses control flow paths.)

To determine the cyclomatic complexity of a program, this formula is used:

$$v(G) = e - n + 2$$

where **e** represents the edge of the graph (i.e., the lines or paths) and **n** represents the nodes (i.e., the points or statements). This translates into

cyclomatic complexity = paths − statements + 2

Again, look at the sample program in Fig. 4.6. There are nine paths (lines) and eight statements (points). Substituting these numbers into the preceding formula gives the following result:

$$v(G) = 9 - 8 + 2$$
$$v(G) = 3$$

which is indeed the number of logic paths in the program.

There is a second way to calculate the cyclomatic complexity number:

$$v(G) = \text{\textbf{enclosed regions on the flow graph}} + \textbf{1}$$

In Fig. 4.6, there are two enclosed regions or spaces on the flow graph: the diamond shaped space and the space just to the right of it.

Finally, there is one more way to calculate cyclomatic complexity. Because a conditional statement creates an enclosed region, it always results in at least two paths that eventually merge. Cyclomatic complexity can be determined simply by counting the conditional statements (IFs):

$$v(G) = \textbf{IF count} + \textbf{1}$$

Extended Cyclomatic Complexity

A variant of the McCabe Cyclomatic Complexity metric is Glenford Myers' **Extended Cyclomatic Complexity** metric.[9] Rather than simply counting IFs, this metric also counts ANDs and ORs, thus recognizing the added difficulty of compound conditional statements (e.g., IF ⟨condition⟩ AND ⟨condition⟩).

Essential Complexity

The **McCabe Essential Complexity** is a metric that measures the degree of structuredness of a program rather than its logic complexity. It measures structuredness by counting the number of times a control path branches outside a module and does not return. In a perfectly structured program, all code is executed via calls or performs, so for every branch there is an automatic return. In effect, essential complexity is a count of the GO TOs in the program, excluding GO TO EXITs. In a perfectly structured program, it is equal to 1, where 1 represents the module exit.

The percent structuredness can be calculated as follows:

$$\text{percent structuredness} = \frac{\text{number of returning branches}}{\text{total branches}}$$

Percent structuredness should be 100 percent.

Box 4.1 summarizes the McCabe complexity metrics.

McCabe's Complexity Threshold

McCabe's strategy is to control complexity by controlling the number of paths through a program. Complexity evaluation is applied at the program or module

BOX 4.1 McCabe complexity metrics

- **Cyclomatic complexity:** Counts the number of logic paths in a module. Should be 10 or less.
- **Extended cyclomatic complexity:** Counts the number of logic paths in a module, plus the number of ANDs and ORs, taking into account the added complexity of compound IF statements.
- **Essential complexity:** Measures the structuredness of a module by counting the number of GO TOs (excluding GO TO EXITs). Should be 1.

level. McCabe uses the cyclomatic number to control the size of a program, and hence its understandability, by limiting the cyclomatic complexity of each module in the program to a maximum of 10. McCabe arrived at 10 as a reasonable limit for cyclomatic complexity after examining several FORTRAN programs. He found that modules (and indeed programs containing modules) whose cyclomatic complexity was greater than 10 were generally more troublesome and less reliable. McCabe suggests that modules with a cyclomatic complexity number greater than 10 should be redesigned and perhaps further subdivided.

Although there is no absolute threshold for measuring software quality,

```
4/3/89                                                           Page:    1

Complexity Report by Procedure for: PROG1.COB
----------------------------------------

Paragraph   n1  n2   N1   N2    N    N^  P/R      V        E   VG1 VG2 LOC <.>  Sp
---------   --  --   --   --    --   --  ---   -----  -------  --- --- --- ---  --
010-main     7  11   23   16    39   58  1.5     163      830   3   3   11  10   1
020-initdi   8  11   31   26    57   62  1.1     242     2288   5   5   16  10   2
030-builda   5   5   10   10    20   23  1.1      66      330   1   1    6   4   0
040-elimin   8   9   30   15    45   53  1.2     184     1227   3   3   14  12   1
045-steps    3   5    7    7    14   16  1.1      42       88   1   1    5   3   0
050-answer   4   5    6    5    11   20  1.8      35       70   1   1    5   3   0
091-errorm   3   3    5    3     8   10  1.3      21       31   1   1    5   3   0
092-errorm   3   3    5    3     8   10  1.3      21       31   1   1    8   3   0
                         Halstead                        McCabe       Other
```

Paragraph Metrics

Figure 4.10 This complexity report includes COBOL complexity values calculated at the program module level automatically by the metrics tool PC-Metric from Set Laboratories. McCabe and Halstead complexity metrics are automated by PC-Metric.

several studies support McCabe's findings. For example, a study was conducted during the development of the AEGIS Naval Weapon System, which was composed of 276 modules with approximately half of the modules at a complexity level above the threshold of 10. Those modules whose complexity was above the recommended level had an error rate of 5.6 errors per 100 source statements, whereas those below 10 had an error rate of only 4.6.[10] There was a significant increase in the error count at a complexity level of 11.

Automatic Complexity Measurement

Several program code analyzers and metrics tools are available to compute automatically the cyclomatic complexity for code written in FORTRAN, COBOL, C, PL/1, Ada, Basic, and Assembler.

Figures 4.10 through 4.12 show reports produced by various metrics tools that automatically calculate the McCabe cyclomatic complexity value at both the

```
4/3/89
PC-METRIC (COBOL)/Version 2.0c
Summary Complexity Report for: PROG1.RPT
-------------------------------------

    Unique Operators (n1):      16
    Unique Operands (n2):       29
    Total Operators (N1):      117
    Total Operands (N2):        85

    Software Science Length (N):            202
    Estimated Software Science Length (N^): 205
    Purity Ratio (P/R):                    1.01       Halstead

    Software Science Volume (V):    1109
    Software Science Effort (E):   26012

    Estimated Errors Using Software Science (B^).^
    Estimated Time to Develop, in hours (T^):    0

    Cyclomatic Complexity (VG1):             9
    Extended Cyclomatic Complexity (VG2):    9    McCabe
    Average Cyclomatic Complexity:           1
    Average Extended Cyclomatic Complexity:  1

    Lines of Code (LOC):                   143
    Number of Paragraphs:           8
    Number of Executable Periods (<.>):48
    0 I/O file(s) were referenced.                Other
    0 copy statements were encountered.
    0 subprogram call(s) were made.
    0 parameter usage(s) encountered.
```

Figure 4.11 This complexity report includes COBOL program complexity values for Halstead and McCabe metrics automatically produced by the metrics tool PC-Metric from Set Laboratories.

SAMPLE QAUDITOR (R) PL/I AUDIT REPORT

① PROGRAM: ABC950   Q/AUDITOR (R)   DATE: 03/03/89
   GRADE: B   (C) COPYRIGHT EDEN SYSTEMS CORPORATION 1989   TIME: 09:06:38
   LICENSED BY: ABC COMPANY - PL/I - IBM MVS   VERSION 1.0.6
② STANDARD: MAINTENANCE STANDARDS - FINANCIAL DIVISION

③ STANDARD	④ #	⑤ GRADE A	B	C	D	F	STANDARD	#	GRADE A	B	C	D	F
VERB COUNTS							**DATA DIVISION ANALYSIS**						
1 DISPLAY	0	000	000	000	020		12 TOTAL INPUT FILES	1	N/A	N/A	N/A	N/A	
2 LOCATE	0	000	000	000	020		13 TOTAL OUTPUT FILES	3	N/A	N/A	N/A	N/A	
3 MAINLINE ASSIGNMENTS (=)	8	020	040	N/A	N/A		14 TOTAL UPDATE FILES	0	N/A	N/A	N/A	N/A	
VERB STATISTICS							**STANDARDS ANALYSIS**						
4 PROCS WITH > 5 LITERALS	4	010	020	N/A	N/A		15 DEFAULT RANGE (*) STATIC	1	001	001	N/A	N/A	
5 CONTROL VERBS	63	N/A	N/A	N/A	N/A		16 ON ERROR CONDITIONS FOUND	2	001***N/A		N/A	N/A	
							17 ON CONDITIONS NOT TOGETHER	0	001	N/A	N/A	N/A	
6 MAXIMUM OPENS PER FILE	1	003	005	007	010		18 COMMENTED CODE IDENTIFIED	9	010	N/A	N/A	N/A	
7 MAXIMUM CLOSES PER FILE	2	003	005	007	010		**STRUCTURE ANALYSIS**						
8 MAXIMUM READS PER FILE	2	003	005	007	010								
9 MAXIMUM WRITES PER FILE	1	003	005	007	010		19 NUMBER OF PROGRAM EXITS	2	001***002		N/A	N/A	
SIZE ANALYSIS							20 NUMBER OF PROGRAM ENTRIES	1	001	N/A	N/A	N/A	
							21 CYCLOMATIC COMPLEXITY	132	350	500	700	N/A	
10 TOTAL PROCEDURES	9	N/A	N/A	N/A	N/A		22 ESSENTIAL COMPLEXITY	1	010	020	030	040	
11 # OF PROC'S OVER 15 STMTS	4	N/A	N/A	N/A	N/A		23 # OF INVALID GO TO'S	0	N/A	N/A	N/A	N/A	
							24 HALSTEAD'S VOLUME METRIC	984	N/A	N/A	N/A	N/A	

THIS FOOTNOTE AREA IS AVAILABLE FOR YOUR USE IN COMMUNICATING CHANGES IN STANDARDS AND UPDATES TO THE PROGRAMMING COMMUNITY.

A BRIEF TOUR OF THE AUDIT REPORT

① **GRADE:** The overall grade assigned to the program based on the standards you set for each metric you choose.

② **STANDARD USED:** Many organizations use different standards for new development and for maintenance.

③ **INDIVIDUAL STANDARDS:** This column lists the metrics being measured. You can easily customize the descriptions printed on the report.

④ **NUMBER:** This column indicates the number of occurrences of each metric.

⑤ **GRADE:** For each metric selected, the report indicates the number of occurrences qualifying for each grade. For example, standard 3, MAINLINE ASSIGNMENTS, receives an A since there were 8 of these in the program whereas up to 20 are acceptable in an A program. The standard would receive a B for 21-40 MAINLINE ASSIGNMENTS.

The standards which contribute to the program's overall grade are highlighted by asterisks (***), as in standard 19, NUMBER OF PROGRAM EXITS. N/A stands for Not Applicable, and indicates either 1) a standard which is reported but not graded (e.g. standard 24, HALSTEAD'S VOLUME METRIC) or 2) a standard that will not take a program below a certain grade (e.g. standard 16, ON ERROR CONDITIONS FOUND. More than one of these will keep the program from getting an A but will not cause it to get lower than a B.)

Figure 4.12 This report includes McCabe and Halstead complexity measures as well as program defect counts for a PL/1 program. It was automatically produced from the PL/1 source code by the re-engineering tool Q/Auditor from Eden Systems Corporation.

program and module levels. In COBOL, a paragraph is considered a module; in C, a function is a module. Figure 4.13 is a tree structure diagram for a program, showing in graphic form that modules 2, 3, and 15 are unmaintainable and unreliable because they have a cyclomatic complexity value above the threshold of 10.

McCabe's complexity metrics have been expanded to include module design complexity, design complexity, and integration complexity metrics.[11] These metrics are used to quantify the complexity of a program design and to develop early in the life cycle a comprehensive test plan that is derived from the design specification. A CASE tool that automatically computes each of these metrics is available.

KNOT COUNT   Another complexity metric of interest is the **Knot Count** metric. Like the McCabe Essential Complexity metric, the Knot Count metric measures program understandability as a function of the degree of structuredness of the program. For example, in the pro-

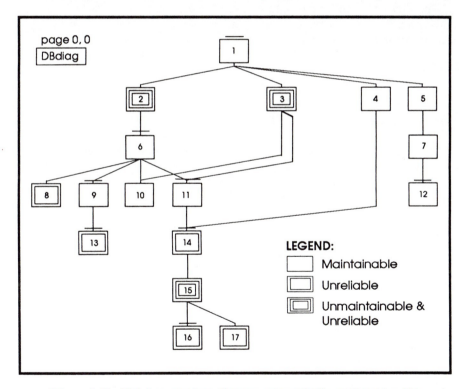

Figure 4.13 This tree structure diagram, automatically produced by Battlemap from McCabe and Associates, shows graphically the modules (2, 3, and 15) that are unmaintainable and unreliable because of their high complexity.

gram in Fig. 4.14, the control paths have been marked with black lines. There is a line from each IF to each ENDIF, and a line from each GO TO to its destination. The "knots" show where control paths intersect. This program has a knot count of 10. Ideally, the knot count should be 0. Figure 4.13 is a metrics report that includes the knot count automatically calculated by a metrics tool.

HALSTEAD SOFTWARE SCIENCE

During the late 1970s, Maurice Halstead developed a set of metrics called **Halstead Software Science** metrics based on a calculation of program keywords and data variables. Numerous studies and experiments from both the academic and industrial communities have shown software science metrics to be amazingly accurate measures of program complexity and effort.[12] In addition to measuring program complexity and overall quality of existing software, Halstead's metrics have been used to measure program reliability, to predict program length, and to estimate programming effort.

Halstead's theory is based on a simple, easy-to-automate count of operators and operands in a program:

- **Operators** are reserved language words, such as ADD, GREATER THAN, MOVE, READ, IF, CALL, PERFORM; arithmetic operators, such as +, −, *, ÷; and logical operators, such as GREATER THAN or EQUAL TO.
- **Operands** are the data variables and constants in the program.

Halstead distinguishes between the number of unique operators and the number of total operators. For example, a program might have one READ, seven MOVEs, and one WRITE; it would therefore have three unique operators,

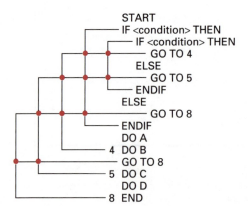

Figure 4.14 The 10 "knots" in this program graphically show that the program is not well structured.

but nine total operators. The same is true for operands. In Halstead Software Science notation

$$n_1 = \textbf{unique operators}$$
$$N_1 = \textbf{total operators}$$
$$n_2 = \textbf{unique operands}$$
$$N_2 = \textbf{total operands}$$

Software science metrics for any program written in any language can be derived from these four basic counts.

Length

Several simple complexity theories have been developed to relate these counts to program properties, such as length, volume, and languages. For example, the **length, N,** of a program is computed as

$$N = N_1 + N_2$$

N is a simple measure of program size. The larger the value of **N,** the more difficult the program is to understand and the more effort required to maintain it. **N** is an alternative measure of program size preferred over counting lines of code. Although it is almost as simple to compute, **N** is a more sensitive complexity measure than a line count because **N** does not assume that all instructions are equally easy or difficult to understand.

In a study of 154 PL/1 programs at General Motors Research Laboratories, Elshoff was able to predict the length of a program quite accurately (the correlation between actual and predicted length was 0.98) merely by knowing the number of unique operators and operands in the program.[13] He calculated the estimated length, $\hat{N}$, according to the following Halstead software science formula:

$$\textbf{estimated length } \hat{N} = (n_1 \times \log_2(n_1)) + (n_2 \times \log_2(n_2))$$

This formula shows Halstead's belief that as the number of unique operators and operands increases, the total number of operators and operands increases logarithmically.

In addition, Elshoff found that the estimated length, $\hat{N}$, more closely equaled the actual length, **N,** for well-structured programs. Based on this finding, he used a comparison of **N** and $\hat{N}$ as a simple check for structuredness. This measure is called the **purity ratio** and is calculated as

$$\textbf{purity ratio} = \hat{N} \div N$$

Volume

Length **N** is used in another Halstead size estimate called **volume**. Whereas length is a simple count (or estimate) of total operators and operands, the volume metric gives extra weight to the number of unique operators and operands in the program. For example, if two programs have the same length **N** but a greater number of unique operators and operands, which would make it naturally harder to understand, then that program would have a greater volume.

The formula is

$$\text{volume } V = N \times \log_2(n) \text{ and } n = n_1 + n_2$$

Because volume is a more accurate predictor of program difficulty, it is used in the effort metric.

Effort

Effort is a measure of the work required to develop a program. The formula is

$$\text{effort } E = V \div L$$

where volume **V** is divided by language level **L**. Language level indicates whether a high- or low-level language is being used. For example, a simple procedure call would have an **L** value of 1; COBOL might have an **L** value of 0.1, and Assembler might have an **L** of 0.01. Therefore, effort **E** increases as the volume **V** increases, but will be decreased by the use of a higher-level language. As we would expect, the volume decreases as we go from lower-level to higher-level languages containing more powerful instruction sets. Halstead's effort metrics gives us a way to quantify the notion that higher-level programming languages, including fourth generation languages, are easier to understand than lower-level languages.

According to several empirical studies, program effort, **E**, is an even better measure of program understandability than **N**. In several different programming experiments, the estimated programming effort calculated using software science metrics was found to match closely the actual programming effort. In a study involving FORTRAN, PL/1, and APL programs, Halstead predicted 22.51 hours for the experiment. Actual time was 20.15 hours.[14]

When applied to individual programs, software science metrics may not always be accurate. However, the great number of empirical results reported thus far significantly indicate that program understandability can be accurately assessed by a simple examination of a few elementary program measurers such as those suggested by Halstead.

The advantages of Halstead Software Science metrics as a measure of program understandability are that

BOX 4.2 Halstead Software Science metrics

- Length $N = N_1 + N_2$
- Estimated length $\hat{N} = (n_1 \times \log_2(n_1)) + (n_2 \times \log_2(n_2))$
- Volume $V = N \times \log_2(n)$ where $n = n_1 + n_2$
- Effort $E = V \div L$

1. Software science metrics are easy to calculate and to automate and do not require resorting to analysis of program features such as depth of statement nesting or detailed flow analysis.
2. Software science metrics are applicable to any programming language and yet are programming language–sensitive.
3. Many different statistical studies of programs from industry demonstrate their validity as predictors of programming effort and mean number of bugs in a program.

Halstead Software Science metrics are summarized in Box 4.2. They have been automated by several re-engineering tools. Figures 4.10 to 4.12 show metrics reports that include Halstead metrics and that were automatically produced by three different metrics tools.

COUNTS AND LISTS

Besides calculating complexity metrics, another simple but effective way to compare programs is to count program characteristics, such as the number of

Lines of code
PERFORMS
IFs
Paragraphs
Files
Databases
Procedure calls

It also is useful to count and list program defects—program characteristics that should *not* be there—such as

ALTERS in COBOL programs

GO TOs

Deeply nested IFs

Control fallthroughs

Uninitialized data elements

Procedure overlaps

Recursive code

Illegal exits

Dead (unreachable) code

Range violations

Figures 4.12 and 4.15 show examples of metrics and counts and a defect list produced by two re-engineering tools. Box 4.3 summarizes program counts produced automatically by program code analyzers and metrics tools.

PORTFOLIO SUMMARY ANALYSIS   The metrics and counts we have seen thus far have been calculated on an individual program basis. It also is useful to gather all these measures together in a meaningful way at the system level. This is done in the portfolio summary analysis. There are three main types of portfolio analysis reports: quadrant report, histogram analysis, and system structure report.

ALL PROGRAMS	UNSTRUCTURED PERCENTAGE	NUMBER OF ALTERS	NUMBER OF GOTOS	APPARENT FALL THRUS	RECURSIVE PATHS
PROGRAM1	100.00	55	133	28	2
PROGRAM2	100.00	0	240	54	0
PROGRAM3	99.50	3	45	29	0
PROGRAM4	78.64	0	97	95	1
PROGRAM5	69.64	0	75	36	0
PROGRAM6	45.43	0	247	101	0

ALL PROGRAMS	COMPLEX PERCENTAGE	NUMBER OF IFS	NUMBER OF PERFORMS	NUMBER OF LINES	NUMBER OF STATEMENTS
PROGRAM1	100.00	104	23	1207	967
PROGRAM2	86.32	239	76	3405	2370
PROGRAM3	97.32	30	12	5062	3289
PROGRAM4	20.53	255	167	3453	2653
PROGRAM5	45.68	34	68	698	423
PROGRAM6	78.03	581	213	7827	5112

Figure 4.15 The metrics tool Inspector, from KnowledgeWare, can produce a report of various metrics and counts for COBOL programs.

BOX 4.3 Program counts

General Counts
- Lines of code
- PERFORMs
- IFs
- Paragraphs
- Files/Databases
- Calls

Defects
- ALTERs
- GO TOs
- Deeply nested IFs
- Fallthroughs
- Uninitialized data elements
- Procedure overlaps

Defect Lists
- Recursion
- Illegal exits
- Dead code
- Range violations

Quadrant Report

Figures 4.16 and 4.17 show two examples of a **quadrant report**. This type of report is produced on a system or library basis by calculating both a complexity and a structuredness metric for each program and by placing each program in one of four quadrants based on whether each metric is "high" or "low."

Any program in the first quadrant (high complexity/low structuredness) will undoubtedly be troublesome, as will any system with a large percentage of programs in that quadrant. Quadrant reports give a bird's-eye look at the overall complexity and structuredness of a system, set of systems, or library.

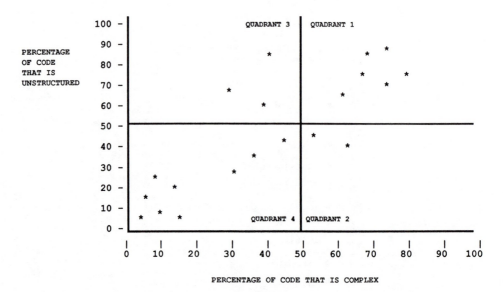

Figure 4.16 This scattergram, automatically produced by the metrics tool Inspector, from KnowledgeWare, shows graphically those systems that cause the most maintenance concern.

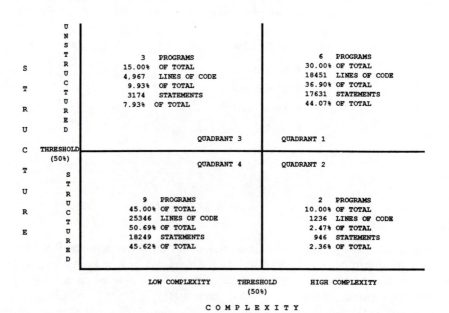

Figure 4.17 This quadrant breakout report, produced by the metrics tool Inspector, from KnowledgeWare, shows what percentage of the application portfolio is difficult to maintain.

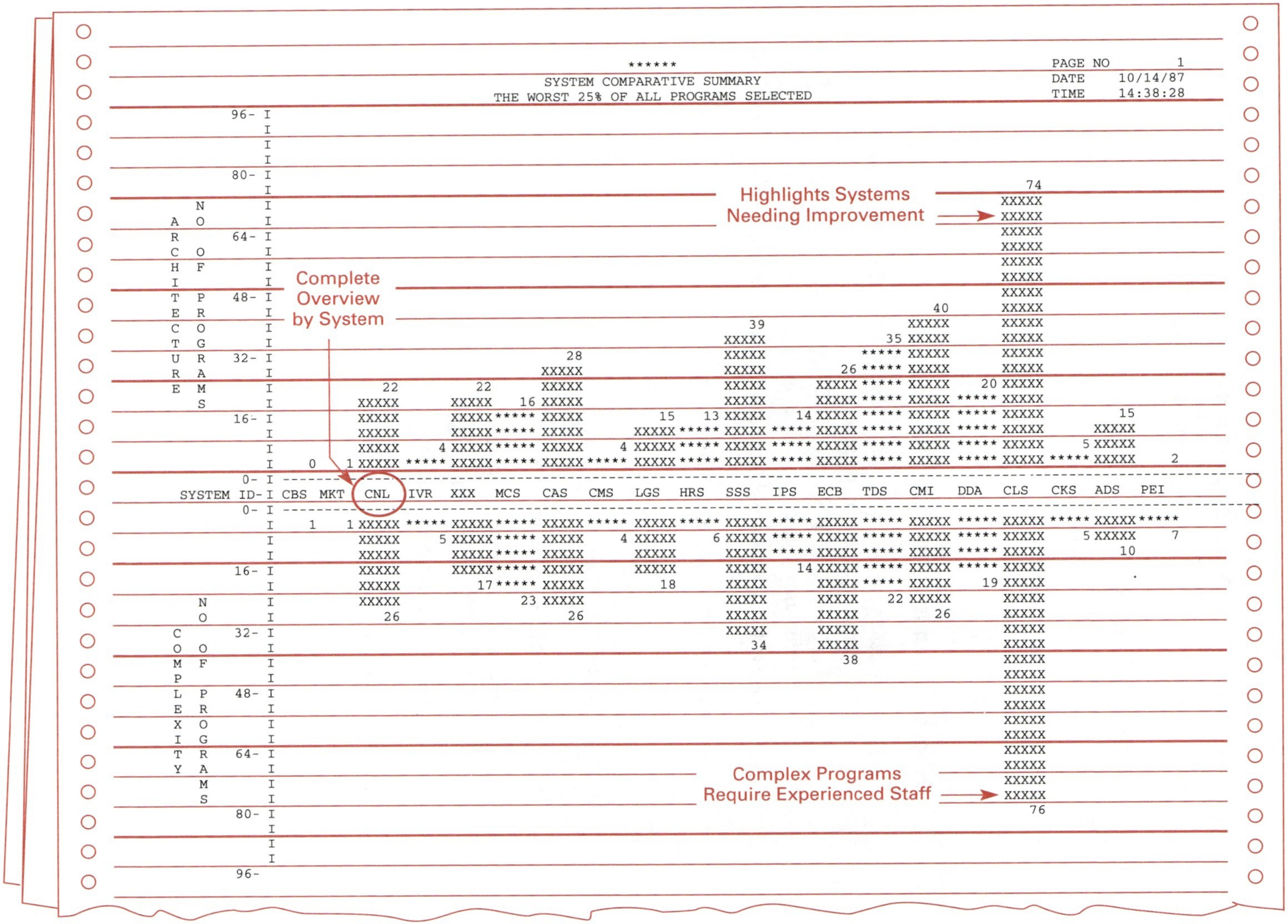

Figure 4.18 This histogram analysis report, produced by the metrics tool Pathvu, from XA Systems, shows graphically those systems that are most difficult to maintain.

BOX 4.4 Program code analyzers and metrics tools features checklist

Complexity Metrics

_____ Flowgraphs/Testpaths

_____ McCabe Cyclomatic Complexity

_____ Halstead Software Science

_____ Knot Count

Program Counts

_____ General counts (lines of code, PERFORMs, IFs, paragraphs files/data elements, function points)

_____ Defect counts (ALTERs, GO TOs, deeply nested IFs, fall-throughs, uninitialized data elements, procedure overlaps)

_____ Defect lists (recursion, illegal exits, dead code, range violations)

Existing System Portfolio Summary

_____ Quadrant report

_____ Histogram analysis

_____ System structure

Program Logic Analysis

_____ Program structure—structure charts

_____ Program structure—online highlighting

_____ Logic trace and problems/defects

Data Analysis

_____ Data element trace

_____ Data element trace—online

_____ Record trace

Histogram Analysis

Another way to measure an entire system or library at one time is with a **histogram analysis.** A histogram is a bar chart where the bars on the chart represent programs in a system or systems in a library. Typically, the size of the bars reflects some sort of metriclike structuredness or complexity or a composite metric that includes complexity, structuredness, defects, and other measures identified and weighted by the user. Figure 4.18 shows an example of a histogram analysis report.

System Structure Report

The system structure report shows not only the structure of the system (i.e., what programs call what other programs) but also some attributes of those programs, such as complexity. Figure 4.13 is an example of a system structure report.

RULERS OF SOFTWARE MAINTENANCE

With program code analyzers, maintainers can better understand the systems they must maintain. With metrics tools, maintainers and managers can measure systems in an objective and quantitative manner. They can measure the complexity, structuredness, and size of individual programs and the modules that they comprise and can count and list program characteristics and defects. Systems and entire libraries can also be measured in aggregate using these same metrics and counts.

Metrics tools are also useful when evaluating vendor-supplied software. When paired with manual system maintenance statistics, they are invaluable for selecting programs and systems that are candidates for restructuring or reverse engineering.

Box 4.4 is a checklist of selection criteria for program code analyzers and metrics tools.

REFERENCES

1. Harlan D. Mills and Peter B. Dyson, "Using Metrics to Quantify Development," *IEEE Software,* 7, no. 2 (March 1990), 15–56.

2. Ibid.

3. B. Boehm, J. Brown, H. Kaspar, M. Lipow, J. MacLeod, and M. Menit, *Characteristics of Software Quality* (New York: TRW/North-Holland Publishing Co., 1978), pp. 3-1–3-26.

4. F. Brooks, *The Mythical Man-Month* (Reading, MA: Addison-Wesley, 1975), pp. 41–50.

5. C. Bohm and G. Jacopini, "Flow Diagrams, Turing Machines and Languages with Only Two Formulation Rules," *CACM*, 9, no. 5 (May 1966), 366–371.

6. Tony Scott and Dennis Farley, "Slashing Software Maintenance Costs," *Business Software Review* (March 1988).

7. Fjeldstad and Hamlen, "Application Program Maintenance Study—Report to Our Respondents," IBM Corporation, DP Marketing Group, 1979.

8. Thomas McCabe, "A Complexity Measure," *IEEE Transactions on Software Engineering*, SE-2, no. 4 (December 1976), 308–320.

9. Glenford Myers, "An Extension to the Cyclomatic Measure of Program Complexity," *ACM SIGPLAN Notices* (October 1977), 61–64.

10. Thomas McCabe and Charles Butler, "Design Complexity Measurement and Testing," *CACM*, 32, no. 12 (December 1989), 1415–1425.

11. Ibid.

12. Maurice Halstead, *Elements of Software Science* (New York; Elsevier North-Holland Publishing Co., 1977).

13. J. Elshoff, "Measuring Commercial PL/1 Programs Using Halstead's Criteria," *ACM SIGPLAN Notices* (May 1976), 38–46.

14. A. Fitzsimmons and T. Love, "A Review and an Evaluation of Software Science," *ACM Computing Surveys*, 10, no. 1 (March 1978), 3–18.

5 RESTRUCTURING

PRODUCTIVITY THROUGH RESTRUCTURING

Software maintenance is expensive and time-consuming because existing software systems are difficult to understand. Most existing software is neither well documented nor well structured, often because it was originally developed before the era of structured programming. A powerful, automated way to increase maintenance productivity while at the same time reduce the risk of changing existing systems is to introduce structure and documentation to existing software through restructuring. Both program logic and data can be restructured to improve the understandability of a software system.

> **Restructuring is the process of standardizing data names, definitions, and program logic structure to improve software maintainability and productivity.**

Restructuring is done primarily for the benefit of the system maintainer, not for the computer. It is aimed at improving the efficiency and effectiveness of the maintenance staff. As shown in Box 5.1, the first objective of restructuring is to improve program readability. However, the other short-term objectives of restructuring in Box 5.1 show that restructuring can improve overall software quality and increase its value to the corporation. Important longer-term goals for restructuring include preparing systems for migration and conversion to newer technologies, such as dictionaries, databases, and online operating mode; and reverse engineering and repository population.

There are two types of restructuring: program code or logic restructuring and data restructuring.

BOX 5.1 Objectives of restructuring

- Improve program readability/simplify logic
- Decrease testing/debugging time
- Enforce programming standards
- Simplify program change/reduce risk
- Reduce software maintenance costs
- Improve response to maintenance requests
- Increase program quality
- Increase user satisfaction
- Improve maintainer morale and job satisfaction
- Reduce dependency on individual maintainers
- Prepare for software conversion/migration
- Protect software asset value

Style and Structure

Style is normally considered a matter of personal preference and a mark of individuality. But whatever the particulars may be, there are some elements common to any good style. Good style is simple, consistent, and complies with standards. Its rules are not so complicated that the reader becomes bogged down in attempting to understand the form of what is written. Above all, it clarifies, not obscures, what the author is communicating.

The rules of good style apply to programming as well as conventional writing because programs must be read by people. If a program is well written using a good programming style, much of the difficulty of reading and understanding the program disappears. Both program logic restructuring and data restructuring offer a means for retrofitting a standardized, easy-to-understand style into existing software systems and programs.

REDUCING THE MAINTENANCE BURDEN   It is estimated that 80 billion lines of COBOL source code running on some 77,000 IBM and non-IBM mainframe computers support business, industry, and governments across the world today. The estimated replacement cost for this code is approaching $2 trillion.[1] Many companies have chosen to address their COBOL maintenance problems through automated restructuring rather than through replacement. Hartford Insurance Company is one example.

In the mid-1980s, most of Hartford's software programmers were involved in the maintenance of its 34,000 existing COBOL programs rather than in new development work.[2] Hartford estimated that all of its 1100 programmers would be devoted exclusively to maintenance by 1991 if its maintenance burden was not substantially reduced. Hartford's solution was to restructure automatically millions of lines of existing COBOL code with an anticipated 25 to 75 percent reduction of its maintenance costs. The restructuring project cost was $3 million, but with an expected savings of $9 million.[3]

Another example comes from another large U.S. insurance company, where 70 percent of its 4000-member MIS staff is devoted to software maintenance work. They are responsible for maintaining approximately 90 million lines of existing COBOL code. Because these systems still serve the business needs and the users are basically happy, the insurance company views its existing systems as a corporate asset. It believes that with the use of re-engineering tools the life of these systems (many of which are already 10 to 20 years old) can be extended another 10 years. The insurance company's immediate re-engineering goal is to upgrade the technology of its COBOL systems, using restructuring tools to standardize the program form by restructuring both the DATA DIVISION and the PROCEDURE DIVISION of its COBOL programs.

This company sees restructuring as a way to increase maintenance productivity and the quality of its existing systems. By restructuring big, old programs, revealing and eliminating dead code and making smaller, well-structured modules, it is much easier for more people to understand the programs. The company is no longer forced to rely on one individual to maintain a system, and that individual is finally free to participate in other projects. Another important benefit is that the tools have opened up a whole new world to the maintenance staff. Re-engineering tools are a good motivator because they offer exposure to new technologies and a way to move toward CASE tools.

The insurance company experience thus far has shown that re-engineering is a complex process that requires the involvement of experienced, knowledgeable system maintainers. You cannot simply push a button and get a re-structured system. Box 5.2 summarizes the benefits that restructuring has provided to several other companies. Based on these and other experiences, we have learned that program logic restructuring is a practical, proven method for controlling software maintenance.

PROGRAM LOGIC RESTRUCTURING

> **Program logic restructuring is the process of reordering source code according to the rules of structured programming to make it more maintainable.**

BOX 5.2 Restructuring successes

Aetna Life & Casualty	Reduce maintenance staff for 3 million line COBOL system from 28 to 8 and reduce data names from 15,000 to 2,000.[4]
Dunlop Tire & Rubber	Change programming focus from error corrections to enhancements.[5]
Northwestern Mutual Life	Make maintenance changes to a PL/1 system in 50 hours instead of 500 hours.[6]
PacBell	Contain support costs in major systems.[7]
Pratt & Whitney	Reduce time to make changes to COBOL systems by 37 percent.[8]

The three basic functions of the program logic restructuring process are

- Reordering the program logic
- Reformatting the source code
- Standardizing the use of the programming language

Each of these functions is supported by program logic restructuring tools, whose beginnings can be traced back to the early 1980s.

STRUCTURED RETROFIT In the late 1970s, Lyons and deBalbine proposed "structured retrofit" as an automated method for introducing structured techniques and their benefits to existing software systems after the fact.[9] The objective was to improve the understandability of existing software and thereby improve their maintainability and extend their useful life. The first restructuring tools, called "structuring engines," were introduced in the early 1980s to transform unstructured FORTRAN (e.g., Caine, Faber & Gordon FORTRAN Engine) and COBOL (e.g., Catalyst Corporation COBOL Engine) into structured FORTRAN and COBOL programs.

WELL-STRUCTURED PROGRAMS Structured programming was introduced to control the quality of a program by managing its complexity. The key to managing complexity is standardization of program control structure and form. Like complexity metrics (discussed in Chapter 4), structured programming has a rigorous, mathematical base because it is founded on graph theory. In the 1960s, it was mathematically proved that all possible program logic control flows can be expressed using the three control constructs: sequence, selection, and iteration. These three control constructs are the basic building blocks for constructing the logic in a well-structured program.

> **Structured programming is a method of constructing a program according to a set of rules requiring a strict style format; a modular, hierarchical control structure; and a restricted set of logic constructs.**

The objectives of creating a well-structured program are to

- Improve program readability and reliability
- Minimize program complexity
- Simplify program maintenance
- Increase programmer productivity
- Provide a discipline for programming

The approaches used by structure programming to accomplish these objectives are to

- Minimize the number of program logic paths
- Limit program path patterns by restructuring the set of allowable control constructs
- Clarify program path meaning by requiring the flow of program control to return to the invoking module

A structured program is a modular program, where each module represents one logical task to be performed by the program. As shown in Fig. 5.1, the modules are hierarchically ordered. Modules performing the most general tasks are placed at the top of the hierarchy; those performing the most detailed tasks are placed at the bottom.

The standardized form of a well-structured program gives the reader one standard road map to follow through any structured program, regardless of its size or inherent complexity. Because of the hierarchical organization of the modules, the reader can understand the program in degrees, dealing with the next level of detail only when necessary. Box 5.3 summarizes the properties of a well-structured program.

Experiences from industry indicate that structured programs have a lower error frequency rate and a lower maintenance cost than equivalent, unstructured programs.[10]

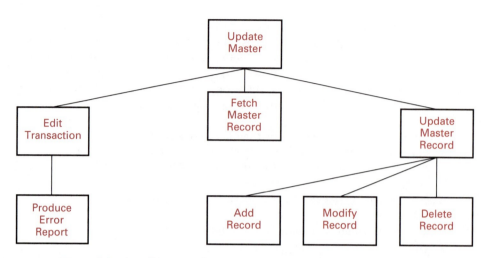

Figure 5.1 A well-structured program is a modular, hierarchically ordered program.

WHEN TO RESTRUCTURE

Restructuring the logic of a program to comply with the rules of structured programming can make it easier to understand and therefore easier to maintain. However, not all programs should be restructured. Programs that are familiar to the maintenance staff, that are infrequently changed, and that have a low error rate regardless of their coding style are probably best left as is. A basic rule of software maintenance is: **If it is not broken, do not fix it.**

BOX 5.3 Properties of a well-structured program

- Program is divided into a set of hierarchically arranged modules.
- Each module represents one logical, self-contained function.
- Program control constructs include sequence, selection, and repetition.
- Execution flow is restricted to one scheme in which control must enter a module at its entry point, leave from its exit point, and be passed back to the invoking module.
- Error processing follows normal control flow except in cases of unrecoverable errors where normal processing cannot continue.
- Each program variable serves only one purpose and the scope of the variable is apparent and limited.

Unfortunately, this rule does not apply to most existing software. Most existing software is broken in the sense that it is fragile, difficult to understand and change. For example, it is estimated that of the 80 billion lines of existing COBOL code, approximately 60 million lines are unstructured, "spaghetti" logic containing:[11]

- Excessive use of iteration loops
- Excessive use of nested IFs
- Embedded constants and literals
- Self-modifying code
- Multiple module entry and exit points
- Gigantic modules
- Multiple modules performing the same task

To replace this poor quality COBOL code will cost about $1.5 trillion.[12] To restructure it would cost a fraction of this amount.

Fragile software systems are the software systems that can most benefit from restructuring. However, not all 60 billion lines of unstructured COBOL are necessarily fragile. In general, fragile programs that are complex and error-prone as well as unstructured are top candidates for restructuring. Box 5.4 summarizes the characteristics of programs that are prime candidates for restructuring.

PROGRAM LOGIC RESTRUCTURING PROCESS

As shown in Fig. 5.2, the program logic restructuring process transforms unstructured source code into well-structured code usually with the aid of restructuring tools. The resulting structured program is functionally equivalent to the prestructured program because both programs per-

BOX 5.4 Candidate programs for restructuring

- Poor quality code
- Difficult (impossible) to read, change, and test code
- High error rate, correction time, and cost
- High/special staffing requirements
- Systems that are strategically important, expensive, and changed frequently

Program Restructuring Steps

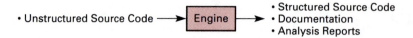

- Unstructured Source Code → Engine →
- Structured Source Code
- Documentation
- Analysis Reports

Steps

1. Automatically Analyze Unstructured Program
2. Review and Correct Unstructured Program
3. Automatically Generate Structured, Documented Program
4. Automatically Optimize Structured Program
5. Automatically Validate Structured Program

Figure 5.2 The program logic restructuring process transforms unstructured source code into well-structured code.

form the same sequence of operations on the same data. Of course, any logic errors contained in the prestructured program will be transferred to the newly structured program. The errors, though, will be easier to find and to repair in the structured version.

The advantage of the program logic restructuring process is that it can be performed by automated tools requiring only a small amount of human assistance. The restructuring process consists of these six basic steps:

1. Program code analyzers are used to analyze the unstructured program and reveal defects, such as dead code and infinite loops.
2. The unstructured program is compiled to identify and correct compilation errors (e.g., "E" level compilation errors).
3. Results of compilation and analyzers are reviewed and errors are corrected in the unstructured program. (This step requires human assistance.)
4. The corrected source code is automatically restructured and/or reformatted with the aid of restructuring tools.
5. The structured source code is recompiled with the aid of an optimizing compiler to enhance the program's efficiency.
6. The structured program is revalidated to ensure that the unstructured and structured versions of the program are functionally equivalent by processing the same data through both versions and comparing the results with comparers.

Benefits and Side Effects

Figure 5.3 is an example of the clean, structured, documented code that automated restructuring tools can produce. Programs such as the one shown in Fig. 5.3 have their complexity reduced to the lowest point possible given the nature of the task they perform, and are consequently easier to maintain. As illustrated in Fig. 5.4, studies have shown that restructured programs may be a third to a

Original FORTRAN-IV

```
        SUBROUTINE ORDSNE(PRI, IC, KAS, RC)
C  PURPOSE
C  IF PRI IS .TRUE. SUBROUTINE ORDSNE ORDERS ELEMENTS
C  OF VECTOR KAS IN INCREASING ORDER OF THEIR VALUES
C  AND VECTOR RC CORRESPONDINGLY. IF PRI IS .FALSE.
C  SUBROUTINE ORDSNE ORDERS ELEMENTS OF VECTOR RC IN
C  DECREASING ORDER OF THEIR VALUES AND VECTOR KAS
C  CORRESPONDINGLY.
        LOGICAL PRI
        DIMENSION RC(IC), KAS(IC)
        ID = -IC/2
10      IF (ID.GE.0) RETURN
        MQ = ID + IC
        DO 40 J=1,MQ
        I = J
20      IF (I.LT.1) GO TO 40
        JJ = I - ID
        IF (PRI) GO TO 50
        IF (RC(I).GE.RC(JJ)) GO TO 40
30      G = RC(I)
        RC(I) = RC(JJ)
        RC(JJ) = G
        II = KAS(I)
        KAS(I) = KAS(JJ)
        KAS(JJ) = II
        I = I + ID
        GO TO 20
40      CONTINUE
        ID = ID/2
        GO TO 10
50      IF (KAS(I).LE.KAS(JJ)) GO TO 40
        GO TO 30
        END
```

Standard FORTRAN-77 Output

```
C  Structured by FOR_STRUCT, v1.0.1
C  Options SET: s=7
        SUBROUTINE ORDSNE(PRI, IC, KAS, RC)
C  PURPOSE
C  IF PRI IS .TRUE. SUBROUTINE ORDSNE ORDERS ELEMENTS
C  OF VECTOR KAS IN INCREASING ORDER OF THEIR VALUES
C  AND VECTOR RC CORRESPONDINGLY. IF PRI IS .FALSE.
C  SUBROUTINE ORDSNE ORDERS ELEMENTS OF VECTOR RC IN
C  DECREASING ORDER OF THEIR VALUES AND VECTOR KAS
C  CORRESPONDINGLY.
        LOGICAL PRI
        DIMENSION RC(IC), KAS(IC)
        ID = - IC/2
10      IF( ID .GE. 0 ) RETURN
        MQ = ID + IC
        DO 40 J = 1, MQ
        I = J
20      IF( I .GE. 1 ) THEN
            JJ = I - ID
            IF( PRI ) THEN
                IF( KAS(I) .LE. KAS(JJ) ) GOTO 51
            ELSE IF( RC(I) .GE. RC(JJ) ) THEN
                GOTO 51
            ENDIF
            G = RC(I)
            RC(I) = RC(JJ)
            RC(JJ) = G
            II = KAS(I)
            KAS(I) = KAS(JJ)
            KAS(JJ) = II
            I = I + ID
            GOTO 20
        ENDIF
51      CONTINUE
40      CONTINUE
        ID = ID/2
        GOTO 10
        END
```

Figure 5.3 The FORTRAN code on the left is not well structured and contains loops formed by GO TO statements. The code on the right, produced by the restructuring tool FOR__STRUCT from Cobalt Blue, is structured to standard FORTRAN-77 and reduces the number of GO TO statements.

half less expensive to maintain than their unstructured predecessors.[13] However, some negative side effects of restructuring must be taken into consideration.

The learning curve for newly structured programs is one of the costs of logic restructuring. It takes time for the maintainers to become familiar with the program in its new form. Another type of cost is associated with program efficiency. Structured programs often are bigger than their unstructured predecessors, and do not run as efficiently. One study reported the average increase in

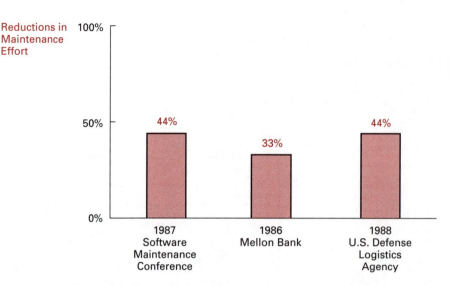

Figure 5.4 Reports indicate that restructured programs may be a third to a half less expensive to maintain than their unstructured predecessors.

the number of source code statements was 26 percent, and an average of 9 percent more CPU time was required by the program after it was restructured.[14]

Furthermore, the restructuring process may resequence program modules (e.g., COBOL paragraphs), and new paragraphs or procedures with unfamiliar or meaningless names may be added. Also, many of the comments from the old program may be rendered meaningless in the newly structured version. Finally, because some restructuring tools cannot handle exceptions, such as multiple exits or forward branching to the module exit point, they can actually make the program logic more complicated by introducing many NOTs and ANDs into the code.

Restructuring Method

Program logic restructurers eliminate GO TOs, fallthrough logic, dead code, recursion, runaway paths, and infinite loops and create modular, hierarchically ordered, well-structured programs. How is this accomplished? Many restructurers use a code restructuring method that is based on a graph theory approach (see Fig. 5.5).

Recall from Chapter 4 that with graph theory we can use a flow graph to model the control flow of logic in a program. The graph is made up of lines and points, where the points represent one or more sequential (i.e., noncontrol) program statement(s) and the lines represent the control paths between the statements.

As we can see in Fig. 5.6, to restructure a program the restructuring tool reads the source code and creates a flow graph of the unstructured program.

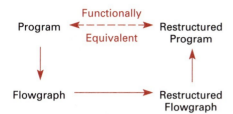

Figure 5.5 Many program logic restructuring tools use a code restructuring method that is based on a graph theory approach.

Then, starting at the point in the flow graph that represents the most deeply nested IF statement (in our example, statement 3), it applies a series of structuring transformations, such as the conversion of a GO TO to a PERFORMed routine. During this transformation, only the lines of the graph are modified, changing the control paths between statements. The points, representing the statements themselves, remain unchanged. Then, the restructuring tool selects the next most deeply nested IF statement (in our example, statement 2) and does the same transformation. This iterative process continues to the outermost IF until all the transformations have been made. The process normally requires one to four CPU minutes.

Besides modifying control paths, restructuring tools also perform actual code modifications. For example, they can create one mainline paragraph (procedure) and extract to it the program's highest-level control logic; they can isolate the program's other control logic from its I/O, consolidating both separately; they can split and combine routines if necessary; and they can remove dead code and other nonstandard constructs such as ALTER statements in COBOL.

Restructuring tools separate form from function. They modify the form, but the function stays the same. Even though the new version is structured and somewhat modified, it is still functionally equivalent to the original, unstructured version. Because the restructuring process is based on graph theory, it is possible to prove mathematically that the prestructured version and the structured version are functionally equivalent.

Once all the transformations and modifications have been made, the restructuring tool generates new source code. This source code reflects all the structured transformations of the flow graph control paths, as well as the code modifications (see Fig. 5.6).

PROGRAM LOGIC RESTRUCTURING TOOLS

Program logic restructuring tools read in program source code, analyze and restructure logic paths using graph theory, and create new source that is clean, structured, formatted, and functionally equivalent to the original unstructured program.

```
1  START
2  IF <condition> THEN
3      IF <condition> THEN
            GO TO 4
        ELSE
            GO TO 5
        ENDIF
    ELSE
            GO TO 8
    ENDIF
4  DO A
   DO B
   GO TO 8
5  DO C
   DO D
8  END
```

Functionally Equivalent

```
1  START
2  IF <condition> THEN
3      IF <condition> THEN
4          DO A
           DO B
       ELSE
5          DO C
           DO D
6      ENDIF
7  ENDIF
8  END
```

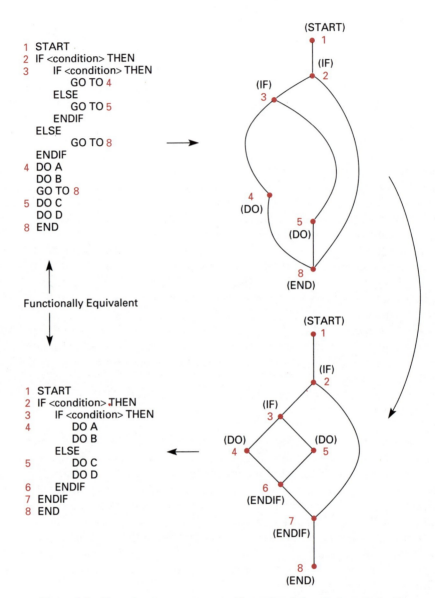

Figure 5.6 To restructure a program, the restructuring tool reads in the source code and converts it to a flow graph.

A logic restructuring tool can be offered as a product or a service. It is language-specific. Most restructuring tools support COBOL or FORTRAN and most are batch tools. Their primary function is the one-time, program-by-program conversion of unstructured source code into its structured form. The structured version of each program then replaces the unstructured

version in the source library and becomes the object of further maintenance.
Program logic restructuring tools perform the following functions:

- Restructure program logic
- Implement user-selected structuring options
- Implement user-selected formatting options
- Produce program analysis reports and documentation

Structuring Options

Restructuring tools make many changes to the form of the program while keeping the function the same. Because they are batch tools, the user does not interact with the tool during the restructuring process and does not see the flow graph form of the program. However, users may make choices about the specific nature of the structuring done by the tool through the selection of various structuring options.

Figure 5.7 is an example of unstructured COBOL code. Figure 5.8 is the equivalent structured code produced by a restructuring tool. Notice that all GO TOs have been eliminated from the code. It follows the strictest rules of structured programming in which the GO TO is not considered a legal control construct. Figure 5.9 is another structured version for the COBOL code shown in Fig. 5.7. Note that in this version a well-behaved GO TO (i.e., a GO TO statement in a module that branches to that module's entry point or exit point) is allowed.

The restructuring tool gives the user a choice on how strictly the rules of structured programming are to be imposed. The user-selected options along with the unstructured source code are the input to the restructuring tool. For example, when restructuring COBOL, users may choose

- *Mainline creation:* Whether or not to extract the highest-level control logic to newly created mainline paragraph.

```
ADD-PROJ.
  IF PROJ-CODE AND NEW-PROG NEXT
  SENTENCE ELSE
  GO TO ADD-PROG.
  IF INDX-P IS EQUAL TO 100 GO TO
  WRITE-REC.
  MOVE EXP-REV-PROJ TO PROJ-TABL (INDX-P).
  MOVE NO-PROG-OR-TE TO MODE-T (INDX-P).
  ADD 1 TO INDX-P.
```

Figure 5.7 An example of unstructured COBOL code containing multiple entry points and exit points and GO TO branches outside of the paragraph.

```
0960-RETOOL.
    *PERFORMED BY 0940-WRITE-GOOD-RECORD.
    IF PROJ-CODE AND NEW-PROJ
      IF INDX-P IS EQUAL TO 100
      PERFORM 0980-WRITE-REC
    ELSE
      MOVE EXP-REV-PROJ TO PROJ-TABL :(INDX-P)
      MOVE NO-PROG-OR-TE TO MODE-T(INDX-:P)
      ADD 1 TO INDX-P
      PERFORM 0970-ADD-PROG
      PERFORM 0980-WRITE-REC
    ELSE
      PERFORM 0970-ADD-PROG
      PERFORM 0980-WRITE-REC.
```

Figure 5.8 This restructured COBOL code for the code shown in Fig. 5.7 was produced by Retool, from Computer Data Systems, Inc. Note that no GO TOs are allowed.

```
0940-SUPERSTRUCTURE.
    * * * * * * * * * * * * * * * * * * * * * * *
    * PERFORMED BY 0930-ADD-PROJ *
    * * * * * * * * * * * * * * * * * * * * * * *
    IF PROJ-CODE
      AND NEW-PROJ
        NEXT SENTENCE
      ELSE
        PERFORM 0950-ADD-PROG THRU 0950-END.
        GO TO 0940-END.
      IF INDX-P IS EQUAL TO 100
        PERFORM 0960-WRITE-REC THRU 0960-END.
      GO TO 0940-END
      MOVE EXP-REV-PROJ TO PROJ-TABL (INDX-P),
      MOVE NO-PROG-OR-TE TO MODE-T (INDX-P).
      ADD 1 TO INDX-P.
      PERFORM 0950-ADD-PROG THRU-0950-END.
0940-END.
    EXIT.
```

Figure 5.9 This restructured COBOL code, produced by Retool from Computer Data Systems, Inc., allows a well-behaved GO TO that branches to the paragraph exit.

- *Nesting:* The selection of the limit of nested IFs allowed before a new paragraph is generated.
- *Logic style:* Whether to use an IF-IF-IF construct or an IF-AND-AND construct; whether to transform negative logic (e.g., AND NOT) to positive logic.
- *Iteration looping style:* Whether to use a DO UNTIL option for paragraph iteration or loop to the top of the paragraph with a GO TO.
- *Perform style:* Whether to use PERFORMs, PERFORM THROUGHs, or SECTIONS for COBOL programs.
- *Paragraph (procedure) names:* Whether the tool automatically assigns new paragraph names or whether the assignment is done manually.
- *Paragraph (module) ordering:* The means of ordering the sequence of modules in the source code listing. The user could choose to keep the existing order, could order the modules so that all the high-level modules come first followed by the next highest-level modules and so on, or could order them so that each high-level module is followed by all the modules it calls.
- *Module size:* The selection of a minimum and maximum size for modules in the new program. If modules are smaller, they will not be created; if they are larger, they will be broken down into series of smaller modules performed sequentially.
- *Paragraph (module) folding:* The selection of a limit threshold that determines whether a repeated chunk of source code is placed in a newly created paragraph or whether the code is simply replicated when needed.

When restructuring FORTRAN, the following FORTRAN constructs can be converted into a structured form:

- Arithmetic IF and block IF converted to an IF-THEN-ELSEIF-ENDIF form
- DO WHILE loops converted from IF-GOTO to DOWHILE-ENDDO form
- Computed GOTO converted from GOTO (S [,s] . . .) [,] Int_expr to IF-THEN-ELSEIF-ENDIF form

With some tools, the user can choose to convert the FORTRAN program to another language, such as C, as part of the restructuring process (see Figs. 5.10 and 5.11).

Besides selecting structuring options to determine the style of a restructured source code, users may also select formatting options.

Formatting Options

For COBOL program restructuring tools, users may select formatting options such as the following:

- *Paragraph prefixing:* Whether to add or delete prefixes to paragraph names to reflect any new paragraph ordering.

FORTRAN
```
      PROGRAM ODE
C     Solve Ordinary D.E. by RUNGE-KUTTA Method
      PARAMETER( NPTS=51 )
      DIMENSION X(NPTS),Y(NPTS)
      WRITE(*,*) 'Please enter the initial condition'
      READ(*,*) Y0
      WRITE(*,*) 'Please enter the range of X'
      READ(*,*) X0, XN
C     Echo the Input values
      WRITE(*,'(" I.C.:" F7.3,/," Indep. Range: ",F7.3," to ",F7.3)')
     & Y0, X0, XN
      AA = RUNGKUT(X0,XN,Y0,NPTS,X,Y)  !solve the ODE
      DO 10 I=1,NPTS
  10  WRITE(*,*) 'X(',i,') =', X(I), ' Y(',I,') =',Y(I)
      STOP
      END

C     This function solves an Ordinary D. E. of the form: Y'=F(X,Y)
C     by a 4th Order RUNGE KUTTA technique.
C     The number of points, N, should include the Initial Condition.
C     The solution to the ODE is returned via the arrays X(I) & Y(I).
C     The function is supplied as a statement function, FXY(X,Y)
      FUNCTION RUNGKUT(X0,XN,Y0,N,X,Y)
      DIMENSION X(N),Y(N)
      REAL K1,K2,K3,K4
      FXY(X,Y) = Y+EXP(-X)    ! ODE to solve
      H= (XN-X0)/(N-1) ! step size
      Y(1) = Y0
      DO 10 I=1,N-1
      X(I)= X0 + (I-1)*H
      X(I+1)= X(I) + H
       K1=FXY(X(I),Y(I))
       K2=FXY(X(I)+0.5*H,Y(I)+0.5*H*K1)
       K3=FXY(X(I)+0.5*H,Y(I)+0.5*H*K2)
       K4=FXY(X(I+1),Y(I)+H*K3)
  10  Y(U+1) = Y(I) + (H/6.)*(K1 + 2.*K2 + 2.*K3 + K4)I)
      RUNGKUT + Y(N)    ! Return last value of Y
      RETURN
      END
```

Figure 5.10 An example of FORTRAN code.

- *IF, CASE alignment:* How to handle the indentation for nested IFs and CASE statements.
- *Verb alignment:* Sets indentation rules for verbs (e.g., MOVE . . . TO . . .).
- *DATA DIVISION leveling:* How to number the data element levels in the DATA DIVISION (e.g., 01, 05, 10 vs. 01, 02, 03).
- *77-level replacement:* Whether to replace all 77-level data elements with 01-level data elements.
- *Reserved word use:* Whether to keep, convert, or remove COBOL reserved words (THEN, NEXT SENTENCE, etc.).

```c
/*Translated by FOR_C, v3.0, on 06/28/90 at 11:25:30 */
/*FOR_C Options SET: cio no=d - prototypes */
#include <stdio.h>
#include <math.h>
#include <f_rt.h>
#include "ode.h"
#include <f_io.h>
#define NPTS    51

main( argc, argv )
int argc; char *argv[];
{
int i, i_;
float aa, x[NPTS], x0, xn, y[NPTS], y0;

        f77_ini(argc,argv);
        /*      Solve Ordinary D.E. by RUNGE-KUTTA Method */
        fprintf( stdout, "Please enter the initial condition\n" );
        fscanld( stdin, "%f ", &y0 );
        fprintf( stdout, "Please enter the range of X\n" );
        fscanld( stdin, "%f %f ", &x0, &xn );
        /*   Echo the Input values */
        fprintf( stdout, "  I.C.:%7.3f\n Indep. Range: %7.3f to %7.3f\n",
         y0, x0, xn );
        aa = rungkut( x0, xn, y0, NPTS, x, y );      /*solve the ODE */
        for( i = 1; i <= NPTS; i++ ){
                i_ = i - 1;
                fprintf( stdout, "X(%d ) =%g    Y(%d ) =%g \n", i, x[i_], i, y[i_] );
                }
        exit(0);
} /* end of function */

/*      This function solves an Ordinary D. E. of the form:  Y'=F(X,Y)
 *         by a 4th Order RUNGE KUTTA technique.
 *      The number of points, N, should include the Initial Condition.
 *      The solution to the ODE is returned via the arrays X(I) & Y(I).
 *      The function is supplied as a statement function, FXY(X,Y) */
double /*FUNCTION*/ rungkut(x0, xn, y0, n, x, y)
double x0, xn, y0;
int n;
float x[], y[];
{
int i, i_;
float h, k1, k2, k3, k4, rungkut_v;

#define FXY(x,y)        (float)((y) + exp( -(x) ))     /* ODE to solve */
        h = (xn - x0)/(n - 1); /* step size */
        y[0] = y0;
        for( i = 1; i <= (n - 1); i++ ){
                i_ = i - 1;
                x[i_] = x0 + (i - 1)*h;
                x[i_ + 1] = x[i_] + h;
                k1 = FXY( x[i_], y[i_] );
                k2 = FXY( x[i_] + 0.5*h, y[i_] + 0.5*h*k1 );
                k3 = FXY( x[i_] + 0.5*h, y[i_] + 0.5*h*k2 );
                k4 = FXY( x[i_ + 1], y[i_] + h*k3 );
                y[i_ + 1] = y[i_] + (h/6.)*(k1 + 2.*k2 + 2.*k3 + k4);
                }
        rungkut_v = y[n - 1]; /* Return last value of Y */
        return( rungkut_v );
#undef  FXY
} /* end of function */
```

Figure 5.11 The FORTRAN code in Fig. 5.10 is converted into C code by the tool FOR__STRUCT, from Cobalt Blue.

- *Period usage:* Whether to add a period where possible at the end of each statement.
- *Comments:* Whether to delete or retain existing comments.
- *Blank line handling:* Whether to maintain existing blank lines, remove them, or add a set number between paragraphs.
- *COMPUTE:* Whether to replace ADD and SUBTRACT statements with COMPUTE statements.
- *Relational operators:* Whether to spell out relational operators or keep them as symbols (e.g., <).
- *Quotes:* Whether to use single or double quotes.

Analysis and Documentation

The main job of logic restructuring tools is to create a clean, structured program from an unstructured one. However, these tools also create program analysis reports and program documentation so that maintainers can quickly learn their way around the newly structured versions of their programs.

Restructuring tools typically produce the following kinds of analysis and documentation:

- Metrics and counts
- Logic analysis
- Structure chart
- Modularization aid

Metrics and Counts

These reports show complexity and structuredness metrics, as well as various counts (e.g., GO TOs, fallthroughs, ALTERs) for the program both before and after restructuring. They are similar to the metrics and counts described in Chapter 4.

Logic Analysis—Trace and Problems

A logic trace creates comments for each paragraph in the newly restructured program. The comments identify for each paragraph all the other paragraphs that call this particular paragraph. Logic problems identify such things as recursion, dead code, premature exits, and nonreturning paragraphs. The logic analysis done here is similar to that described in Chapter 4.

Structure Chart

This is an indented narrative structure chart that shows the paragraph calling hierarchy of the new program.

BOX 5.5 Program code restructure features checklist

Level of Restructuring

_____ Program _____ Online

_____ System _____ Batch

_____ Library

Language(s) Restructured

Input to Tool

_____ JCL

_____ Source code

_____ Load modules

_____ Copy books

Output from Tool

_____ Revised source code

_____ New copy books

_____ Standardized data names

       _____ Record level

       _____ Element level

_____ Standardized data definitions

       _____ Record level

       _____ Element level

_____ Where used/cross-reference reports

Code Restructuring

_____ Create one mainline paragraph with single entry/exit

_____ Eliminate GO TOs, ALTERs, FALLTHROUGHS

_____ Isolate and consolidate I/O

_____ Split and combine routine if necessary

_____ Remove dead code

Restructuring Options

_____ Mainline creation

_____ Permissible levels of nesting

(Continued)

BOX 5.5 *(Continued)*

_____ IF-IF-IF vs. IF-AND-AND
_____ PERFORM UNTIL vs. GO TO TOP OF PARAGRAPH
_____ PERFORM vs. PERFORM THRU
_____ Paragraph ordering
_____ Paragraph folding vs. separation (determines whether replicated or performed)
_____ Automatic vs. manual assignment of new paragraph names
_____ Elimination of negative logic

Code Formatting

_____ Verb alignment
_____ DATA DIVISION leveling
_____ 77-level replacement
_____ IF, CASE format alignment
_____ ADD/SUBTRACT vs. COMPUTE
_____ Paragraph prefix removal
_____ Deletion/Retention of old comments

Analysis and Documentation

Modularization Aids

    _____ Identification of procedures to remove or duplicate in new program
    _____ Identification on a paragraph basis of all code that can be reached via this paragraph

Logic Trace

    _____ Comments in code for each paragraph
    _____ Identifying all locations from which control could come
    _____ Structure chart showing paragraph/module calling sequence

Metrics and Counts

    _____ Complexity metrics
    _____ ALTERs
    _____ GO TOs
    _____ FALLTHROUGHs
    _____ PERFORMs

Modularization Aid

Often, programs selected for restructuring are not only complex but also extremely large. Consequently, the newly restructured program is also large and would be easier to maintain if it were broken down into a set of smaller programs. When this is the case, the modularization aid helps analysts figure out how to divide the program into a set of smaller, more manageable programs. It identifies blocks of the program (e.g., a paragraph and all the other paragraphs it calls) that can be removed and placed in a new program. For each program block recommended for removal, it also identifies the paragraphs in the old program that must be duplicated in the new program.

A KNOWN RE-ENGINEERING TECHNIQUE Logic restructuring tools are the most mature and most used type of re-engineering tool. Hundreds of organizations have successfully used restructuring as a practical means of improving the understandability of their existing programs. Box 5.5 provides a checklist of the features to look for in logic restructuring tools.

REFERENCES

1. Ralph Carlyle, "Fighting Corporate Amnesia," *Datamation,* February 1, 1989, pp. 41–44.

2. Karen Guillo, "Automating Software Support Is the Cause Celebre in IS Shops," *Datamation,* January 1, 1988, pp. 19, 22.

3. Parikh Girish, "Restructuring Your COBOL Programs," *ComputerWorld Focus,* February 19, 1987, pp. 39–42.

4. Johanna Ambrosio, "Finally Coming into Its Own—Reverse Engineering Technology Makes Headway in IS Organizations," *ComputerWorld,* October 22, 1990, pp. 25, 36.

5. William M. Ulrich, "The Evolutionary Growth of Software Re-engineering and the Decade Ahead," *American Programmer,* 3, no. 10 (October 1990), 14–20.

6. Ambrosio, "Finally Coming into Its Own."

7. Ulrich, "The Evolutionary Growth of Software Re-engineering and the Decade Ahead."

8. "A Success Story at Pratt & Whitney: On Track for the Future with IBM's VS COBOL II and COBOL Structuring Facility," *IBM US Marketing & Services Report,* 1989.

9. M. J. Lyons, "Salvaging Your Software Asset (Tools-Based Maintenance)," *AFIPS Conference Proceedings on 1981 National Computer Conference* (Chicago), vol. 50 (Chicago, May 4–7, 1981), pp. 332–342.

10. James Martin and Carma McClure, *Software Maintenance: The Problem and Its Solution,* (Englewood Cliffs, NJ, Prentice Hall, 1983), pp. 75–105.

11. R. J. Martin and W. M. Osborne, "System Maintenance vs. System Redesign," in *Tutorial on Software Restructuring,* (Washington, DC: IEEE Computer Society Press, 1986), pp. 258–261.

12. Eric Bush, "A CASE for Existing Systems," *Language Technology White Paper,* Salem, MA (1988), p. 27.

13. "Application Re-engineering," MP-1411, *Guide 72,* 1989.

14. C. Babcock, "Restructuring Eases Maintenance," *ComputerWorld,* November 30, 1987, pp. 21–22.

6 DATA RESTRUCTURING

ROAD BLOCKS TO UNDERSTANDABILITY It is obvious that meaningful names and standard definitions for program data improve program readability. For example, consider the following two COBOL COMPUTE statements:

COMPUTE EXPENSES = TRANSPORTATION + MEALS + LODGING

COMPUTE E = E1 + E2 + E3

The first COMPUTE statement conveys substantially more information about the program than does the second because of the choice of data element names.

Below are three different names and definitions for employee number. Which is correct and which is the one the maintenance programmer should use?

```
01 EMPLOYEE-NUMBER  PIC X(4).
05 CP-EMP-NO         PIC 9999.
02 EMPL-NUM          PIC 9(9).
```

Standardizing data names and definitions will greatly lessen maintenance confusion, effort, and errors. This may be the single most important key to program readability. The results of several programming experiments point out that the larger and more complex a program, the more important meaningful, standardized data names and standardized data definitions become.[1] Many system maintainers waste a great deal of their time trying to make sense out of programs that are full of meaningless, "cute" data names (e.g., TOMS-PLACE) and inconsistent data definitions.

DATA RESTRUCTURING

Like program logic restructuring, data restructuring improves the maintainability of existing systems by improving their understandability. Logic restructuring standardizes program logic; data restructuring standardizes program data. But, unlike logic restructuring, which is normally done at the program level, data restructuring is a form of system-level restructuring. To optimize understandability, the data used in a system should always be defined in the same way and called by the same name across the system.

Data restructuring is the process of standardizing data names and data definitions across a system(s).

Data restructuring is performed to position existing systems for migration to new technologies, such as dictionaries and repositories, data modeling, database management systems, and software reusability. Besides making systems easier to understand, data restructuring offers other benefits, such as enforcing corporate standards and conventions and reducing maintenance effort and costs. Box 6.1 lists the benefits of data restructuring.

Candidates for Data Restructuring

Systems with the following characteristics are prime candidates for data restructuring:

- Nonstandard, meaningless data names
- Inconsistent data definitions

BOX 6.1 Data restructuring benefits

- Improves understandability of existing systems
- Enables cost-effective system maintainability
- Increases productivity of system maintainers
- Enforces corporate standards and conventions
- Eliminates inconsistent record definitions, field sizes, and redundant data elements
- Supports creation of data dictionaries and data modeling
- Improves data documentation
- Positions systems for technology migrations
- Enables reuse of existing data structures (meta data)

- Hard-coded literals and record definitions
- Lack of auditability

If data restructuring is done prior to such projects as creating a corporate data dictionary, populating a CASE repository, migrating to a database management system, or even simply expanding a data field size, millions of dollars and many staff-years of effort potentially can be saved. Some organizations have abandoned seemingly simple projects such as increasing the zip code field to nine digits after determining that the project would require a staff-year to change, hundreds of programs would be affected, and many programs were likely to crash as a result of the change. By restructuring the program data, and using other re-engineering tools, such as program code analyzers, to determine everywhere in the programs where zip code was defined and referenced, such a change can be made safely within a few weeks.

DATA RESTRUCTURING TOOLS

Like program logic restructuring, data restructuring can be most efficiently and effectively performed when aided by automated re-engineering tools. Data restructuring tools gather, group, analyze, and modify record and program data element names and definitions across programs and systems to ensure that all data used in a system are defined in the same way and called by the same name. They also are able to populate the corporate data dictionary with these newly formed standard names and definitions and other attribute and where-used information produced by the restructuring process.

The ability to populate the data dictionary is very important because it can help an organization not only to clean up and restructure its data but also to keep it that way. Data dictionaries provide an automated mechanism for managing data definition changes and enforcing consistent use of data across the corporation. Being able to find easily information describing the location, edit criteria, and description of each data element will help shorten the time needed to understand and to change the system.

As shown in Fig. 6.1, automated data restructurers read in source code, JCL, load modules, copy books, and data descriptions and create as their output revised source and new copy books with standardized data element and record names. They also produce analysis reports and create files for export to data dictionaries, CASE tools, and repositories.

Data restructurers do their job by performing four functions:

- Data record analysis and updating
- Data element trace and updating
- Data dictionary load
- Operations environment analysis

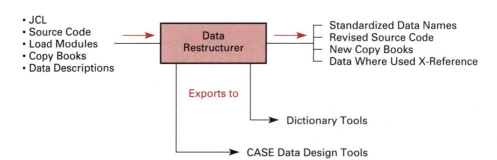

Figure 6.1 Data restructuring tools read in source code, JCL, load modules, copy books, and data definitions to create revised source code with standardized data names and definitions.

Data Record Analysis and Updating

Data record analysis and updating is a step-by-step process that requires a knowledgeable system maintainer. First, the data restructuring tool reads in all of its inputs and pulls from them all the record definitions (i.e., FDs, database segments) identified in the various input source and copy libraries. It then separates these record definitions by length and format, with the goal of grouping together all the various descriptions from different programs of the same physical file. For example, a payroll master file might appear in ten different programs under ten different FD names, but each program's file definition would have the same length and would have the same sequence of format types (alpha, numeric, etc.). This fact would be a clue that they are all referencing the same physical file. Because this operation is not foolproof, the maintainer steps back into the process at this point to make the final determination.

The data restructuring tool outputs a list of records grouped by length and format type, as shown in Fig. 6.2, and the maintainer reviews and corrects the groupings to ensure that all record definitions grouped together truly reference the same physical file. Then the tool creates a "composite record" for each correct grouping. As you can see in Fig. 6.3, the first field in the top two records, C-ACCOUNT-NUM and ACCT-NUM, appears in the composite records as XXX-C-ACCOUNT-NUM. These automatically assigned data element names can then be changed by the maintainer to more complete and meaningful names that meet corporate standards.

After the composite record for each physical file has been verified by the maintainer, the data restructuring tool completes the job by

- Replacing all the old record definitions in all of the involved source code and copy libraries with the new composite record definition.
- Propagating the new names through the PROCEDURE DIVISION of all the involved programs by changing all the references from the original names to the new composite record names.

```
RECORD
LENGTH   PROGRAM-ID   RECORD NAME            USAGE


 115     PROG0011     CUSTOMER-RECORD        INPUT,READ
         PROG0019     CUST-REC               INPUT,READ

 140     PROG0002     MONTHLY-ADJ            INPUT,READ
                      MONTHLY-CASH           INPUT,READ
                      MONTHLY-CHG            INPUT,READ
         PROG0005     MONTH-CHARGE-RECORD    INTO
         PROG0012     MONTHLY-CHARGE         MOVE
                      MONTHLY-IN             INPUT,READ
         PROG0014     MTHLY-CHG              INTO
         PROG0015     MONTHLY-CASH-OUT       OUTPUT,WRITE

 175     PROG0026     BKUP-RECORD            OUTPUT,WRITE

 180     PROG0006     TRANSACTION-INPUT      INPUT,READ
                      TRANS-IN               INTO
         PROG00009    TRANS-OUT              OUTPUT, WRITE
         PROG0015     WS-TRANS-REC           FROM
         PROG0020     PASS-TRANS             LINK
                      WK-TRANSACTION         MOVE

 220     PROG0017     TAPE-OUT               OUTPUT,WRITE
         PROG0031     TAPE-IN                INPUT,READ
         PROG0032     TAPE-REC               INPUT,READ

 500     PROG00007    MASTER-DETAIL-REC      INPUT,READ
                      MASTER-HEADER-REC      INPUT,READ
                      MASTER-INQUIRY-REC     INPUT,READ
                      MASTER-SUMMARY-REC     INPUT,READ
         PROG0014     PRODUCT-RECORD         INTO
         PROG0016     PROD-REC               INPUT,OUTPUT,READ,WRITE
                      INQ-REC                MOVE
         PROG0019     PRODUCT-MASTER         OUTPUT,WRITE
         PROG0022     MASTER-RECORD          FROM
         PROG0024     WS-PRODUCT-AREA        CICS
         PROG0027     PRODUCT-MASTER         OUTPUT,WRITE
         PROG0031     DTL-REC                INPUT,READ
                      HDR-REC                INPUT,READ
         PROG0032     PRODUCT-MASTER         INTO

 740     PROG0016     WS-PASS-PARMS          CALL
         PROG0018     CAL1-PARMS             CALL
         PROG0023     PARAMETER-LIST         LINK
         PROG0026     T40AC1-PARMS           LINK
         PROG0034     PASS-PARMS             CALL

 960     PROG0005     SCREEN1                CICS
                      SCREEN0                CICS
         PROG0006     QUERY1                 CICS
                      QUERY0                 CICS
```

Figure 6.2 Example of a record grouping analysis performed by the data restructuring tool DataTEC, from XA Systems.

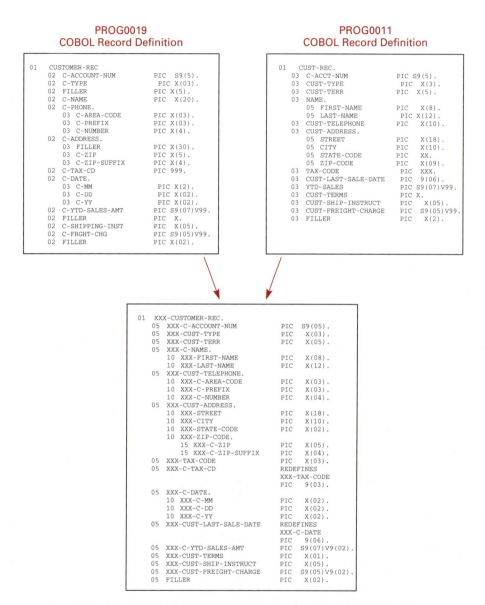

Figure 6.3 Example of a composite record built by the data restructuring tool DataTEC, from XA Systems.

After this operation, the maintainer must then verify all the changes and test all the programs to ensure that no errors were introduced. In this way, an entire system or portfolio of systems can have all the data elements in its records standardized with consistent, meaningful names and format definitions.

Because this process applies only to the data elements that happen to be in a system's records, the next function standardizes the rest of the data elements in the system: those defined, not in records, but in WORKING-STORAGE SECTION.

Data Element Trace and Updating

This function allows the maintainer to identify, trace, and update the name of any data element in a program, as well as the names of all the data elements related to it. If, for example, a data element named INPUT-PAY is defined in a record and its value (e.g., 1000) is moved to a data element named GROSS-PAY, then INPUT-PAY and GROSS-PAY are related data elements because they both contain the same value. If the name of the INPUT-PAY data element is changed to RO1-WEEKLY-GROSS-PAY, the maintainer should know that GROSS-PAY is a related data element so that its name could also be changed to RO1-WEEKLY-GROSS-PAY if appropriate. By analyzing the program's data handling (MOVEs, REDEFINEs, WORKING-STORAGE groupings, etc.), the data element trace function lists the related data elements for each data element that the maintainer specifies. In this way, it is possible to trace the path that a particular data value takes through a program. Figure 6.4 shows an example of a data element trace.

Data element trace is useful in many situations. For example, as a result of data record analysis and updating, the names of many composite record data elements will change. This function allows the maintainer to trace the movement of the values in these data elements, so related data element names may also be changed if appropriate to maintain consistency. Also, if the size of any data element must change, the related data elements can be identified so that their size can be changed as well.

The data element trace also is generally useful for restructuring data elements not specifically related to input records. For example, it can identify a data element that is used for more than one purpose (i.e., a homonym); it can identify two or more data elements that are used for the same purpose (i.e., a synonym); it can identify mismatched source and target field lengths; and it can be used to analyze the impact of any field length expansion.

Once all the data element names requiring change are known, the maintainer builds a list of the old names and new names, and the data restructuring tool uses it to change the names in WORKING-STORAGE and propagate them throughout the PROCEDURE DIVISION. An example of such a list is shown in Fig. 6.5.

Data Dictionary Load

Both the data record analysis and updating function and the data element trace and updating function allow the maintainer to convert inconsistent and meaningless data element names to ones that are standardized and meaningful. During

```
                                              DATA ELEMENT TRACE REPORT
PROGRAM ID: PROG0019



                              ┌─── Data element
                              │
                              ▼
STANDARD NAME: CUST-ACCOUNT-NUMBER
 MOVE I01-CUST-ACCOUNT-NUMBER IO WS-NUM(1,5,X)
 MOVE HOLD-ACCOUNT91,5,X) IO I01-CUST-ACCOUNT-NUMBER
 MOVE I01-CUST-ACCOUNT-NUMBER TO ACCT-NO(1,5,X)
 MOVE I01-CUSTOMER-MASTER-RECORD(I01-CUST-ACCOUNT-NUMBER) TO SAVE-REC(1,5,X)
    MOVE HOLD-ACCOUNT(1,5,X) TO WK-FIELD(1,5,X)                     Related data
    MOVE HOLD-ACCOUNT(1,5,X) TO ACCT-HIST-NUMBER(1,5,G)             elements
    MOVE ACCT-NO(1,5,X) TO C-A(1,5,X)                               and source
       MOVE ACCT(1,5,G) TO C-A(1,5,X)
       MOVE C-A(1,5,X) TO SAVE-NUM(1,5,X)
          MOVE SAVE-NUM(1,5,X) TO WK-FIELD(1,5,G)

STANDARD NAME:  CUST-TERRITORY
 MOVE I01-CUST-TERRITORY TO CR-TERRTY(1,5,X)
 MOVE I01-CUSTOMER-MASTER-RECORD(I01-CUST-TERRITORY) TO SAVE-REC(9,13,X)

STANDARD NAME:  CUST-LAST-NAME
 MOVE I01-CUST-LAST-NAME TO P-NAME(1,12,X)
 MOVE I01-CUST-NAME(I01-CUST-LAST-NAME) TO SV-NAME(SV-LAST-NAME)
 MOVE CUST-IDENT(9,20,X) TO I01-CUST-NAME(I01-CUST-LAST-NAME)
 MOVE CUSTOMER-N(9,20,X) TO I01-CUST-NAME(I01-CUST-LAST-NAME)
 MOVE I01-CUSTOMER-MASTER-RECORD(I01-CUST-LAST-NAME) TO SAVE-REC(22,33,X)
    MOVE SV-LAST-NAME(1,12,X) TO P-L-NAME(1,12,X)

STANDARD NAME:  CUST-ZIP-CODE
 MOVE I01-CUST-ZIP-CODE TO WK-ZIP(1,9,X)
 MOVE I01-CUST-ADDRESS(I01-CUST-ZIP-CODE) TO SV-ADDR(SV-ZIP)
 MOVE I01-CUSTOMER-MASTER-RECORD(I01-CUST-LAST-SALE-DATE) TO SAVE-REC(74,82,X)
    MOVE WK-ZIP(1,9,X) TO P-Z(1,9,X)
    MOVE NUMBER(1,5,X) TO WK-ZIP-FIRST-PART(1,5,X)
    MOVE SV-ZIP(1,9,X) TO P-Z(1,9,X)

STANDARD NAME:  CUST-LAST-SALE-DATE
 MOVE I01-CUST-LAST-SALE-DATE TO DATE(1,6,G)
 MOVE I01-CUSTOMER-MASTER-RECORD(I01-CUST-LAST-SALE-DATE) TO SAVE-REC(86,91,X)
    MOVE MONTH(1,2,X) TO WS-MM(1,2,X)

STANDARD NAME:  CUST-YTD-SALES-AMOUNT
 MOVE I01-CUST-YTD-SALES-AMOUNT TO AMOUNT(1,9,X)
 MOVE I01-CUSTOMER-MASTER-RECORD(I01-CUST-YTD-SALES-AMOUNT) TO SAVE-REC(92,100,X)
    MOVE ACCUM-DOLLARS(1,4,B) TO AMOUNT(1,9,X)
    MOVE AMOUNT(1,9,X) TO P-YTD(1,9,X)
```

Figure 6.4 Example of data element trace report produced by the data restructuring tool DataTEC, from XA Systems.

```
        OLD DATA NAME                    OLD DATA NAME
--------------------------------  --------------------------------
SAVE-REC                          R01-CUSTOMER-MASTER-RECORD
WS-NUM                            R01-CUST-ACCOUNT-NUMBER
SAVE-NUM                          R02-CUST-ACCOUNT-NUMBER
ACCT                              R03-CUST-ACCOUNT-NUMBER
ACCT-NO                           R04-CUST-ACCOUNT-NUMBER
HOLD-ACCOUNT                      R05-CUST-ACCOUNT-NUMBER
C-A                               R06-CUST-ACCOUNT-NUMBER
ACCT-HIST-NUMBER                  R07-CUST-ACCOUNT-NUMBER
WK-FIELD                          R08-CUST-ACCOUNT-NUMBER
CR-TERRTY                         R01-CUST-TERRITORY
SV-NAME                           R01-CUST-NAME
CUST-IDENT                        R02-CUST-NAME
CUSTOMER-N                        R03-CUST-NAME
SV-LAST-NAME                      R01-CUST-LAST-NAME
P-L-NAME                          R02-CUST-LAST-NAME
SV-ADDR                           R01-CUST-ADDRESS
WK-ZIP                            R01-CUST-ZIP-CODE-G
P-Z                               R02-CUST-ZIP-CODE-G
SV-ZIP                            R03-CUST-ZIP-CODE-G
WK-ZIP-FIRST-PART                 R01-CUST-ZIP-CODE
SAVE-INS                          R01-CUST-SHIPPING-INSTRUCTIONS
DATE                              R01-CUST-LAST-SALE-DATE
MONTH                             R01-CUST-MM
YEAR                              R01-CUST-YY
WS-MM                             R02-CUST-MM
AMOUNT                            R01-CUST-YTD-SALES-AMOUNT
AMOUNT                            R01-CUST-FREIGHT-CHARGE
TERM                              R01-CUST-TERMS
WK-TX-CD                          R01-CUST-TAX-CODE
ACCUM-DOLLARS                     R01-CUST-YTD-SALES-AMOUNT
P-ACCT                            R02-CUST-ACCOUNT-NUMBER
P-NAME                            R02-CUST-NAME
P-ADDR                            R02-CUST-ADDRESS
P-YTD                             R02-CUST-YTD-SALES-AMOUNT
C-TYPE                            R01-CUST-TYPE
CCM4-TAX-IND                      R02-CUST-TAX-CODE
CCM4-TERMS                        R02-CUST-TERMS
```

Figure 6.5 Example of a data element update list produced by the data restructuring tool DataTEC, from XA Systems.

this process, the data restructuring tool creates files containing record and data element names, formats, and definitions. These files can be exported and used to load the corporate data dictionary, CASE tool, or repository. The comprehensiveness of these export files is a function of the data restructuring tool and the nature of its internal repository.

Operations Environment Analysis

Operations environment analysis is the final function a data restructuring tool can perform. Again, because the tool has read and mechanized information from source, database, load, and procedure libraries, this information can be used to generate operations analysis reports. These reports fall into three categories:

- Job, program, and database lists and diagrams
- Cross-reference reports
- Exception reports

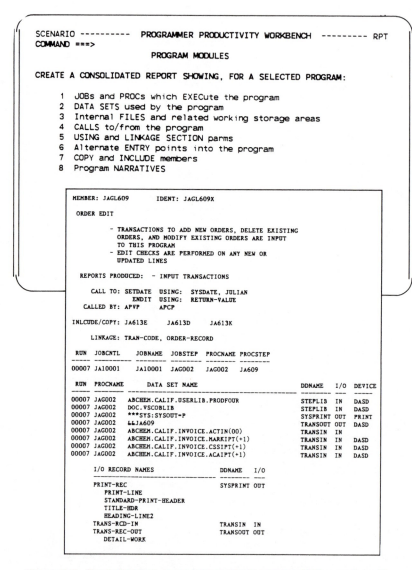

Figure 6.6 Example of an operations analysis program listing produced by the re-engineering tool PM/SS, from Adpac Corporation.

BOX 6.2 Data restructure features checklist

Analyze Environment
_____ Parse operations libraries
_____ Produce job and job step lists and diagrams
_____ Produce cross-reference reports
_____ Produce exception reports
_____ Produce run books
_____ Database information (CICS screens, etc.)

Standardize Data Record
_____ Create composite data record
_____ Create meaningful data names
_____ Replace old record definitions with new composite record
_____ Change all program record references

Standardize Data Elements
_____ Trace flow of data element through program
_____ Identify synonyms, homonyms, aliases
_____ Identify mismatched source and target lengths
_____ Standardize name: _____ element _____ record
_____ Standardize attributes: _____ element _____ record
_____ Propagate changed data element names throughout source code
_____ Data where-used cross-reference

Export To
_____ Data dictionary
_____ CASE tools
_____ Repository

Job, program, and database lists and diagrams provide a complete inventory of all production system components. They list and diagram job and procedure contents, create up-to-date run books, identify inputs, outputs, and calls for individual programs (see Fig. 6.6), and list and diagram database segment relationships. This information is useful for audit purposes, for disaster recovery, for conversion or migration preparation, and to enforce operations naming conventions.

Cross-reference reports provide production component cross-reference information so that system maintainers can determine ahead of time the operations impact of a change to a particular component. For example, if a file were converted to a database, this report can identify all the jobs, procedures, and programs that read or write that file.

Exception reports identify missing components or unresolved references in the operations environment. For example, they note that a certain load module had no associated source file, or that a program made a call to a load module that did not exist.

SUMMARY

Both logic and data restructuring tools can reduce maintenance time and expense by returning programs to their lowest natural level of complexity through structuring logic and creating standard and meaningful data element names. Box 6.2 is a checklist of features offered in data restructuring tools.

REFERENCE

1. Ben Shneiderman, *Software Psychology* (Cambridge, MA: Winthrop, 1980).

7 REVERSE ENGINEERING

FACT OR FANTASY   Reverse engineering is one of the most common buzzwords in current software vocabulary, and one of the most talked about aspects of re-engineering. Yet, because it is one of the less mature parts of the re-engineering technology, there is much confusion about reverse engineering. Exactly what is software reverse engineering? How real is it? What practical benefits can it deliver?

WHAT IS REVERSE ENGINEERING?   **Software reverse engineering** is the process of examining physical level descriptions of software, such as source code or database/file descriptions, to rediscover or reconstruct specification level information describing the process and data components of the software. This information is used as an aid in better understanding the software in terms of what it does and how it works. To maintain software effectively, one must first understand the software. Because understanding software often requires a major portion of the maintenance effort (47 percent according to the Fjeldstad-Hamlen study[1]) reverse engineering has the potential to improve software maintenance productivity significantly.

Reverse engineering tools play a major role in making the reverse engineering process practical, expedient, and accurate, and permanently capture the results of the process in a form that can be reused. Therefore, they should be considered an integral part of the reverse engineering process.

> **Reverse engineering is the process of deriving a conceptual or logical description of a software system's contents and components from its physical level description with the aid of automated tools.**

REVERSE ENGINEERING BENEFITS

Reverse engineering is used to maintain software systems, to aid system migrations and conversions, and to discover reusable software components. Box 7.1 lists the benefits of reverse engineering.

Reverse engineering aids software maintenance by documenting existing software systems and enabling systems to be maintained at the design specification level with the use of CASE tools. The software maintainer can view the system at varying levels of detail and use such graphics as structure charts and entity relationship diagrams to show software structure and component interrelationships. The software maintainer not only can examine the system at the design specification level but also make maintenance changes to the design specification and then use CASE code generators to produce the new code automatically. Maintaining systems at the specification level with CASE tools can substantially increase maintenance productivity.

Reverse engineering extends the useful life and value of existing systems by converting them to newer software technologies, such as higher-level and standard programming languages and databases, and by migrating them to other operating platforms, such as personal computers and workstations.

The knowledge that is captured about existing systems by the reverse engineering process can be reused in the development of new systems. For example, the design of an existing system can be the prototype for building the new replacement system. Because there may be as much as a 60 to 75 percent over-

BOX 7.1 Benefits of reverse engineering

- Recaptures knowledge about existing systems by automatically providing up-to-date documentation.
- Speeds up maintenance and makes it more controllable by providing an efficient way to analyze an existing system's data and logic.
- Aids in analyzing vendor-provided software.
- Allows the maintainer to implement enhancements at the design level.
- Allows for forward engineering of changed designs.
- Allows for reuse of logic and data designs.
- Aids in system conversion and migration efforts because data and logic can be forward engineered to the new environment.
- Positions systems to be supported with CASE tools.
- Populates the repository with information about existing systems.

lap between the functions of the existing system and its replacement,[2] reusing components of the existing system can substantially cut development costs and risks.

Benefits for Software Development

The benefits of reverse engineering are not confined to the software maintenance phase. Reverse engineering can both directly and indirectly assist software development. Reverse engineering provides the means to mine a wealth of information buried in existing systems that can be used to guide and speed up new development efforts. For example, system analysis and design can be speeded up by reusing system design architectures that were discovered by reverse engineering existing systems. The reverse engineered design can be used as a design starting point and then be modified to meet the requirements of the new system.

Also, understanding the architectures of existing systems to which a new system must interface will help ensure that the new and existing systems will work together properly.

After a new system is built, its actual design architecture can be reverse engineered from the source code as a requirements checking exercise. The reverse engineered system design is compared to the original design to determine if the system produced fully meets requirements.

ONE, TRUE SOURCE CODE The primary reference source for understanding a software system is its source code. Although accompanying documentation such as design specification documents and user manuals may be available, software maintainers more often turn to and trust only the source code as the true description of the software. An existing software system that has complete, up-to-date documentation is indeed a rare find because the documentation was maintained independently from the implemented system.

However, reading a thousand-page source listing to learn about the components and architecture of a software system is a formidable, extremely time-consuming challenge. Sometimes it is an impossible task because a maintenance programmer's "span of understanding" is only 7000 to 15,000 source code lines; and to understand this amount of code requires about three to six months of time.[3]

To understand the software by reading the code, the maintainer must somehow reconstruct a higher-level view that abstracts away unnecessary implementation details to reveal the software control structure and architecture. Reverse engineering is this process and is a normal part of software maintenance. However, reverse engineering left as a manual process borders on the impossible for large, complex systems. Even for small systems, reverse engineering tries the human mind beyond its capabilities and should most definitely be supported by powerful, automated tools.

Reverse engineering is not simply the process of redocumentating software to explain what the source code does. Reverse engineering captures the essence of the system in terms of a high-level, less implementation-specific description that is easier for the human mind to grasp. An inherent part of reverse engineering is to transform a lower-level representation of software system (source code, DDL, JCL) into a different but equivalent representation at a higher level of abstraction (logical data model).

Although reverse engineering most often is thought of in terms of transforming a physical, implementation level system description into a design level representation, reverse engineering also can be applied at other system representation levels, such as transforming a design-level representation into a requirements specification describing the business rules.

Reverse engineering does not change what the system does; it only transforms how the system is represented into a form that is easier to understand or may more clearly reveal the system from one perspective, as from its data or function side.

Figure 7.1 shows the reverse engineering process from the physical level to the logical design level. The input to the process is the physical-level description of the software system, such as JCL, source code, DBMS data description language, file descriptions, and copybooks. The output is the logical description of the software represented by logical data models in the form of entity relationship diagrams and hierarchical data structures; process models in the

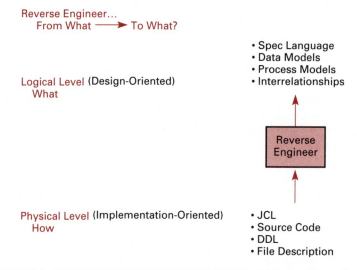

Figure 7.1 The reverse engineering process can be used to transform physical level software information into a logical level description of the software.

form of structure charts; action diagrams and program specification languages describing what each module does; and interrelationships among the various system components, such as data and module cross-reference reports.

Reverse engineering tools can automate much but not all of this process because not all of the design information is contained in the physical description of the software. Such information as design issues and design decisions can only come from personal experience and knowledge of the application domain, the semantic meaning of system components, and the organizational context. Thus, reverse engineering should be viewed as an interactive process that requires a partnership between humans and tools.

REVERSE ENGINEERING AND FORWARD ENGINEERING

Reverse engineering frequently is performed as one part of a two-part process that entails, first, reverse engineering an existing system to position it to be redesigned and then forward engineering the system to redesign it and implement the design changes (see Figure 7.2).

During the reverse engineering part of the process, the current physical level description is examined to produce a higher-level view and higher-level form (i.e., process and data model components) of the system. This allows redesign work to be performed on the logical, implementation-independent design model, which is easier to understand and can be supported by powerful CASE tools. Forward engineering CASE tools can be used to generate automatically a new physical level system description from the revised design model. Thus, reverse engineering is an important first step in system redesign or replacement.

Why Reverse Engineer?
- Work at a Logical, Implementation-Independent Level
- Automate System Maintenance and Development Tasks
- Reuse Existing System Designs

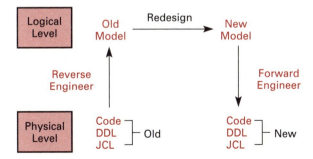

Figure 7.2 Reverse engineering is one part of a two-part process, which also includes forward engineering to redesign and reimplement a software system.

FUTURE SOFTWARE MAINTENANCE AUTOMATION

A view of software maintenance automation in the future is that eventually all software maintenance work will be performed at the design specification level rather than at the code level. This will greatly simplify maintenance and reduce maintenance costs. Reverse engineering is the vehicle for moving software maintenance work up to a higher level of abstraction.

REVERSE ENGINEERING INTO A REPOSITORY

The reverse engineering process produces valuable information as well as process and data model components about existing software systems that can be shared and reused. Therefore, an important part of the reverse engineering process is to store the information recovered in a **repository**. The repository offers not only a data store and automated information management facilities but also a standard representation form for reverse engineered information. This makes it possible to share the information across a team and across CASE and re-engineering tools and to reuse it in new applications. The common representation (the repository meta model) will allow all users (both tools and team members) of the information to share a common understanding of what the information means.

As shown in Fig. 7.3, the repository can be used to store information de-

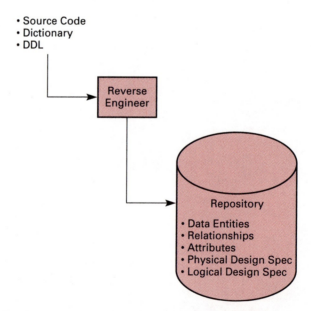

Figure 7.3 An important part of the reverse engineering process is to store the information recovered in a repository where it can be shared and reused.

scribing a software system. Storing the reversed engineered information in one logical data store greatly increases the integrity of that information and greatly reduces software maintenance costs.

REVERSE ENGINEERING TOOLS

There are two types of reverse engineering tools: **data** reverse engineering tools and **logic** reverse engineering tools. Data reverse engineering tools provide a fairly complete reverse forward engineering capability. Many logic reverse engineering products, because of the additional complexities of handling logic, provide a full redocumentation capability but only a partial reverse forward engineering capability.

DATA REVERSE ENGINEERING

Data reverse engineering can be used to understand existing systems and to enable the organization to migrate to new technologies. For example, data reverse engineering can be used not only to modify an existing database but also to migrate to a new database management system, such as from IMS to DB2. Also, data reverse engineering can be used as the first step in building an enterprise-wide logical data model. By reverse engineering and consolidating the data models embedded in existing systems, an organization can quickly build a current logical data model. This data model then becomes the starting point for building the data model that is required by the enterprise's IS strategic plan. Data reverse engineering allows the organization to use a combination top-down, bottom-up approach to expedite and improve its enterprise-wide data modeling process.

The data reverse engineering process is shown in Fig. 7.4. It involves extracting entities, data relationships, attributes, and physical design specifications from source, data dictionaries, and data definition languages (DDL). It includes creation, modification, consolidation, and verification of physical database diagrams and logical diagrams, such as entity-relationship (ER) diagrams, and online graphics presentation of the diagrams. Also, it involves the recreation of DDL schema from the updated logical and physical diagrams.

First, the reverse engineering tool reads in source code, data descriptions, and DDL. Then this information is reverse engineered first into physical (i.e., record-based) design diagrams, which are stored in the repository. These diagrams can be modified and used to regenerate new DDL reflecting the modifications. Or they can be further reverse engineered into a higher level of abstraction such as logical entity-relationship diagrams, which are also stored in the repository. These ER diagrams are modified and forward engineered into physical design diagrams and then into new DDL reflecting both logical and physical changes. The tool also provides diagram-specific verification and expert advice,

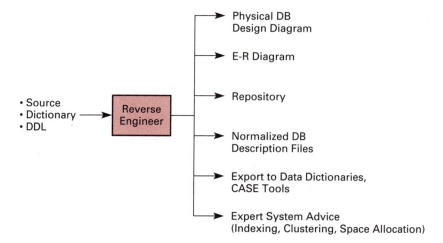

Figure 7.4 The data reverse engineering process involves extracting conceptual and logical data structure information from physical data descriptors.

as well as generates documentation and export files upon request and creates normalized database description files based on the information in the repository.

Bachman Reverse Engineering Process

The data reverse engineering process as supported by Bachman Information Systems includes four functions, which are explained in detail:

- **Reverse engineering**
- **Diagram manipulation**
- **Expert advisor**
- **Forward engineering**

Figures 7.5 through 7.10 illustrate the typical sequence of the data reverse engineering process.

Reverse Engineering

The first function in the process reads existing source code (e.g., COBOL FDs), data descriptions from data dictionaries or other CASE tools, and DDL (e.g., IMS, DB2, IDMS schema and statements). It extracts the inherent design information and loads it into the repository.

The physical design information is record- or segment-based and is database-specific (e.g., IMS, DM2, IDMS). It includes such information as the record or segment length, the key, the fields, pointer relationships, indexes, and space allocation. The logical design information is database-independent and is

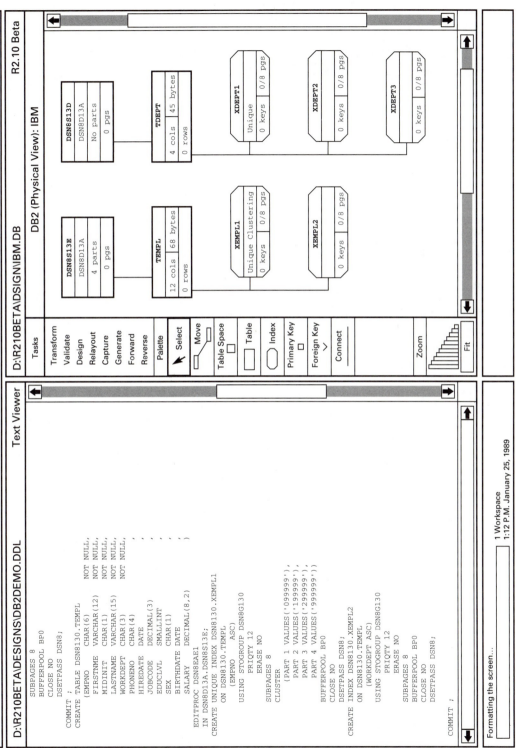

Figure 7.5 The DDL for a DB2 database shown on the left side of the screen has been reverse engineered into a physical database diagram shown on the right by the Re-Engineering Product Set, from Bachman Information Systems, Inc.

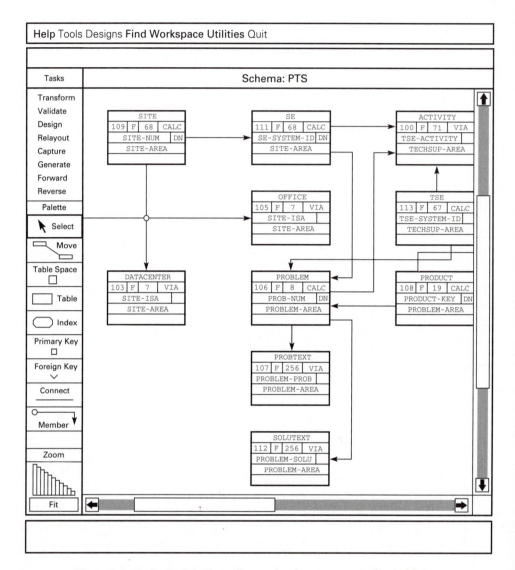

Figure 7.6 A physical database diagram has been reverse engineered into an entity-relationship diagram by the Re-Engineering Product Set, from Bachman Information Systems, Inc.

stored in a format capable of producing entity-relationship diagrams. Box 7.2 explains ER diagrams.

Some tools reverse engineer source, data descriptions, and DDL directly into the repository; others reverse engineer the information first into a physical repository and from there into a logical ER-based repository.

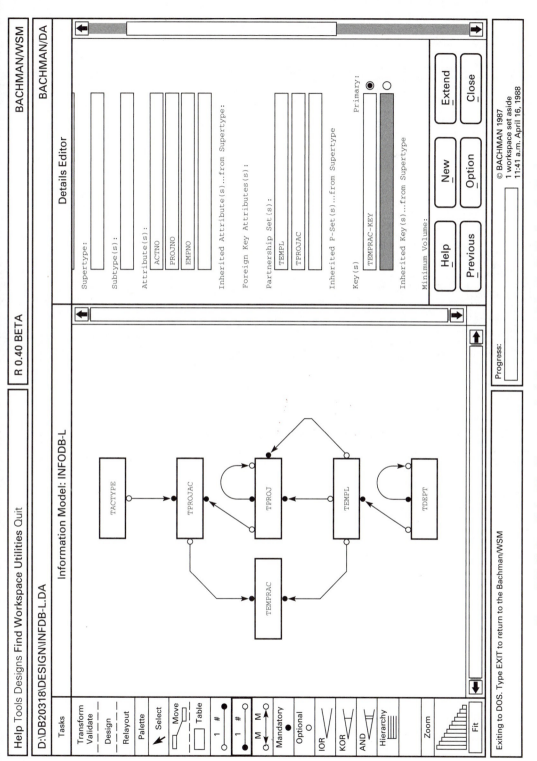

Figure 7.7 Entity-relationship diagram manipulation performed by the Re-Engineering Product Set, from Bachman Information Systems, Inc.

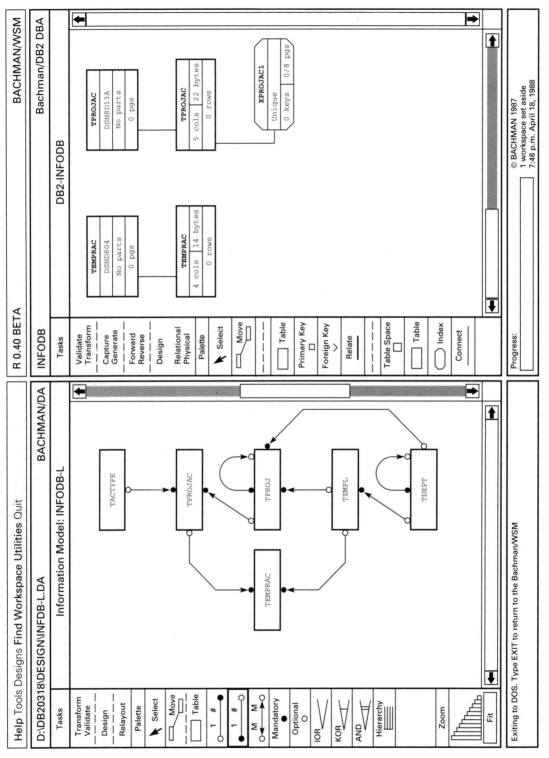

Figure 7.8 An entity-relationship diagram forward engineered to its physical database diagram by the Re-Engineering Product Set, from Bachman Information Systems, Inc.

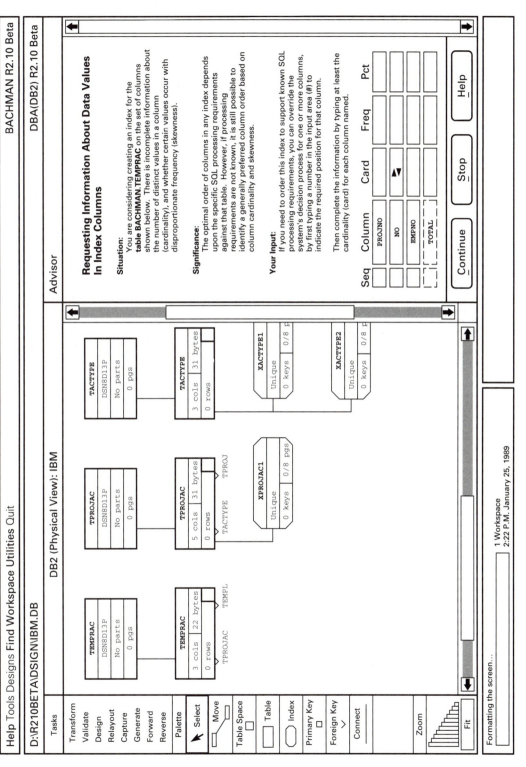

Figure 7.9 An example of the expert Advisor feature of the Re-Engineering Product Set, from Bachman Information Systems, Inc., raising an indexing question on a physical database diagram.

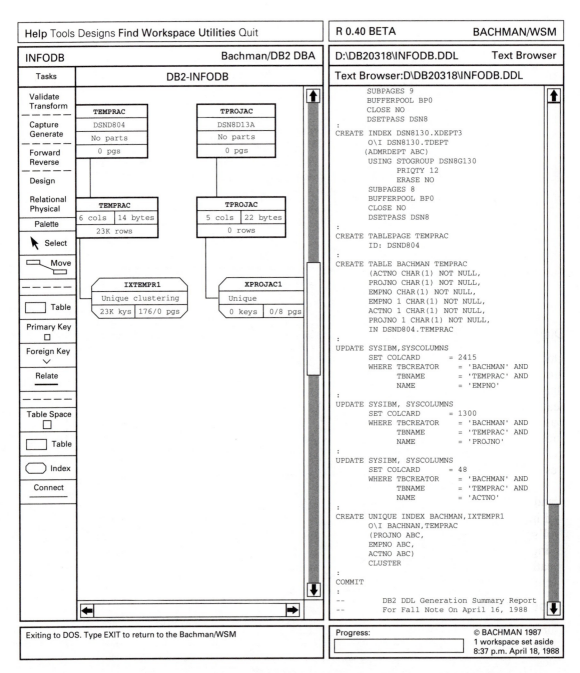

Figure 7.10 The final step of forward engineering to the updated DDL performed by the Re-Engineering Product Set, from Bachman Information Systems, Inc.

BOX 7.2 Entity-relationship diagrams

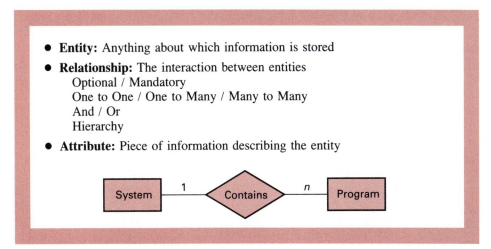

Diagram Manipulation

Once the design information is reverse engineered into the repository, diagrams are generated and presented on an online, full-screen editor. Using the editor, diagrams can be created, modified, and consolidated with existing ones. This feature, especially for logical ER diagrams, is a good tool for integrating database information from various sources and building an enterprise-wide data model bottom-up from the information that is used in current software systems.

After modification, all diagrams are verified for completeness and correctness.

Browsing through the diagrams helps the developer or maintainer understand the databases and their relationships, and makes it easier to fix problems and implement enhancements. Developers and maintainers are also aided by the tool's ability to print the diagrams and associated data dictionary information. Using the diagrams to modify databases, rather than modifying them directly, greatly reduces a time-consuming, error-prone task.

Expert Advisor

During diagram manipulation, the tools provide guidance to the developer or maintainer through an expert (AI-based) rule set. For logical ER modeling, the rules prompt the user to follow sound data modeling principles. For physical database modeling, the advisor gives guidance based on database-specific physical design rules (e.g., indexing, clustering, space allocation) to ensure proper database design and performance optimization.

Forward Engineering

Once the diagram has been modified and verified, the information in the repository is forward engineered. Information can be forward engineered to create database-specific design diagrams and to produce updated DDL schema and statements (IMS, DB2, IDMS, ORACLE, etc.).

Data reverse engineering tools perform two other important functions: normalization and exporting. The *normalization function* generates third normal form (3NF) data files from information in the repository. It can also verify existing database schemas for 3NF compliance and suggest corrected schemas for those databases not in 3NF. The *export function* creates export files based on information in the repository for loading into mainframe dictionaries and other CASE tools.

Figures 7.5 through 7.10 illustrate the reverse engineering process applied to the task of updating a DB2 database. In Fig. 7.5, DDL for a DB2 database, shown on the left side of the screen, has been reverse engineered into a physical database diagram shown on the right. Figure 7.6 shows that same physical database diagram reverse engineered into an ER diagram. Figure 7.7 shows the ER diagram after the analyst had added a new component and related information. Figure 7.8 shows the updated ER diagram forward engineered to its physical database design diagram, and Fig. 7.9 is an example of the expert advisor raising an indexing question on the physical diagram. Figure 7.10 shows the final step of forward engineering to updated DDL.

CGI Systems Reverse Engineering Process

PACBASE, from CGI Systems, approaches data reverse engineering in a different way. The functions of this reverse engineering process are

- Load and analyze source data definitions
- Create a logical data model
- Refine model
- Import to the repository

Load and analysis includes decomposing all the source into its parts to create objects such as source files, source records, and source data (group and elementary). Then a cross-reference of all these parts to each other and all their uses in other data definitions or logic is done. Next, alias analyses, using mathematical algorithms and semantic analysis, within and across all sources on all of these parts is performed, and a proposed logical data model consisting of unique data elements, data views, and all the interrelationships between these objects and the logic using them is created. Additionally, the data elements and views are given fully qualified business names that are automatically built from the applications "vocabulary." The application's vocabulary comes from the data names in the source and words developed in a thesaurus created for forward engineering or earlier reverse engineering of other sources.

An interactive environment and database are provided to allow analyst intervention to enrich the data model. Additionally, the analyst can add documentation and logical structure to source programs to enhance maintenance in the repository environment.

The last function in the CGI Systems reverse engineering process is to import the source into the PACBASE repository, synchronizing the logic sections to the logical data model. Additionally, any source identified as reusable is automatically converted to a program template form called a "parametrized macro structure." These can be used in maintenance and forward engineering simply by calling them by name and providing appropriate generation time parameters.

LOGIC REVERSE ENGINEERING

Logic reverse engineering is the process of extracting the process design specifications from source code or logical designs, populating the repository, and creating, modifying, consolidating, and verifying information in the repository. Once the physical design specifications are in the repository, they can be used to regenerate partial or full programs, to document the system, to do change impact analysis, and to migrate the system to new environments.

If we compare logic reverse engineering with program code analysis (discussed in Chapter 4), we can see many similarities. The input to both processes is the physical description of the program. Also, the output from both is documentation that describes the process logic components. Figure 7.11 shows an

```
─────────────────── SALES ───────────────────
   PRODUCE-SALES-SUMMARY.
       DISPLAY "ENTER PASSWORD:  ".
       ACCEPT
           PASSWORD
           WITH CONVERSION.
       PERFORM VERIFY-PASSWORD THRU VERIFY-PASSWORD-EXIT.
       IF VALID THEN
           PERFORM SETUP
           PERFORM PROCESS-A-RECORD UNTIL MORE-INPUT IS EQUAL TO "N"
           PERFORM END-OF-FILE-PROCESSING
       ELSE
           NEXT SENTENCE.
   END-SALES.   ...
   GET-PASSWORD SECTION.   ...
   SETUP SECTION.   ...
   PROCESSING SECTION.
   PROCESS-A-RECORD.   ...
   WRITE-A-BACKUP-ENTRY.   ...
```

Figure 7.11   An example of process logic from a COBOL program.

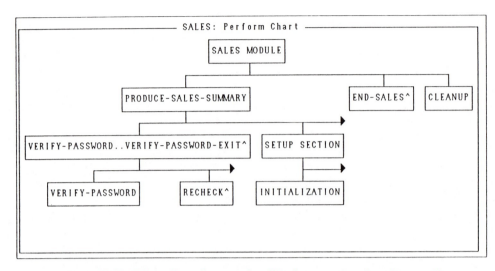

Figure 7.12 This perform chart, produced by the program code analyzer tool Application Browser from Hypersoft Corporation, shows the control structure for a COBOL program.

example of process logic from a COBOL program. Figure 7.12 and Figure 7.13 show the perform chart and performed-by chart produced by a COBOL program code analyzer tool. Perform charts and performed-by charts show the control structure for the program from the perspective of which paragraphs invoke and which are invoked by other paragraphs in the program.

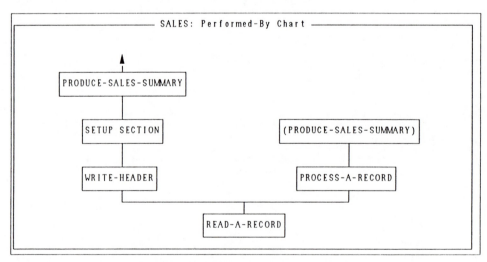

Figure 7.13 This perform-by chart, produced by the program code analyzer tool Application Browser from Hypersoft Corporation, shows all paragraphs that invoke a particular paragraph in a COBOL program.

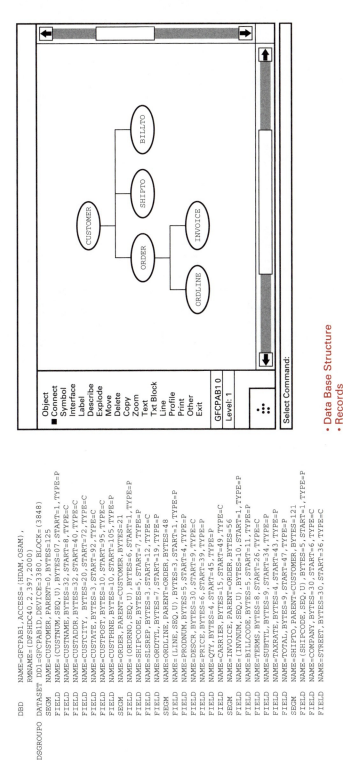

Figure 7.14 Design Recovery, from Intersolv Corporation, is used to create design information from an IMS database definition and to store it in the Excelerator repository.

Even though producing this type of documentation is the primary output of logic analysis, reverse engineering goes beyond producing documentation by placing this design information in a repository and in a form in which it can be manipulated and used in forward engineering activities. This marks an important way to differentiate program code analysis from reverse engineering.

The logic reverse engineering process can be supported by a separate product or service. It can also be implemented as a feature of an existing CASE tool, where the feature reverse engineers source code into the CASE tool's repository and the maintainer or analyst uses the tool's error-checking, documentation, and forward engineering features to complete the process.

One such example for reverse engineering COBOL programs is the Design/Recovery product from Intersolv Corporation. Design/Recovery is used to extract design information from an existing COBOL program. It reads COBOL data definitions, IMS/MFS, CICS/BMS, and IMS database definitions and produces logical data definitions and structured diagrams that are stored in the repository of the CASE tool Excelerator (see Figure 7.14). From COBOL code, it produces structure charts, screen designs, and data definitions, which are also stored in the Excelerator repository (see Figs. 7.15 and 7.16). Once in the repository, Excelerator can be used to manipulate, analyze, and create reports about how the program is structured and its quality (e.g., dead code, unused data, complexity).

Another example are the KnowledgeWare CASE tools Information Engineering Workbench and Application Development Workbench, which include utilities for reverse engineering existing CSP applications. CSP/AD programs (MSL applications and processes) can be reverse engineered into the KnowledgeWare repository, Encyclopedia, and then viewed as structure charts and actions diagrams using the KnowledgeWare CASE tools.

LOGIC REVERSE ENGINEERING PROCESS

Logic reverse engineering tools may have not one but really three repositories to support the logic reverse engineering process (see Figure 7.17). The **physical design repository** is the most important of the three, and its level of detail, error checking, and documenting features determines the nature of the logic reverse engineering process.

As shown in Fig. 7.17, source code is reverse engineered into the physical design repository, as are designs from the logical design repository. Once in the physical repository, these designs can be modified and the changes verified. The maintainer or the analyst can generate graphics and reports to analyze and document the physical specifications, and can forward engineer the changed diagrams to the source code repository by generating partial or full source code reflecting the physical design. Note that the process does not reverse engineer the designs from the physical level to the logical level, but only forward from the logical to the physical level.

```
OEORDR   FMT      TYPE=(3270),FEAT=IGNORE
         DEV      TYPE=INOUT
         DIV      CURSOR=((04,19))
         DPAGE
         DFLD     'DISTRIBUTOR ORDER INFORMATION',  POS=(01,25)
         DFLD     'ORDER NUMBER:',                   POS=(04,05)
ORDRNO   DFLD     LTH=006,                           POS=(04,19),  EATTR=(HREV)
         DFLD     'ACCOUNT NUMBER:',                 POS=(04,28)
ACCTNO   DFLD     LTH=009,                           POS=(04,44),  EATTR=(HREV)
         DFLD     'ORDER DATE:',                     POS=(04,55)
DATE     DFLD     LTH=008,                           POS=(04,67),  EATTR=(HREV)
         DFLD     'TAKEN BY:',                       POS=(06,05)
SOLDBY   DFLD     LTH=004,                           POS=(06,15),  EATTR=(HREV)
         DFLD     'PO #:',                           POS=(06,21)
PONUM    DFLD     LTH=010,                           POS=(06,27),  EATTR=(HREV)
         DFLD     'TERMS'',                          POS=(06,39)
TERMS    DFLD     LTH=008,                           POS=(06,49),  EATTR=(HREV)
         DFLD     'DUE DATE:',                       POS=(06,57)
SHIPBY   DFLD     LTH=008,                           POS=(06,67),  EATTR=(HREV)
         DFLD     'DISTRIBUTOR NAME:',               POS=(08,05)
WHOBY    DFLD     LTH=032,                           POS=(08,23),  EATTR=(HREV)
         DFLD     'SALES REP:',                      POS=(08,61)
SLSREP   DFLD     LTH=003,                           POS=(08,72),  EATTR=(HREV)
         DFLD     'BILLING LOCATION CODE:',          POS=(10,05)
SOLDTO   DFLD     LTH=005,                           POS=(10,28),  EATTR=(HREV)
         DFLD     'SHIPPING LOCATION CODE:',         POS=(10,46)
SHIPTO   DFLD     LTH=005,                           POS=(10,70),  EATTR=(HREV)
         DFLD     ',-------------------------------------------X
                                                                  X
                   POS=(11,05)
         DFLD     'CATALOG NO          DESCRIPTION          QTY   X
                   PRICE   TAX',                                  X
                   POS=(13,05)
         DFLD     '======  ============================  =====   =X
                   =====  =====',                                 X
                   POS=(14,05)
         DO       03
CORDER   DFLD     LTH=010,  POS=(15,05),  EATTR=(HREV)
PDESCR   DFLD     LTH=032,  POS=(15,17),  EATTR=(HREV)
QTYORD   DFLD     LTH=005,  POS=(15,51),  EATTR=(HREV)
UPRICE   DFLD     LTH=008,  POS=(15,59),  EATTR=(HREV)
TXRATE   DFLD     LTH=005,  POS=(15,69),  EATTR=(HREV)
         ENDDO
```

Figure 7.15 Design Recovery, from Intersolv Corporation, is used to create screen design by reading IMS/MFS and CICS/BMS and to store it in the Excelerator repository.

- Field Definitions
- Records
- Elements

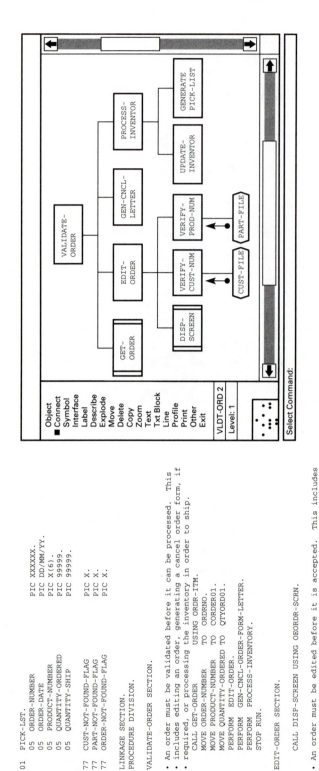

```
01  PICK-LST.
    05  ORDER-NUMBER              PIC XXXXXX.
    05  ORDER-DATE                PIC DD/MM/YY.
    05  PRODUCT-NUMBER            PIC X(6).
    05  QUANTITY-ORDERED          PIC 99999.
    05  QUANTITY-SHIP             PIC 99999.

77  CUST-NOT-FOUND-FLAG           PIC X.
77  PART-NOT-FOUND-FLAG           PIC X.
77  ORDER-NOT-FOUND-FLAG          PIC X.

LINKAGE SECTION.
PROCEDURE DIVISION.

VALIDATE-ORDER SECTION.

• An order must be validated before it can be processed. This
  includes editing an order, generating a cancel order form, if
  required, or processing the inventory in order to ship.
    CALL GET-ORDER    USING ORDR-ITM.
    MOVE ORDER-NUMBER    TO ORDRNO.
    MOVE PRODUCT-NUMBER  TO CORDER01.
    MOVE QUANTITY-ORDERED TO QTYORD01.
    PERFORM EDIT-ORDER.
    PERFORM GEN-CNCL-ORDER-FORM-LETTER.
    PERFORM PROCESS-INVENTORY.
    STOP RUN.

EDIT-ORDER SECTION.

    CALL DISP-SCREEN USING OEORDR-SCRN.

• An order must be edited before it is accepted. This includes
  verifying the customer number and the product number to make
  sure they are valid.

    PERFORM VERIFY-CUST-NUMBER.
    PERFORM VERIFY-PRODUCT-NUMBER.
    EXIT.
```

Figure 7.16 Design Recovery, from Intersolv Corporation, is used to create structure charts from COBOL source code and to store them in the Excelerator repository.

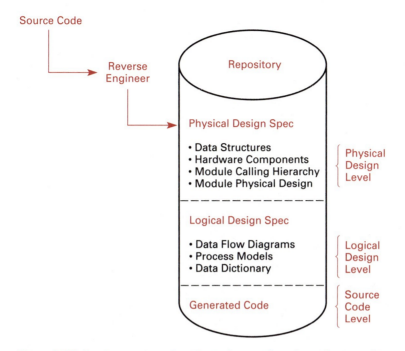

Figure 7.17 Logic reverse engineering tools sometimes have three repositories to support the logic reverse engineering process and to hold source code and physical and logical program design information.

Logical Design Repository

The **logical design repository** is usually that part of a CASE tools environment that captures logical system designs: data flow diagrams (DFD), process descriptions, and the DFD data dictionary. This tool typically has a graphic interface for manipulating data flow diagrams, as well as error-checking facilities to ensure DFD balancing, completeness, and consistency. It generates reports to create the logical system specifications, and extracts and forward engineers (exports) relevant process, dictionary, and relationship information into the physical design repository.

Tools aimed at the engineering/defense/aerospace market also typically support realtime structured analysis, narrative hardware and software requirements, and hardware component design.

Physical Design Repository

The **physical design repository** is the centerpiece of the tool. It contains program level physical designs that have been either forward engineered from the logical repository or reverse engineered from source code. When the design is forward engineered, design facts (e.g., function names, relationships, inputs and outputs, as well as data structure information) are extracted from the logical design repository and stored in the physical design repository. This ensures that the logical design remains intact during its conversion to physical specifications.

When source is reverse engineered, similar design facts are extracted from the source and likewise stored. Once designs are in the physical repository, they can be modified or combined in any manner necessary.

The physical design repository typically contains the following information about how the system modules are organized, how they interact, and what information they exchange:

- **Data structures:** The length and type of each data element in the system; data elements that make up each record; the physical characteristics of each record.
- **Module calling hierarchy:** The name of each module in the system, and the hierarchy defining what modules call what other modules.
- **Module physical design:** For each module in the system, a narrative description, a list of the parameters that are passed to it, and the module's inputs and outputs.
- **Module control logic:** For each module in the system, its control logic (typically pseudocode), as well as timing, sequencing, and trigger information. Sometimes this pseudocode is language-independent, and sometimes it is language-specific.
- **Hardware components:** Any hardware components required to complete the system.

This information is illustrated in Figure 7.18.

The physical design repository of a logic reverse engineering tool typically has the following functions and features:

- Design language
- Design modification
- Error checking
- Documentation
- Code generation (forward engineering)

Design Language

The mechanism for representing design information in the physical repository is a formal design language. These languages are either object-based, similar to the entity-relationship paradigm, or they are pseudocode-based.

In an **object-based** language, objects are typically modules, records or events; relationships are typically data flows, control flows, or other relation-

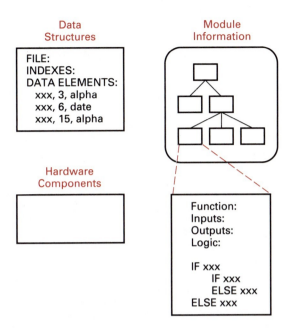

Figure 7.18 The physical design repository holds information about how system modules are organized, how they interact, and what information they exchange.

ships, such as subparts or triggers. Here are some examples of objects and relationships:

Object	Relationship
Process	Subparts are . . .
Group	Consists of . . .
Attribute	Values are . . .
Condition	Triggers . . .

A data object might look like this:

```
DEFINE GROUP XXXXXX
       CONSISTS OF XXXXXX, XXXXXX, XXXXXX, XXXXXX
```

And a process object might look like this:

```
         DEFINE PROCESS XXXXXX
                GENERATES XXXXXX
                RECEIVES XXXXXX
                SUBPARTS ARE XXXXXX, XXXXXX
```

If processing logic is included in the repository, it is typically defined as part of a process object.

When logical designs are forward engineered, relevant parts of the design are extracted and translated into the design language. When source is reverse engineered, it too is translated into the design language. Figure 7.19 shows some examples of an object-based design language.

While some repository design languages are primarily object-based, others are primarily pseudocode-based. In **pseudocode-based** languages, module hierarchy and processing logic are represented using pseudocode. Data structures may also be represented in pseudocode or just stored as information in the repository.

There are two basic types of pseudocode: general purpose and language-specific. Language-specific pseudocode holds more information because it maps more closely to the specified language, thereby allowing greater accuracy and comprehensiveness during code generation. Figure 7.20 shows an example of FORTRAN being reverse engineered into a FORTRAN-specific pseudocode design language, and Fig. 7.21 shows an example of procedure options (i.e., processing logic pseudocode) for a COBOL-specific design language.

Design Modification

After physical designs have been forward engineered, reverse engineered, or entered manually into the repository, the analyst or maintainer can display, modify, and consolidate them. Some tools have a graphic interface; others provide for updating of the design language via a text editor. All changes are verified for accuracy, completeness, and consistency.

Error Checking

All the physical designs in the repository are verified in a number of different ways some of which are

- Syntax
- Completeness
- Function interface consistency
- Data type consistency
- Flow control consistency
- Low complexity
- High cohesion
- Low coupling
- Deadlock

```
 12 >
 13 >DEFINE ENTITY          Raw-Material-Storage;
 14 >     CONSISTS OF:
 15 >         Material-Location, Material-On-Hand;
 16 >


 22 >DEFINE GROUP           Number-of-Finished-Parts-Reqd;
 23 >     SYNONYMS ARE:  NoFPR;
 24 >     DESCRIPTION;
 25 >       The Production department must calculate the number of finished parts
 26 >       required based on the number ordered, number on hand and the raw
 27 >       material on hand.  This number is then used to determine the size
 28 >       of a production run.;
 29 >     ATTRIBUTES ARE:
 30 >       Priority-Level 'Required', Required-Accuracy 'Exact';
 31 >     KEYWORDS ARE:  'Production', 'Calculations';
 32 >     RESPONSIBLE-PROBLEM-DEFINER IS;
 33 >       'RJW, Chief Executive Officer';
 34 >




104 >DEFINE SET             Inventory-File;
105 >     COLLECTION OF:
106 >       Packaging-Slips, Raw-Material-Storage;
107 >
108 >DEFINE SET             Production-Log-File;
109 >     COLLECTION OF:
110 >       Inspection-Statistics, Production-Run-Statistics,
111 >       Size-of-Production-Run;




 36 >DEFINE INPUT           Purchase-Orders;
 37 >DEFINE OUTPUT          Customer-Invoices;
 38 >DEFINE OUTPUT                    Raw-Material-Orders;
 39 >DEFINE PROCESS                   Ann-Arbor-Production-Company;
 40 >     SYNONYMS ARE:  AAPC;
 41 >     DESCRIPTION;
 42 >       The Ann Arbor Production Company is in business to produce parts
 43 >       for the automotive business.  Three major departments exist to
 44 >       streamline AAPC's ability to produce parts efficiently:
 45 >          1.  Receiving, Handling and Storage
 46 >          2.  Part Production
 47 >          3.  Inspection and Shipping
 48 >       ;
 49 >     GENERATES:
 50 >       Customer-Invoices, Raw-Material-Orders;
```

Figure 7.19 In object-based languages, objects include modules, records, and events; relationships include data flows, control flows, and triggers. Examples of an object-based design language produced by REVENGG (PSL/PSA), from ASTEC.

FORTRAN

```
C         Initialization of four tables.
C         The first two of them contain 50 elements,
C         the other two contain 90 elements.
          SUBROUTINE INITTABLES (TAB1, TAB2, TAB3, TAB4)
          DIMENSION TAB1 (50),TAB2(50),TAB3(90),TAB4(90)
          DO 1 J=1,50
          TAB1(J)=0
          TAB2(J)=0
    1     CONTINUE
          DO 2 N=1,90
          TAB3(N) = 0
          TAB4(N) = 0
    2     CONTINUE
          END
```

To Proprietary Design Language

```
ACTION INITTABLES .

DESCRIPTION :

PURPOSE : "

            Initialization of four tables.
            The first two of them contain 50 elements,
            the other two contain 90 elements.


DESCRIPTIONEND

DECOMPOSITION :
   REPEAT "J=1,50" DO
       "    TAB1(J)=0" ;
       "    TAB2(J)=0"
   OD ;
   REPEAT "N=1,90" DO
       "    TAB3(N)=0" ;
       "    TAB4(N)=0"
   OD .

INPUT : TAB1 ,
        TAB2 ,
        TAB3 ,
        TAB4 .

OUTPUT : TAB1 ,
         TAB2 ,
         TAB3 ,
         TAB4 .

ACTIONEND
```

Figure 7.20 An example of FORTRAN-specific pseudocode produced by EPOS/RE-SPEC, from Software Products and Services, Inc.

Procedure Options
(Processing Logic Pseudocode)
Display Screen
Accept Screen
Pass Control
Branching
Get Information
Put Information
Conditional Tests
Program Remarks
Print Reports
Process Extensions
Variable Manipulations
Mathematical Functions
Date Functions
Debug Options

Figure 7.21 Some COBOL-specific reverse engineering procedure options provided by ARRAE, from Price Waterhouse.

The error-checking feature can be used to model maintenance changes (i.e., perform change impact analysis). First, the maintainer makes the changes associated with the maintenance request. Then the error checker is run to verify the correctness of the change and uncover any unknown ripple effects. Finally, once the true extent of the change to each module is verified, the maintainer can make an accurate estimate of the time and resources needed for the change.

Documentation

Logic reverse engineering tools generate graphics and reports to analyze, document, and diagnose the physical design of the system. These include the following:

- Formal design specification documents
- Standard DOD-STD-2167A reports
- Module hierarchy reports
- Methodology-specific design diagrams
- Structure charts
- Data model reports
- Control flow diagrams
- Complexity reports
- Where-used/cross-reference reports
- Audit trail and requirements tracing reports

Figures 7.22, 7.23, and 7.24 show examples of physical design documentation in the form of a flowchart, hierarchy diagram, and structure chart produced by a logic reverse engineering tool.

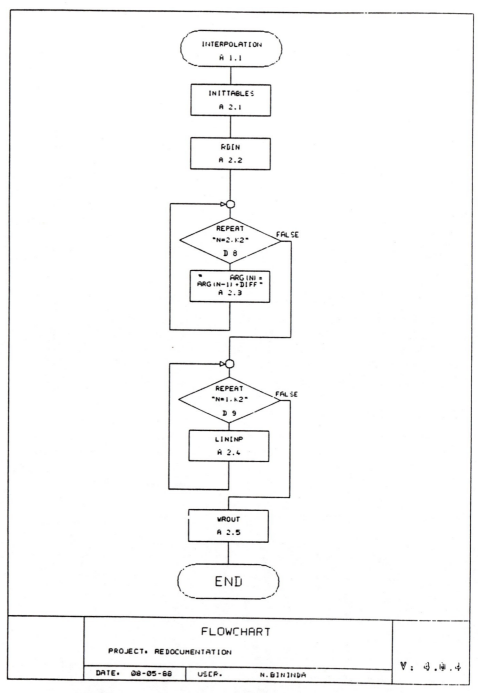

Figure 7.22 An example of graphic documentation produced by reverse engineering tool EPOS/RE-SPEC, from Software Products and Services, Inc.

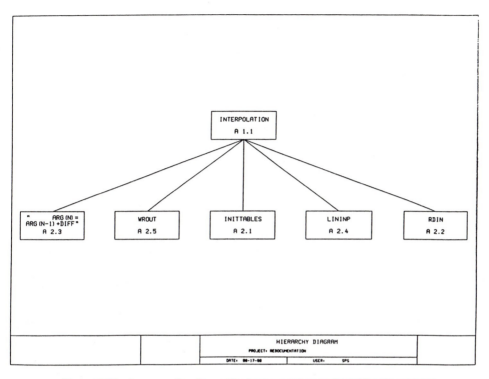

Figure 7.23 An example of graphic documentation produced by the reverse engineering tool EPOS/RE-SPEC, from Software Products and Services, Inc.

Code Generation (Forward Engineering)

Once the physical design has been entered, modified, and verified, the tools will generate new source code based on the updated physical design. The comprehensiveness of the generated source code is a function of two things: (1) the mapping between the logic constructs in the repository design language and the constructs of the generated language, and (2) the degree of logic and data detail in the physical repository. Some tools are able to do 80 to 100 percent code generation. Typically, these are from repositories with language-specific pseudocode. Otherwise, code shells occur for all the modules in the system. These shells contain syntactically correct control structures reflecting the module hierarchy of the physical design, as well as data and type definitions, I/O, and comments. Code shell generations are most often found in tools that handle block-structured languages like C, PASCAL, and Ada. The tool can generate source in any language that it handles (typically one to three languages), making it useful for migrations to other languages and environments.

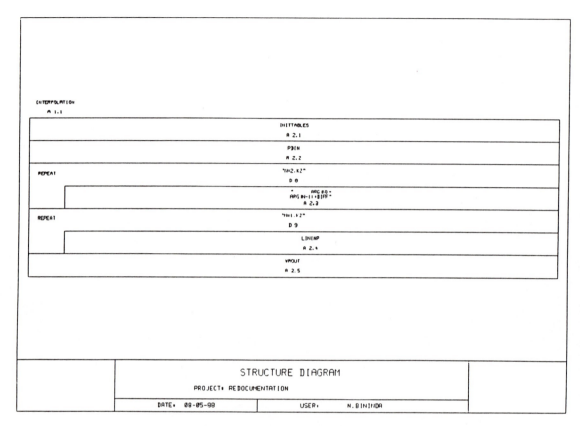

Figure 7.24 An example of graphic documentation produced by the reverse engineering tool EPOS/RE-SPEC, from Software Products and Services, Inc.

Source Code Repository

Logic reverse engineering tools typically provide a way to store and manipulate the source code once it is generated, either in a separate source code repository or in a special part of the physical repository. The tool provides a text editor to modify the source code and a report generator to create documentation; it may also provide error-checking facilities.

Of particular interest is the code feedback report. This report compares the source code of a program that has been modified with its original physical design and identifies any differences in interfaces, names, calls, and parameter usage. This report helps to ensure that errors are not inadvertently introduced when code is modified manually.

BOX 7.3 Practical uses of logic reverse engineering

- Verification of newly coded programs to ensure that the programs match their physical specifications.
- Analysis, documentation, and diagnosis of existing systems to increase maintenance productivity.
- Change impact analysis; modeling maintenance changes in the repository before they are implemented to ensure change is completely understood and controlled.
  _____ Make proposed change to physical design repository.
  _____ Run error checker to uncover problems and omissions.
  _____ Estimate cost of change based on verified physical design.
- Migration to another language or environment.
- Reuse of physical specifications and code shells.
- Integration of two separate systems into one.

Export

Information in the logical, physical, and source code repositories can be exported to other CASE tools or dictionaries, and some tools provide a direct interface to specific CASE tools and thus offer an important function not found in the tool itself, namely, code generation. While it is true that these tools only reverse engineer logic to the physical design level, and may generate only partial source code, they still are powerful tools that maintainers can use to diagnose, document, model, and migrate their systems. Box 7.3 summarizes the practical uses of logic reverse engineering tools.

DATA VERSUS LOGIC REVERSE ENGINEERING

A comparison of data and logic reverse engineering tools offers some interesting insights. One difference is in the nature of the problem each tool is trying to solve. It goes without saying that logic reverse and forward engineering are a task at least one or two orders of magnitude more complicated than data reverse and forward engineering. This difference in the complexity of the problem explains the differences in the tools themselves.

Data reverse engineering tools forward and reverse engineer from source to the physical level to the logical level and back again. It is a clean, contained process with a friendly graphics interface that can be used to implement ongoing database maintenance changes. The logic side is a bit more complicated and a bit more messy. Tools only reverse engineer to the physical level and may only generate (forward engineer) partial source code. The process of reverse and forward engineering requires the maintainer's involvement and "tweaking." After forward engineering from the logical level, the maintainer will have to fill in the details of the physical design not inherent in the logical design. After reverse engineering from source code to the physical repository, the maintainer may also have to supplement the physical design. After forward engineering (generation) of source code, the maintainer must understand the particular design language the repository uses.

The benefit of the tool is more in its ability to redocument the system and model maintenance changes than in its ability to implement the maintenance changes themselves. Yet, given the complexity of the problem, this is no small achievement.

How might logic reverse engineering tools evolve? Some are now offering 100 percent code generation by getting the physical repository detailed enough (e.g., with language-specific pseudocode) to handle the inherent logic complexities. Some COBOL-specific physical repositories are planning to or are now offering code restructuring as well as code reverse/forward engineering. Most tools should offer a full graphics interface rather than a text editor for manipulating the repository's design language.

As they evolve in the 1990s, data and logic reverse engineering tools will most certainly contribute some interesting and very important additions to the re-engineering technology and to software reusability.

REFERENCES

1. Fjelstad and Hamlen, "Application Program Maintenance Study—Report to Our Respondent," IBM Corporation, DP Marketing Group, 1979.

2. A. J. Travis, "Re-engineering Business Systems," *Catalyst Group White Paper,* Peat, Marwick, Mitchell & Co.

3. Fletcher J. Buckley, "Some Standards for Software Maintenance," *IEEE Computer,* 22, no. 1 (November 1989), 69.

8 CONFIGURATION AND CHANGE MANAGEMENT

THE FACT OF CHANGE
"Changing an application already in production is like changing the tires on an automobile—moving at 50 miles an hour," according to one bewildered application manager.[1] Underestimating the need to change and the difficulty of changing software systems is a major contributor to the high cost of software. Business demands that application systems must be frequently changed to continue serving business needs. The best way to deal with software change is to

- Admit that software change is a normal, frequent activity.
- Build software systems that are easy and safe to change.
- Apply software automation to manage the change process.

The re-engineering tools discussed in previous chapters automate key parts of the change process. Complementary to these are configuration management tools. These tools help manage the often overwhelming logistics of modifying software by automating the storage, change, assembly, and movement of software components.

Because many organizations have thousands of programs that change thousands of times, it is a task worth automating and, really, a task that demands automation. If we think of CASE as automating the development process and re-engineering as automating the maintenance process, we should think of configuration management as automating the software change process.

Configuration management functions also are an integral part of a CASE tools environment. However, in this environment, our notion of configuration management must broaden to include not only the management of physical level software components (e.g., source code and object code) but also the management of logical level components (e.g., specification components, design diagrams).

In the 1980s, CASE tool users learned that without proper configuration management of all software components stored in the repository, it is impossible to manage system components even within a CASE tools environment. Configuration management is needed during the development process and during maintenance to manage change across the entire life cycle. Unfortunately, although powerful configuration and change management tools are available, they are not integrated into CASE tools environments. This situation must change in the 1990s. It is likely that configuration and change management functions will become part of the repository services provided by integrated software tools environments. Also, using configuration and change management tools will make the transition to the repository much easier. This is discussed in Part II of this book.

CONFIGURATION MANAGEMENT FUNCTIONS

Today, configuration management tools perform two main functions: library management and change control. **Library management** creates and manages a core of software inventory information; **change control** manipulates that core.

LIBRARY MANAGEMENT

When we consider the **components** of a software system, the following come to mind:

- Program design documents
- Source code modules
- Object code modules
- Copy libraries
- File descriptions
- Screen definitions
- JCL
- User manuals

The library management function of a configuration management tool provides for classifying, storing, and accessing these components, as well as any other machine-readable files, in a way that protects the integrity of the system and eases the job of the system developer and maintainer.

The library management function has five features:

- Component identification
- Logical representation
- Revision control

- Version control
- Parallel development (branching)

Component Identification

A system's components are stored in many different libraries and in many different physical formats, so the first task of library management is the obvious one of identifying all of these physical components and classifying them into component types (e.g., source, object module, JCL). The physical data set names of the components and their component types are then stored in the internal directory of the configuration management tool. Regardless of component type, the tool handles storage, change, and movement in much the same way.

Many configuration management tools also integrate commercial library systems (e.g., Panvalet). They do this by cataloging every item in the commercial library system as a component in the configuration management tool and automatically providing the necessary library interfaces when the component is accessed.

Logical Representation

After a system's physical components are identified, the library management function allows users to logically define and redefine them. Physical components are typically defined in three different ways:

- Grouped into programs/subsystems/systems/applications
- Assigned to individuals/work groups
- Associated with work requests/enhancements/projects

For example, a physical component such as "COBOL program KG500" could be identified as part of the "Accounts Payable" subsystem of the "Journal Entry" application, which is being worked on by the "Accounting Group" as part of its "Online Enhancement." These logical groupings are then added to the internal directory of the tool.

Grouping components logically does two things: (1) It keeps users from having to remember hundreds of physical data set names, because the tool automatically converts the logical identifier to the correct physical data set name; and (2) it links all the components together into a system hierarchy that is used later in the system building feature.

Revision Control

Each software component in a system can change hundreds or possibly thousands of times during the life of the system. It is the job of revision control to manage this change. Revision control handles the naming and storage of each original component and all of its revisions and can produce any revision upon request. Typically, revisions are identified by number (e.g., 1.2), with the leftmost number changing when major revisions are made and the rightmost number or numbers changing when minor revisions are made.

Because storing complete copies of each original and all of its revisions would waste tremendous amounts of space, most configuration management tools employ a **delta** method of storage. Using this method, the tool compares the new version of the component with the old one, identifies the changes, and stores only the identified changes. For each component, then, the tool stores only one full copy and a series of change deltas, each with its own revision number. When a particular revision is requested, the tool generates the revision by applying to the full copy all change deltas up to and including the requested revision. Sometimes the full copy is the very first version and the changes are applied in a forward fashion. More frequently the full copy is the most recent version and the changes are backed out. In either case, the tool can recreate any revision of any component upon request (see Fig. 8.1).

Each time a revision is made, the tool also captures relevant change information, such as the author of the change, the reason, and the date and time.

Version Control

There is often a need to group specific revisions of certain components together in a **version**. For example, a developer might want to group all the "Journal Entry" programs together for a beta test version of the system, or a maintainer might want to group a subset of revised programs together for the "Online Enhancement." This requires a level of identification one step beyond revision control. Not only must all revisions to all components be identified, but one specific revision of a set of components must be identified as being a part of some particular version. This identification allows users (system developers and maintainers) to move entire versions among libraries (e.g., test to production) with the confidence that everything is indeed being included. Figure 8.2 shows an example of version control.

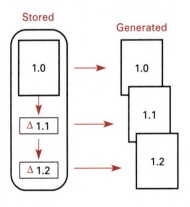

Figure 8.1 Delta method for storage and generation of software component revisions saves a tremendous amount of storage space.

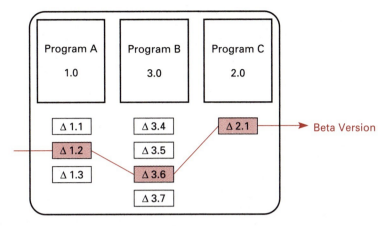

Figure 8.2 Version control—selecting specific revisions for inclusion in a version.

Parallel Development (Branching)

During development and maintenance, it is necessary to make multiple revisions to software components and also to group together specific revisions into versions. Revision and version control features take care of these needs. Users may need to maintain separate copies of entire versions as well. For example, a user may need to identify the test, beta, and production versions of a system for two separate hardware environments. The parallel development or branching feature takes care of this need.

A **branch,** or **parallel development,** version is created when the user identifies a component or set of components (each at a specific revision number) and begins to change them, creating a revision branch, which is basically a revision (or set thereof) of a revision. As we can see in Fig. 8.3, revision 2.1 of program C has branched into two separate versions: 2.2 and 2.1.1. Revision 2.2 is included in the beta version, and 2.1.1 is included in the parallel beta version (2.1.1 might contain some hardware-specific code not required in 2.2).

There is not really that much difference between a branch and a regular revision. The main things that distinguish the two are (1) a means of naming the revision to identify it as a subset of a mainline revision and (2) a means of logically grouping the branch into a parallel version.

Some configuration management tools also allow these branches to be incorporated back again into the mainline revision series. If, for example, a user starts a branch of a particular program at a particular revision to provide a feature to a special client and then decides to provide that same feature to all clients, the tool will merge the latest branch revision back into the mainline and will identify any code conflicts that may have developed (e.g., duplicate data names, missing file references).

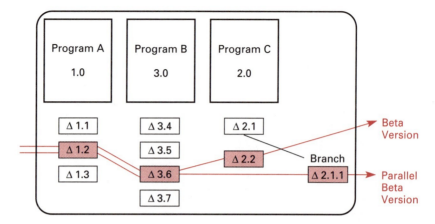

Figure 8.3 Parallel development (branching).

In summary, the library management function creates an inventory of software components, groups them logically in many different ways, manages the storage and retrieval of component revisions, allows grouping into versions, and manages the creation and merging of branches to accommodate parallel developments.

CHANGE CONTROL Whereas the library management function handles the inventory of software components, the change control function manages the modification of a software system. Change control authorizes, controls, and tracks component modification and moves changed components through the life cycle to implementation.

The change control function has four features:

- Security
- Check-out/check-in
- System building
- Reporting

Security

Security controls user access to software components. The project administrator identifies the components involved in a development or enhancement and names the users with read access and write access. The administrator can also limit user access to specific project phases and can preset online approval requirements for activities such as moves to production libraries. Figure 8.4 shows two screens an administrator might use to set up a project and its approvals. Most configuration management tools incorporate and extend existing security pack-

```
------------------------ Project Administrative Menu -----------------------
Option ===>

Project name ===> CMN           (Leave it blank for project list)

    1   PARMS          -   Generate project parameters
    2   STAGING        -   Configure staging libraries
    3   LANGUAGE       -   Configure language names
    4   PROCEDURES     -   Configure compiling procedures
    5   COMPLETE APRV  -   Configure complete approval list
    6   ABBREV. APRV   -   Configure abbreviated approval list
    7   PROMOTION      -   Configure promotion libraries
    8   REMOTE SITE    -   Configure Remote Site List
    B   BASELINE       -   Configure baseline libraries
    C   COMPONENT      -   Update component information
    D   DELETE         -   Delete a project
    P   PRODUCTION     -   Configure a production libraries
    R   REPORTS        -   Generate project batch reports

Enter END command to exit.
```

```
------------------------ Complete Approval List -----------------------
Command ===>

Line commands:  I - Insert, R - Repeat, D - Delete
Enter CANCEL to cancel changes and exit
Enter END command to finalize change

Line    Approver                            Entity      Interfacing
Cmd     Description                         Name        Approver
                                                        (YES or NO)
 ,,,,   Section Head_____ MVSSH___      ___
 ,,,,   Sub-Section Head_____ MVSSSH__      NO_
 ,,,,   Operation Analyst_____ OPS_____      YES
 ,,,,   Change Management_____ CGMUSER_      ___
 ,,,,   Quality Assurance Group_____ QAG_____      ___
```

Figure 8.4 Two administrative setup screens produced by configuration management tools Change-Man, from Optima Software.

ages, such as RACF, ACF2, and Top Secret, so that the user's existing security setup is not compromised. The security feature also logs all activity by user, project, date, and time.

Check-out/Check-in

When an authorized user checks out a software component (i.e., program), the configuration management tool generates a working copy of the most recent revision of the program, logs change information such as user ID, date, and time, and identifies the program as being under modification. Then, if someone else attempts to check out the same program, the tool provides notification of the first user's action and typically will not check out the program again without special authorization.

When the program has been modified, it is checked back in. At this time, the tool collects information from the user describing the nature of the change. Then the library management function compares the new copy with the existing one, creates the delta, kicks up the revision number, and incorporates the new revision as the most current.

It is sometimes necessary to check in two different working copies of the same program. The check-in merge facility takes care of this need. The two copies are compared, multiple changes are integrated, and conflicts are identified. When the conflicts are resolved, one new revision is checked in, reflecting the changes of both working copies.

System Building

The system building feature automatically controls the compiling, linking, and movement of changed components between libraries (e.g., test, beta, production). It is used not only to move projects forward through development to production but also to automatically back out versions quickly when problems are encountered in the live environment.

In order for the system building feature to work, the user must create a "build list." This is a system blueprint that identifies all the components in the system, all of their interdependencies, and the sequence of actions taken to put the components together (e.g., copy Table-X from TABLE.LIB to program A). This list, plus the component revision numbers linked to a specific version or enhancement, controls what gets compiled, moved, backed up, or restored.

The example in Fig. 8.5 shows a build list and an action request. As you can see, the build list is for a compile and link of program X. The system building feature copies in two components from COPYLIB, compiles the program, creates an output component in OBJLIB, links the program, and creates an output component in LOADLIB.

The action request shows a move of components (previously identified on a build list) from test to production.

When a version or enhancement is built or moved, the system building feature automatically checks the date and time stamps on the affected components to make sure that they are current. For example, when moving a system from test to production, the feature will check that every object module in the system has a date and time stamp that matches the date and time stamp of the source code from which it was compiled. If the source has been changed, the tool will automatically recompile the updated source so that its changes will be reflected. It will also recompile or relink any other component that depends on the changed component. For example, as you can see in Fig. 8.6, the source for

ACM Component List

	Configuration Type	Name	Footprint Information	Step	Library
Element Information	ELEMENT	PROGRAM X	v1.3		
Processor Information	PROCESSOR RECORD	COMPLINK	v1.8		
Input Components	INPUT	COPYRECA	v2.1	COMPILE	COPYLIB1
	INPUT	COPYRECB	v2.5	COMPILE	COPYLIB2
Output Components	OUTPUT	PROGRAM X	v1.3	COMPILE	OBJLIB
	OUTPUT	PROGRAM X	v1.3	LINK-EDIT	LOADLIB

```
LIST          ELEMENT           *
FROM          ENVIRONMENT       TEST
              SYSTEM            FINANCE
              SUBSYSTEM         *
              TYPE              *
              STAGE             1
TO            DSNAME            'USER,SRCLIB' MEMBER 'FIX01'
WHERE         CCID EQUALS  'FIX01'
              INPUT COMPONENTS EQUAL '*'
BUILD         WITH COMPONENTS ACTION MOVE.
```

Figure 8.5 Example of a build list and action request produced by Endevor, from Business Software Technology.

DATE-FUNCTION is more recent than its object. So, before moving program A to production, the system building feature will recompile DATE-FUNCTION, create an updated object module for it, and only then link it to program A.

The system building feature controls the movement of systems between libraries as well. Based on the build list and action request, it will move a system to production, back it up, or back it out and restore a previous version if a problem appears.

The feature works equally well with an enhancement as with a complete version. The administrator declares an enhancement project, identifies the components involved, and creates a partial build list. This is used with the action

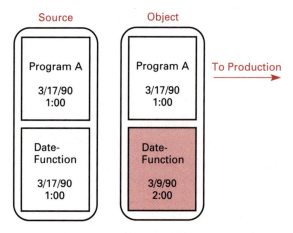

Figure 8.6 Module currency checking.

request to move a set of changes through development and production and to back up or back out the changes as needed.

Many configuration management tools also handle remote sites by distributing components to the appropriate libraries across installation networks. They handle microcomputer-based development and/or operations environments as well.

```
  BROWSE -- ZZLB.ZZLB.XREFRPT2.LIST -------------- LINE 00000003 COL 001 080
  COMMAND ===>                                              SCROLL ===> CSR
REPORT OF COMPONENTS THAT CALL A GIVEN COMPONENT            03/02/89  11:22
     CROSS-REFERENCE CRITERIA ENTERED:
     COMPONENT TYPE ===> COPY    COMPONENT NAME ==> AB*
==============================================================================

>>>>>>>>>>>>>>> CROSS-REFERENCE FOR ABAUDREC
PROG PCSA001

PROG PCSA099

PROG PCSA237


>>>>>>>>>>>>>>> CROSS-REFERENCE FOR ABBEMPI
PROG PCSA001

PROG PCSA034

PROG PCSA099
```

Figure 8.7 Cross-reference query produced by ISPW, from Benchmark Technologies.

The system building feature documents a system's software interdependencies and allows the system to be built and moved quickly and accurately. It also enforces monitoring and approval of all moves and retains a history of build lists as they evolve through time.

Reporting

This feature generates a number of reports based on the activity log file and other configuration management information. Users can generate fixed reports, SQL-like ad hoc reports, and online queries. Some typical reports are

- *Activity reports:* These show work in progress by listing all the active components, who has access to them, and for what project.

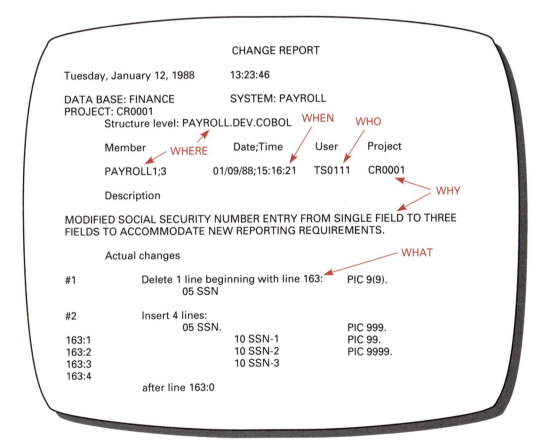

Figure 8.8 Change report, showing actual source changes, produced by CCC, from Softool Corporation.

- *Version report:* This shows all the components (and their revision numbers) included in a particular version or branch. It also lists all the versions and branches in which each component revision is a part.
- *Interdependency report:* Based on build lists, this shows the complete component hierarchy for a system: all the components that make up a program, all the programs that make up a system, and all the interconnections. It also shows all the programs where an individual component is used.
- *Change impact analysis report:* This identifies via cross-reference all the other components in a system that will be affected by a change to one particular component (see Fig. 8.7).
- *Change activity report:* This lists changes by various attributes, such as component, date and time, analyst, and project (see Fig. 8.8).

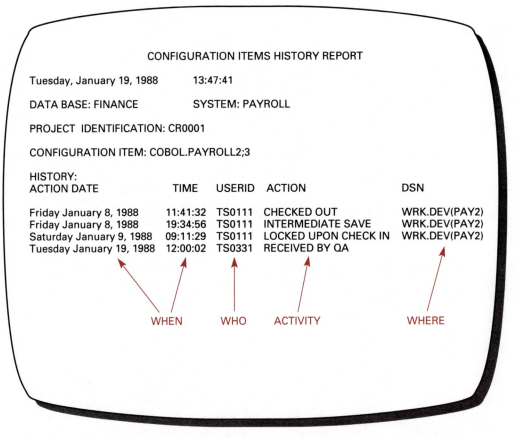

Figure 8.9 Change history report, produced by CCC from Softool Corporation.

- *Change history report:* This shows changes through time. One report might show the change description entered by the user, as well as actual code differences between revisions; another might show all changes made to all components between one version and another (see Fig. 8.9). These reports are useful for tracking change, analyzing trends in system modification, creating audit history, and debugging, by identifying exactly where a bug may have been introduced.

Box 8.1 summarizes configuration management functions and features.

SUMMARY

If software never changed, there would be little need for automated configuration management. But it does change, and frequently. We have described configuration management functions and features separately to make them more understandable, but they all interact to help software developers and maintainers handle the logistics of software management and change. Let us briefly chart how an enhancement would be implemented using a configuration management tool.

First, the project administrator uses the library management function and security feature to define the project by assigning a change ID, selecting the software components involved in the change, and defining users, access levels, and approval requirements. The user (software developer or maintainer) then runs a change impact analysis report to identify any ripple effects of the change

BOX 8.1 Configuration management

Library Management

Component identification
Logical representation
Revision control
Version control
Parallel development (branching)

Change Control

Security
Check-in/check-out
System building
Reporting

BOX 8.2 Configuration management features checklist

Library Management

_____ Serial developments
_____ Parallel development
_____ Integration
_____ Component-based
_____ Logical representation
_____ Version control

Change Control

_____ Impact analysis
_____ Enhancement support
_____ Sign-out/sign-in
_____ Security
_____ Reporting
_____ History

System Builder

_____ Builder
_____ Approval
_____ Backout
_____ History

and incorporate them in the project if necessary. As the user checks out, modifies, and checks in the affected programs, the administrator can review and track all activity. When it is time for testing, the user uses the system building and version control features to compile and link automatically the appropriate revisions of all programs affected by the change. After testing and after obtaining approvals, the user moves the changed components to the beta and then production libraries and backs up and backs out the changes as necessary. Throughout the project, the user and the administrator use the version reports, interdependency reports, and change reports to manage the change.

Configuration management tools not only handle the logistics of software management and change but can enforce an entire user-defined change control process. This can make software development and maintenance a much less expensive and less error-prone undertaking.

Box 8.2 lists the features to look for in configuration management tools.

REFERENCE

1. Dave Thewlis, "Change Management Challenge of DB," *Software Magazine* (January 1989), 34–50.

9 RE-ENGINEERING CASE STUDIES

RE-ENGINEERING IN PRACTICE

The three case studies presented in this chapter show that re-engineering is a broad technology that can be practiced in different ways by different organizations. In each case study, a different aspect of re-engineering served to initiate the organization to the technology and open the way for bringing in other types of re-engineering. At Shearson Lehman Brothers, the creation of a maintenance workbench consisting of a variety of third-party–supplied re-engineering tools resulted in a 30 percent increase in maintenance productivity. At Integral, reverse engineering allowed the capture of the data model from the current system, which was demanded by their software package customers. At PacBell, the use of restructuring tools transformed their technically outdated payroll system into a system that was safe and easy to maintain.

Although they provide different views of re-engineering in practice, the three case studies show how re-engineering can help make a company more viable and competitive in the 1990s. They also show the importance of training and a support structure to make re-engineering work in practice. Finally, each company's experience points out that tools alone cannot do the job of bringing about productivity and quality improvements. Planning an evolutionary move to re-engineering technology and instituting a metrics program to measure results are important ingredients to ensure success.

RE-ENGINEERING AT SHEARSON LEHMAN BROTHERS

Shearson Lehman Brothers (SLB), a subsidiary of American Express, is the second largest U.S. brokerage firm.[1] SLB views itself as an information-driven business and therefore believes that IS can be used to achieve a competitive advantage.

Currently, SLB has six mainframe computers running primarily COBOL II applications under VSAM, nearly 15,000 networked PCs running C programs under MS-DOS and OS/2, and 1000 SUNs running C and C++ under Unix. There are 600 developers involved in both software development and maintenance activities at SLB. In 1990, mainframe application work was split, with 80 percent in maintenance and 20 percent in new development. The maintenance work breakdown was

- 25 percent corrective maintenance
- 15 to 20 percent adaptive maintenance (e.g., migration from VSAM to DB2)
- 60 percent enhancement (much of which is regulatory-driven)

Although its mainframe application portfolio is quite young (average application age is less than five years), the quality is quite low, according to SLB.

Maintenance Automation Focus

Two years ago, SLB began to look at upper-level CASE tools to be used in new development projects. However, because of the economic slowdown, which put more and more new development on the back burner, SLB decided to shift the software automation focus to its existing systems. In such a no-growth period, the biggest improvement at the bottom line can be made by making the current environment as efficient and effective as possible. For example, SLB runs approximately 5000 batch programs each night. Converting these programs to on-line mode could greatly enhance user productivity, thus positively impacting the bottom line.

SLB began by conducting a survey and screening of re-engineering products that perform portfolio analysis and aid software modification. The results of the survey were used to select one or two re-engineering vendors which then assisted the SLB planning group in trying out the tools in a live project. The project experience pointed out that the tools were not really being used for two reasons:

1. Training was needed to teach the staff how to use the re-engineering tools.
2. Tool differences made the tools difficult to learn to use.

Maintenance Workbench

To solve these problems, SLB decided to build its own maintenance workbench consisting of a variety of vendor-supplied tools whose differences were masked by an SLB-designed common user front end. The SLB front end provides options for the use of its batch tools. The workbench user can either directly choose the wanted tools or choose the desired function and have the workbench suggest the tool(s) to be used. When the user selects a task to be performed and multiple tools are needed to accomplish this task, the workbench specifies the order in which to use the tools. Also, the workbench provides online help and online tutorials.

In addition to the maintenance workbench, a support structure was created at SLB. For each of the five major development areas, there is one full-time tool coordinator who acts as the first point of inquiry on how to use the tools. A second line of support is provided by a six-person group each member of which is an expert in one or two tools. Also, the group hosts a quarterly tools fair during which brief training sessions are held.

The SLB maintenance workbench contains a variety of re-engineering tools: PathVu and DataTec from XA Systems, Inspector and Recoder from KnowledgeWare, ViaInsight and SmartEdit from ViaSoft, Pretty Printer from Blackhawk, Scan COBOL from CDSI, and the Re-engineering Toolset from Bachman. Training is provided for both managers and maintainers. For example, two hours of required training plus tutorials on ViaSoft's products are given to every maintainer. These tools are used daily to analyze and modify COBOL programs. PathVu, which is particularly valuable at the manager level, requires one day of training. Recoder, the COBOL restructuring tool, also requires one day of training.

SLB claims that use of its maintenance workbench has resulted in a 30 percent improvement in maintenance productivity. SLB measures software productivity by counting function points and quality in terms of mean time to repair and mean time between failures. SLB stated that re-engineering tools have helped it to keep up with user requests, which previously it was not able to do. SLB also stated that re-engineering tools have helped to discover errors that previously had eluded users. For example, after using PathVu to analyze a COBOL program, a previously undetected logic fallthrough that was the source of an error was discovered by the tool. Recoder was used to restructure a 14-page IF statement in a COBOL program that was impossible for any human being to understand.

Using Re-engineering Tools

SLB has about 10 million lines of COBOL code to maintain. However, not all of it can or should be restructured. Some programs have certain characteristics that will cause them to grow enormously in size if they are restructured. Other programs need to be redesigned, not simply restructured. SLB has developed a set of heuristics to determine if and how to re-engineer existing programs. The output of PathVu is used in this determination.

The general order of using re-engineering tools at SLB is to begin with PathVu or Inspector to measure the quality of the program, followed by Recoder to restructure the program, then PathVu again to measure quality and capture measurements in a metrics database, and finally Scan COBOL to produce updated program documentation. ViaSoft's tools are used daily to perform online analysis (e.g., change impact analysis) and testing. Re-engineering tools have become so indispensable at SLB that they are now standard tools. SLB plans to substitute PathVu for the COBOL compiler because of the program metrics it produces, and to make SmartEdit its standard COBOL editor.

Re-engineering Future Wish List

Looking toward the future, SLB has several requests on its re-engineering wish list. For example, SLB would like to perform program level reverse engineering to extract physical design information from its existing COBOL programs. This design information could then be used to identify reusable, repeating patterns for use in building new systems, to convert path applications to online mode, and to feed the repository.

Like many other organizations, SLB views the repository as an important component in building an integrated tool environment in the 1990s. However, SLB also recognizes that for the repository to deliver promised productivity and quality benefits, it must be populated with high-quality system information. An important preparation step in feeding the repository with information about existing systems is to clean up and rationalize data names and definitions with the help of re-engineering tools.

Also, SLB is looking forward to re-engineering tools that provide better CICS and VSAM support to aid migration efforts. Above all, SLB would like its multivendor-supplied tools to fit and work together better. A major re-engineering issue is that each vendor's tools attack only a part of the maintenance problem. The SLB plan is to build a full life cycle tool environment where the developer's workbench feeds into the maintainer's workbench and both are enabled to the repository.

Finally, while the re-engineering tools of today provide program level support, what SLB is looking forward to in the future is a system level view.

SLB has observed that evaluating and buying tools represent only 50 percent of the re-engineering effort. It advises looking beyond buying a re-engineering tool at management, training, and user issues. An integrated re-engineering tool environment makes the difference in ensuring the delivery of the maximum benefits from the tools. Giving the tools a common look and feel is the first step in achieving this environment. Also, an extremely important part of support is staff training. SLB's final piece of advice is to **plan, plan, plan.**

REVERSE ENGINEERING AT INTEGRAL

Integral was formed 18 years ago as a payroll consulting organization.[2] As it evolved over the years, Integral produced packaged software systems for the areas of payroll, personnel, human resources, and finance. Initially, these packages were developed for CICS and VSAM mainframe-based environments. Later, they were migrated to IDMS, IMS, Data-

Com, and Adabas. Most recently, Integral acquired a line of PC/workstation-based packages.

Two years ago, Integral began surveying the CASE and re-engineering tools market. The company had noted that clean-slate application development was rare and most of its software work concentrated on product enhancement. Although the value of system code decreased over time, many of the business rules and data embedded within existing systems were worth saving.

CASE for Existing Systems

Integral's focus on existing systems was contrary to the widely held belief that applying CASE to existing systems was not worth the effort. However, Integral's position was driven by very practical reasons. Its clients were demanding that the package be delivered with accompanying documentation that included a data model. Because Integral had not produced a data model when the product was originally developed, the easiest and fastest way to produce one after the fact was with the aid of re-engineering tools, and in particular reverse-engineering tools. Integral's goal was twofold:

1. Capture the DDL from the current system and reverse engineer it to a data model.
2. Thereafter use the data model to update the system and as input to CASE tools to forward engineer it to the next release.

One sale of the package that depended on having a data model would provide the payback for the investment in CASE. Integral chose the Bachman re-engineering product set because it could be used to achieve both parts of its goal.

The Bachman learning curve was short at Integral. It required only one day for the Integral staff to learn how the tool worked, how to cope with it, and how to apply a re-engineering life cycle, because the staff already had experience in DB2 and in entity-relationship data modeling. The re-engineering life cycle steps are

1. Capture DDL and reverse engineer back to the ER model.
2. Make change to the ER model.
3. Forward engineer by generating the DDL from the ER model.

New development also uses the Bachman tools. New development begins with building the ER model and then generating DB2 DDL from the ER model.

Re-engineering Mistakes

Although the concept is good, its implementation fell short of Integral's goals. The Integral developers changed the generated DDL for performance reasons but failed to introduce the changes back into the ER model. Because it was not properly updated, the ER model soon was out of sync with the DDL. The developers claimed they could not maintain the proper re-engineering cycle because it took too long to do so. Also, they did not readily accept or trust the generated code.

Integral believes that its re-engineering mistake was to attempt to change the culture too quickly. This frightened the staff and caused them to mistrust and resist the new technology and the re-engineering life cycle process. As a result of its experience, Integral suggests a more evolutionary move into re-engineering technology and makes the following points:

1. There is a need for a re-engineering champion who is a member of the staff to tout the benefits of the new technology.
2. It is important to show short-term benefits to gain initial interest in and acceptance of the new technology.
3. It may require one to two years to see longer-term benefits. (For example, Integral was able to shorten the delivery cycle for regulatory changes.)
4. A system of metrics showing estimated versus actual project results should be introduced.

Like many other organizations, Integral agrees that cost justifying CASE technology is extremely difficult. It was able to get management support for CASE because it needed to produce a data model. However, Integral warns against trying to cost justify solely on the basis of productivity improvements. Instead, it suggests that CASE users take a page out of the Japanese book and emphasize quality. According to the Japanese, the most important long-term cost savings will come from producing the best quality product.

Re-engineering Experiences

Integral found another application for re-engineering technology in a product that required the merging of two different product lines developed by two different companies. It was necessary to integrate the data so, for example, there would be only one definition for employee, account number, and so forth. With the aid of Bachman re-engineering tools, an integrated ER model was built by first extracting the two separate models and then using file capture to create detail level information. Next, the models were merged to create an integrated model across the product lines.

Although Integral's first reverse-engineering experiences were on the data side, process reverse engineering has great appeal as well at Integral. Integral's latest reverse engineering experience is to reverse engineer CSP (IBM's Cross System Product) into External Source Format (ESF). The ESF files are imported into the KnowledgeWare Encyclopedia where a consolidation file is created. Then, using the KnowledgeWare CASE tools, functional decomposition diagrams and screen maps for the application are produced. Unfortunately, there is no bridge to import Bachman data structures into the KnowledgeWare Encyclopedia, commented Integral. The ideal situation, according to Integral, is to reverse engineer an entire CSP application into the KnowledgeWare Encyclopedia where it can be modified, forward engineered, and thereafter enhanced and maintained. However, this is beyond current state of the art.

Business Point of View

Integral advises that the place to begin when adopting a new technology such as CASE or re-engineering is with the **business.** Where do you stand from a business point of view? How do you do business today, what are your business problems, and what is your future direction?

First, build a model of your business. Then look at what the technology provides today, what its future direction is likely to be, and how this technology fits your business needs. Look beyond today and plan two to three years out, remembering that it will take time to realize the benefits from the technology. Planning the use of a technology from the business perspective is likely to gain the most support from management.

RESTRUCTURING AT PACIFIC BELL

Re-engineering made its way into Pacific Bell (PacBell) virtually unnoticed, without fanfare, glamour or management bother.[3] PacBell began on a small scale with expenditures that were not visible to upper-level management. It worked directly with internal clients who were the direct re-engineering tool users, and these clients in turn obtained any needed support from their immediate superiors. In the beginning, PacBell specialists approached potential clients to sell the technology. Today, clients seeking re-engineering assistance usually come to them. Re-engineering has remained a quiet movement that to date has never gained or really needed high-level sponsorship.

The history of re-engineering at PacBell dates back to 1985 when it needed a new payroll system. Although much of the functionality needed already existed in the old payroll system, it was in dire need of reorganization. It no longer made sense to attempt to add new functionality or even to continue maintaining the old system unless its technical condition could be upgraded and improved. However, the estimated rewrite replacement cost for the payroll system was $44 million and the estimated time was seven years. The package replacement option was not any more acceptable than the rewrite option because of the special regulations required.

After looking at its business needs and restructuring technology, PacBell decided to restructure rather than replace the payroll system and enlisted the Peat Marwick restructuring service. The restructuring effort was successful and it resulted in re-organizing the payroll system into a form where new functionality could be safely and efficiently added. One important benefit from restructuring was to reduce substantially the testing costs for the payroll system.

System Renewal Group

Following this first successful re-engineering experience, PacBell created the System Renewal Group in 1986. The function of the group is to research re-engineering tools and apply them where appropriate at PacBell. The group consists of three renewal technicians who serve more than 3000 software maintainers by providing consulting services, training, and re-engineering planning.

Much of the initial work focused on application portfolio analysis to learn about existing systems—their components, interfaces with other systems, and quality. Re-engineering tools such as PathVu from XA Systems and Inspector from KnowledgeWare were employed to assist in the analysis.

Quality Measures

PacBell now uses PathVu as a standard quality assurance tool. At PacBell, quality means continued improvement every time the software is modified or enhanced. PathVu provides a quantitative measure of quality by applying software complexity metrics (e.g., McCabe and Halstead metrics) to systems maintained by outsourced groups, to packages being evaluated for purchase, and to newly developed systems. PathVu's diagnostic indicators tell programmers and management whether maintenance changes meet company standards or have introduced potential problems such as backward branches. PathVu also is used to determine the level of maintenance difficulty for a piece of software to enable proper task assignment based on the level of experience and expertise required. Although not used to evaluate employees, PathVu analysis results can help pinpoint what additional staff training is needed. Because PathVu is used to measure the work product, everyone is trained in it.

In addition to analysis tools, PacBell also makes good use of other re-engineering tools. Retrofit from XA Systems and Recoder from KnowledgeWare are used to restructure COBOL code. VIA/Insight and VIA/Renaissance from ViaSoft are also used. For example, VIA/Renaissance is used in code splitting to extract common functionality out of existing systems so that it can be reused in new products. Prior to VIA/Renaissance, PacBell did code splitting manually. What required one week to do manually now can be done in ten minutes with VIA/Renaissance.

Most recently, PacBell has acquired DataTec from XA Systems to perform data name rationalization. In some instances, PacBell has 25 to 35 data names for one data element. Cleaning up data names and definitions is an important preparation step in PacBell's migration to repository technology.

Gaining a Competitive Advantage

PacBell has very strong feelings about the need for re-engineering. The company believes that it is a technology that can help an organization **gain a competitive advantage**. One example is its billing system. PacBell found it could bring a product to market faster than it could bill for it. What was needed was the ability to reuse and adopt existing billing functionality with new products, such as call forwarding, as they were introduced. Re-engineering gives PacBell this ability.

REFERENCES

1. From an interview with author and Ira Morrow, vice president for technical planning, Shearson Lehman Brothers, New York, NY.

2. From an interview with author and Bill Bagnell, product manager, Integral, Walnut Creek, CA.

3. From an interview with author and Patricia Seymour, systems renewal manager, Pacific Bell, Camino, CA.

PART II REPOSITORY

10 REPOSITORY CONCEPTS

REPOSITORY—BASED The key software technology for the 1990s is a workstation-based software tools environment. CASE technology introduced and brought this technology to the forefront. The software developer now expects a full-function CASE tools environment—not just a set of powerful CASE tools to support software development but rather an assembly of integrated CASE tools that link together and provide automated support for the phases across the entire software life cycle. The repository is now recognized as an important component in an integrated CASE tools environment. As a matter of fact, it is the single most important component, because the repository is the basis for software tools integration and the major productivity gains that we hope CASE will bring.

The 1990s will be the era when the repository is viewed as a core technology in building integrated software tools environments and reaching higher levels of software automation. In the 1980s, software tools environments and in particular CASE tools were viewed from the outside in with an emphasis on user interfaces and graphical system representations. In the 1990s, the perspective on tools has changed to an inside out view with the emphasis on the repository. Advances in software technology require not simply the creation and use of integrated software environments but **repository-based,** integrated software environments.

REPOSITORY The repository is the heart of an integrated CASE tools environment. It is the basis for

- Integration of tools
- Standardization of software system descriptions and form

- Sharing of software system information
- Software reusability

The *repository* is the mechanism for defining, storing, accessing, and managing all the information about an enterprise, its data, and its software systems.

The repository allows software system components and information about software systems to be shared **and reused** across software systems, life cycle phases, teams, and the organization. A key to increasing software productivity is getting information to software developers and maintainers when it is needed and in a form that is directly usable by software tools.

Before the term was standardized, the repository component of a CASE tools environment was referred to as a design dictionary or database, object-oriented database, knowledgebase, or encyclopedia. However, regardless of what it is called, the basic purpose is the same. The repository provides one place in which enterprise information can be entered once, kept up to date, and made available to everyone (users and tools) who needs it.

REPOSITORY BENEFITS

In general, a repository enhances communication and sharing of software system information across tools, life cycle activities, users, and applications. It greatly simplifies software development and improves the quality of system information by controlling access to the information and eliminating redundant definitions. Also, because the repository supports an open architecture environment, it allows the mixing and matching of tools provided by multiple vendors and allows tools to be used across multiple computing platforms. Furthermore, users can easily update and add new tools to an open architecture environment as they become available. Finally, the repository can help improve the consistency, validity, and integrity of software system information.

Longer-term benefits of the repository that should be emphasized are (1) simplification of software system maintenance because system components and system information are managed by the repository and (2) software reuse because the repository provides an inventory of reusable software components along with the means of easily accessing and understanding the components. Simplifying maintenance and enabling more software reuse have a direct impact on greatly reducing software costs.

Box 10.1 summarizes the most important benefits to be reaped by using the repository. It is important to note that the major benefits sought from integrated CASE tools environments are those directly derived from the repository.

BOX 10.1 Repository benefits

- Share system information across applications, tools, and system life cycle.
- Enable a multiuser, integrated software tools environment.
- Enhance user communication and information sharing.
- Consolidate and eliminate redundant corporate data.
- Increase system integrity.
- Simplify system maintenance.
- Enable combining tools from multiple vendors.
- Enable reuse of information across life cycle systems.
- Simplify migrations/conversions.

REPOSITORY CONTENTS

The repository supports the entire software life cycle from planning through maintenance by holding the information and system components used by and produced during each life cycle phase. To support planning, information about the corporation—organizational structure, business goals, business processes—is needed. System design information includes process models, data models, screen and report definitions, and algorithms. During the implementation phase, such system components as programs, load modules, subroutines, tables, files, and records are created. Impact analysis information, such as all users of a particular piece of information, aids the software maintainer when changing and revalidating existing systems. Project management information concerning project plans, schedules, audit trails, cost estimates, and quality assurance metrics is used across the phases of the life cycle. Also, information that describes the software life cycle process, such as process steps, deliverables, and quality control checks, is needed across the life cycle.

As shown in Box 10.2, several kinds of information must be stored in the repository:

- Information about the corporation (enterprise)
- Information describing the software system at various levels of abstractions/each phase of the life cycle
- Information describing the operating environment(s) for the system.
- Information for project management
- Information for software life cycle process management

BOX 10.2 Kinds of information in repository

- Logical data and process models
- Physical definitions and code
- Enterprise models
- Business data
- Business rules
- Relationships
- Repository meta model and validation rules
- Project management and auditing information
- Life cycle process model

Not only does the repository contain many types of information (structured diagrams, screen and menu definitions, report layouts, record descriptions, process logic, organization models, business rules, project management forms, data structures), but it also contains the **relationships** among the various information components (e.g., process explodes to subprocesses) and the **rules** for validating and using these components (e.g., diagram notation syntax rules, naming standards, redundancy and consistency checking). It is not unusual for a repository to maintain hundreds of types of information components and relationships. Including relationship information in the repository is a very important capability because it supports system understanding and change management.

Each repository component (also referred to as an entity or object) is described in terms of its **properties** or attributes. Properties typically include ID, alias names, type, narrative description, subcomponents, range values, edit and derivation rules, size, and language, as well as audit information. The properties used to describe a component will vary, depending on its type. Relationship properties or characteristics include cardinality (one-to-many, many-to-many), mandatory source and/or target, controlling for source and/or target, and order for source and/or target information.

Audit information is concerned with ownership identification and change history information for a repository component. For example, audit information includes who created the component, the project in which the component was created, when the component was originally created, and when the component was last updated.

MORE THAN A DICTIONARY

Like a dictionary, the repository holds physical, implementation level descriptions of data used in software systems. And, like a dictionary, the repository is responsible for maintenance, security, and access to its contents. However, the repository is a much more encompassing data store than a dictionary because it holds information and the processes (or methods) that operate on this information. The repository holds enterprise information, the corporate data model, and software system descriptions and components (see Fig. 10.1). The repository not only contains data (or information), but also (and most importantly) it contains the meaning of its data through the properties associated with each information component.

The repository serves more types of users than a dictionary. While the dictionary is a data/database administration tool, the repository is a tool for application developers and maintainers, quality assurance staff, project managers, and system planners. The repository potentially can consolidate all enterprise data and information resources (i.e., all the resources needed to produce information for an enterprise—data, systems, organizational context) and their descriptions into one collection and management point.

The repository is the successor to the dictionary. Tools such as the IBM Dictionary Model Transformer will be used to migrate data from corporate dic-

Figure 10.1 The repository contains enterprise information, the corporate data model, and software system descriptions and components.

tionaries (e.g., IBM OS/VS DB/DC Data Dictionary) to repositories (e.g., IBM Repository Manager).

MORE THAN A CASE REPOSITORY

Much of the interest in the repository thus far has centered around its role as the focal point for integrating CASE tools. As a matter of fact, the integration of CASE tools cannot be achieved without a repository. It is a required part of any CASE strategy, because without a repository, CASE tools cannot easily exchange and share data. The repository stores information in an implementation-independent, standardized form that can be understood in terms of its underlying meta model. This gives tools a common frame of understanding of what is stored in the repository. Furthermore, the repository provides common data access and manipulation services that can be shared by CASE tools.

However, the repository is more than a CASE repository because it integrates CASE tools and also re-engineering tools, project managers, configuration managers, and so forth. The repository supports all software system activities not just development. It serves application development, maintenance, system management, and operations (see Fig. 10.2). In effect, it holds and is responsible for managing all information needed to create, modify, evolve, execute, and maintain a software system.

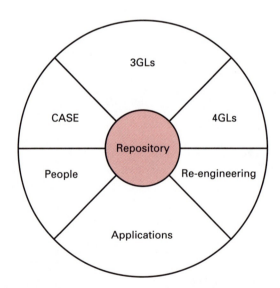

Figure 10.2 The repository is more than a CASE repository because it integrates CASE tools, re-engineering tools, third-generation, fourth-generation, and fifth-generation tools.

ENTERPRISE REPOSITORY

The repository concept is evolving toward a full-enterprise repository. Because most corporations now view all corporate information as an invaluable corporate asset that is crucial to its functioning and competing, a powerful mechanism is needed to protect and manage all corporate information and the systems that produce it. The repository is that mechanism.

By the end of the 1990s, corporations will have enterprise repositories. Enterprise repository users will include data/database administrators, software developers and maintainers, business analysts, managers, and **end users.** The enterprise repository will be responsible for the integrity of corporate information, the quality of software systems that produce corporate information, and the safe and easy access to corporate information (including access by tools and end users).

The repository will become the single source for all corporate information and the chief enterprise information integrator. That is

- Dictionary integrator
- Software tool integrator
- Software system integrator
- Software life cycle process integrator

Dictionary Integrator

Today, corporations often support multiple, incompatible dictionaries. For example, one dictionary can be required for each database management system, another used with a fourth generation language, and others for various CASE tools.

Because the information is fragmented across incompatible data stores, such as libraries, directories, dictionaries, and catalogs, it is impossible to ensure that information is consistently defined, that it is kept up to date, and that redundancies are controlled. The repository eventually will eliminate the need for multiple dictionaries, provide a single point of definition and management for corporate information, and a practical way to ensure information integrity.

Tool Integrator

The repository is required to integrate CASE tools and eventually all software tools that support software life cycle activities. It acts as the control point for sharing information among tools.

System Integrator

A goal for most corporations is to be supported by a set of integrated application systems. Integrated application systems are built on top of the same data model that logically describes how information is used and shared across a corporation. This enterprise-wide data model establishes a common information infrastructure for uniting systems used throughout the corporation. This model is stored in the enterprise repository.

Process Integrator

Software process integration is concerned with linking the phases of the software life cycle process—integrating across the steps of developing and maintaining software systems and integrating across the levels of abstraction used to represent the systems. Two bridges provide process integration: the repository and the methodology.

The repository provides one controlled source for system information and life cycle process information. It also provides a common representation of system information as described by the repository meta model to ensure a common understanding of that information as it is passed from tool to tool and phase to phase. Furthermore, the repository provides a means for tracing the information through its transformations across levels of abstraction as it evolves from initial system requirements definition form to its production-time executable form.

A methodology drives the software process by providing and ordering the overall framework for defining the software process steps, deliverables, and quality control checks. Information about the methodology can be stored in the repository and used to guide users in proper use of the methodology and in the selection of tools needed to support various methodology steps and tasks.

WHAT DOES TOOL INTEGRATION MEAN?

An important requirement of CASE technology is tool integration. Why is integration so important? What are the properties of integrated tools? What role does the repository play in integration?

Integration lies at the very foundation of the CASE concept because it is the key to making the use of powerful software tools practical. Tools in an integrated tools environment interact with each other in a consistent, intuitive way and conform to a set of industry standards concerning user interfaces and data exchange. To the tool user they appear to be cooperating with each other and are coordinated enough not to duplicate functions or data. Integrated tools increase both software productivity and quality. They reduce the need for redundant data entry when the same information is needed by different tools and thereby reduce the opportunity for user data entry errors. Integrated tools link the phases of the life cycle by automatically passing data on to the next phase in the form in which the data are needed.

An integrated, full-function CASE tools environment is an assembly of CASE tools that provide full-function support across the entire life cycle and possess the following properties:

- All CASE tools share a common user interface.
- All CASE tools share a common data interface.
- All CASE tools feed and access a common repository.
- All CASE tools represent information in terms of the same underlying meta model.
- All CASE tools support the same life cycle process model.

A **common user interface** is a bridge connecting CASE tools in an integrated software environment. Because it gives all tools "a common look and feel," it reduces the learning curve for the tools. Acquiring experience with one CASE tool in the environment can be applied to learning other CASE tools in the environment. Several standards, official and de facto, are emerging for graphic user interfaces, such as Motif from OSI, Windows from X-11, Presentation Manager of IBM SAA, and DEC windows from DEC (1).

A **common data interface** is another kind of bridge connecting CASE tools. It should be easy to pass data from tool to tool because it is expected that the output of one CASE tool in the environment will become the input to another.

In order for tools to share data, they must recognize and understand the data received from other tools. The **repository meta model** gives the tools a common frame for understanding the data form and meaning. Integrated tools interpret the meta model in exactly the same way and conform to the same information rules and constraints. This ensures that nonsensical, invalid information is not passed to a tool.

REPOSITORY META MODEL

The repository contains information about an enterprise, its software life cycle process, and its application systems, as well as the components of its application systems. It is the repository meta model that defines what kinds of information can be stored in the repository, the format and descriptive properties of the information and the relationships, as well as the rules for accessing and validating the information. The meta model is the overall conceptual view of the entire repository contents. Individual user (tool) views are derived from it.

The meta model is the basis of tools integration and the integrity of repository information. It allows tools to share both common data and methods that operate on the data. It can offer broad support for multiple tools and techniques because it is capable of supporting all the views required by all tools accessing the repository. For tools to share information, they must define that information in a compatible way (i.e., in terms of the same types of entities and relationships). For example, if a tool needs to pass information about a data flow diagram to another tool, the tools must use a consistent means of specifying the representation of a data flow diagram and its elements (e.g., processes, data flows, data stores) and abide by the same validation rules.

Furthermore, the meta model determines what software life cycle processes and methodologies can be supported by the repository-based CASE tools environment. The repository contains the information produced by and fed to the phases of the software process. The methodology defines the specifics of the information in terms of when it is used, the form it must take, and the validating rules. For the repository to support the methodology, its meta model must include the types of information produced by and used by the methodology.

Rules and constraints to ensure semantic integrity of the model and control use of the repository contents can be included within the meta model. This enables automatic enforcement of the rules when repository data are entered or manipulated. Some rules may be enterprise-wide, and some can be specific to a particular tool.

Entity-Relationship Model

Many repository meta models are represented in the form of an entity-relationship (ER) model. As shown in Fig. 10.3, the basic entity-relationship model includes entities and relationships between entities.[2] An **entity** is anything about which data can be stored, such as a person, a business process, or a data element. A **relationship** is a directed association between two entities, such as an employee belongs to a department or a program calls a subroutine. An entity type is a category to which many individual entities or instances belong (i.e.,

Entity:

    Anything About Which Information Is Stored

Relationship:

    Interaction Between Entities

      • Optional / Mandatory
      • One to One / One to Many / Many to Many
      • And / Or
      • Hierarchy

Attribute:

    Piece of Information Describing the Entity

Figure 10.3 The entity relationship model frequently is used as the repository meta model and to model software application systems.

inventory control program and payroll program are instances of the entity type *program*). Likewise a relationship type is a category grouping individual relationships. Relationship types are described in terms of their sources and targets. For example, in the relationship type *Program Calls Module,* program is the source and module is the target. An example of a relationship instance (or occurrence) is PAYROLL PROGRAM CALLS SALARY-COMPUTE-ROUTINE.

In its simplest form, only binary relationships are allowed in the ER model. A binary relationship allows at most two types of entities (relationships) to participate in the relationship (ex. payroll program calls a tax calculation subroutine) and multiple instances of only one entity type (1:M). However, the ER model may be extended to allow multiple instances of both entity types (M:M) and *n*-ary relationships (multipart relationships between entities). **Cardinality** refers to the number of instances involved in the relationship and is a property of relationship type.

Also, the ER model can be extended to include attributes associated with entities and relationships. For example, some of the attributes associated with the entity *program* are its name, author, language, description, version number, input and output, and quality indicator.

Entity and relationship types can be collected into a single hierarchical construct called an **aggregation type**.

The ER model is used as the repository meta model because it is frequently also used to model software application systems (business process, data structure, database). Using a similar model to represent the application system and the repository that contains application system information should simplify our understanding of software systems and the contents of the repository.

The ER model is a powerful modeling technique because the meaning of the information defined by the model carried in attributes and relationships is also contained in the model. It is a simple, but semantically rich, model.

Object-Oriented Model

The basic components in an object are the **object data** and **methods** (or operations) that operate on the data. Both the object data and the methods can be viewed independently of their physical implementation. This offers the advantage of defining and changing implementation details separately from their higher-level descriptions. Examples of object data are source code and business processes. Examples of methods include data manipulation operations, such as create, edit, copy, and delete.

The repository can be viewed as a collection of objects that are arranged in a type hierarchy and are defined in terms of an entity-relationship model.[3] The object is the basis for

- Control and extensibility
- Management and manipulation

- Allowing different views of repository contents
- Handling of complex data

An object is similar to an entity because an object definition includes a data definition. But, unlike an entity, it also includes process definitions. This enables sharing of both data definitions and processes for manipulating the data.

Whereas entity-relationship modeling allows the definition of low-level, distinct kinds of information, the object model allows the collection of information, such as ER aggregation and the work or operations associated with it. Object data can be stored in the repository or some other data store, and the repository services and control can be extended to these data via an object level interface. Tools manipulate object data (stored in the repository or elsewhere) by calling the repository (sending a message) and specifying the name of the object and the methods to be performed.

Object type is a collection of information, such as a program. Individual instances of the object type program include COBOL, PL/1, and C. The object type includes a set of methods that each instance can share. When a new instance (such as Ada) is added, it also can share these methods. The sharing and reusing of methods can greatly reduce the effort needed to change and enhance systems and the functions that tools provide.

Some repositories provide both an ER view and an object-oriented view of their contents. For example, the IBM repository meta model, called the Information Model, has both an object level and an ER level.[4] The object level provides a high-level view of application and enterprise-related information in terms of objects (program source, object code, large documents) and the methods that operate on these objects. The ER level provides a detailed view of the information in its ER format that can be directly processed by tools and methods.

The DEC repository, called CDD/Repository, also uses an ER model for its repository meta model, repository information model. In addition, an object-oriented layer is provided on top of the ER level to allow entities to be treated as objects. The object-oriented layer makes it easier to change and add new objects and new tools to meet future needs and requirements.[5] It also simplifies tools by allowing them to share common methods rather than creating their own individual tool logic.

Extensibility

The vendor providing a repository also will provide a predefined repository meta model along with supporting repository services for defining, accessing, manipulating, and controlling repository contents. Figures 10.4, 10.5, and 10.6 show examples of the meta models in ER form for three repository-based CASE tools. The predefined repository meta model will include definitions for entity types, relationship types, attributes, rules for manipulating and validating repository

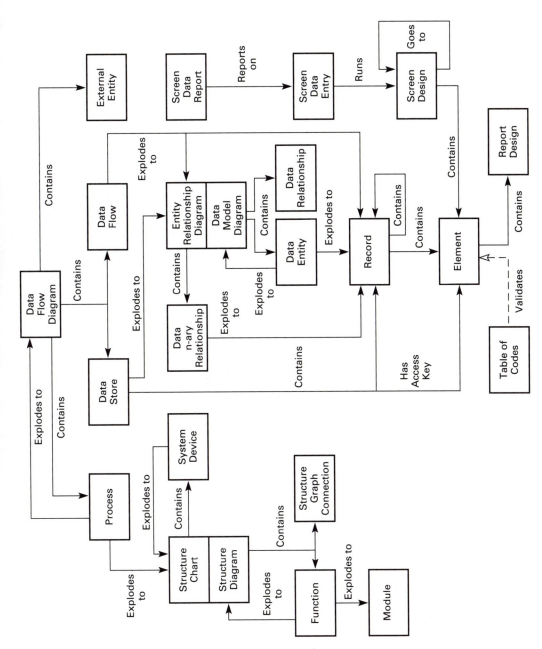

Figure 10.4 Example of the underlying meta model for a CASE front-end analysis/design tool kit. This model has 32 entity types.

169

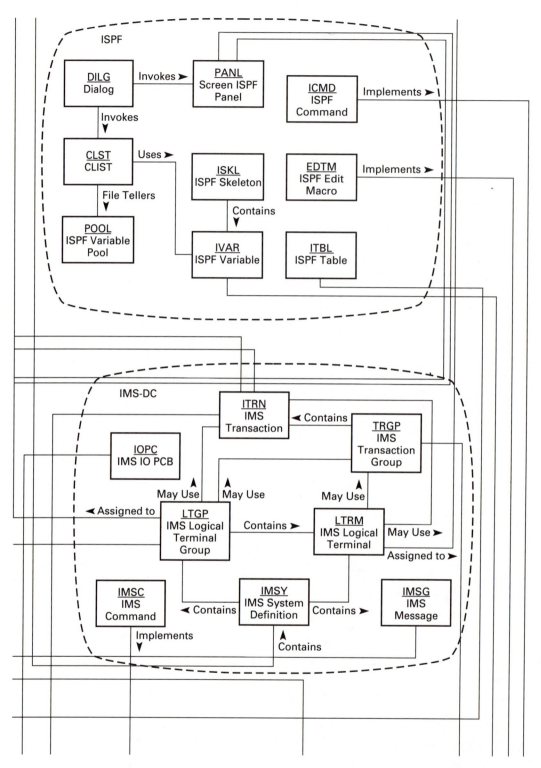

Figure 10.5 Example of a portion of the underlying meta model for a CASE COBOL code generator. The complete model has 200 entity types and 500 relationships.

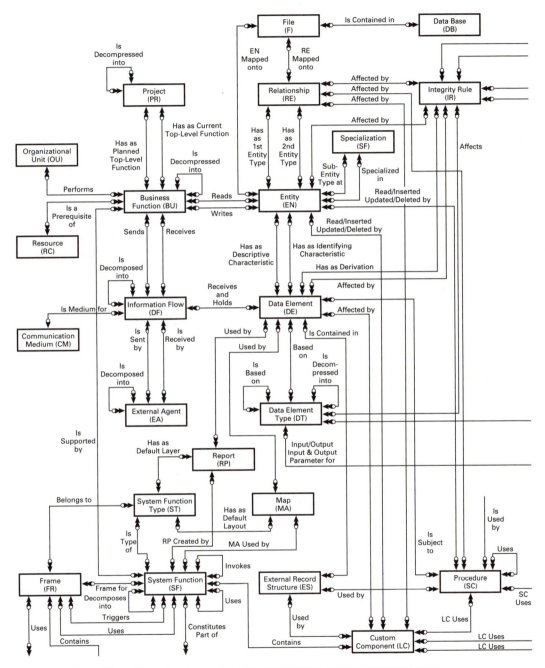

Figure 10.6 Example of a portion of the underlying meta model for a CASE workbench that supports application analysis, design, and implementation.

data called policies or constraints, object types and methods, depending of course on its meta model. Frequently used information types, such as process model, database, and data structures, will be included in the meta model.

The meta model restricts the information that can be used by tools and methodologies and stored in the repository to the format and meaning of information it has defined. To accommodate different and additional information requirements of new tools, technologies, and methodologies, it must be possible to change the meta model. An **extensible meta model** allows users (software tool builders) to add new object types, methods, and descriptions of repository information.

REPOSITORY IMPLEMENTATION

A layered architecture based on the ANSI SPARC three-level schema is most commonly used to implement a repository. As shown in Box 10.3, the three levels or layers are

- **External (logical) model: individual user's view**
- **Conceptual model: comprehensive view of entire contents**
- **Physical model: physical implementation for data storage**

BOX 10.3 Repository implementation

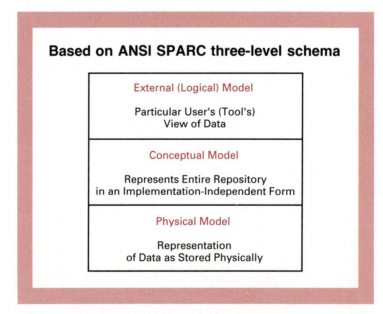

This layered architecture gives the repository its ability to present different views of its contents to different users.

The repository meta model is at the conceptual level in this schema. It is most commonly modeled in ER form. The physical level of the schema describes how the contents of the repository are actually stored. It is most commonly a relational model.

Repository Engine

Currently, the physical data store for most repositories is a relational store. Along with the relational store, a relational database management system is used to supply data management facilities, such as data recovery, logging, and distribution for the repository. Examples of commercial DBMS that are commonly used for repository implementation include DB2, Oracle, Ingres, and DEC Rdb. SQL-based databases are often chosen to provide SQL, the de facto database access language.

There is a question about the ability of a relational DBMS to meet the performance requirements demanded of a repository and to support the rich, complex variety of entity and relationship types stored in the repository.[6] Object-oriented DBMSs are suggested as an alternative to relational DBMSs. However, because the object-oriented DBMS technology is less mature than relational, the use of object-oriented DBMSs should be considered a future trend more than a current implementation choice.

To provide object-oriented capabilities an object-oriented layer is included over the relational DBMS level. For example, the DEC repository CDD/Repository includes an object-oriented interface based on ATIS, a proposed repository interface standard, on top of the relational DEC DBMS Rdbs/VMS.[7] This approach combines the desired object-oriented capabilities with the practical implementation solution provided by a relational DBMS.

REPOSITORY INFORMATION MANAGEMENT

Automatic management of all system information is the primary reason for storing it on the computer and one of the primary benefits that the repository offers.

It is impossible to maintain the integrity of corporate and system information with only manual, informal methods, especially in a large project team or across systems. To ensure safe, controlled sharing of information, a formal, automated information management facility is needed. The types of functions that should be provided by the repository information management facility are summarized in Box 10.4.

Security

Security controls in the form of passwords restrict access to contents (or selected portions of the contents) of the repository. Access privileges limit user

BOX 10.4 Repository information management facilities

Security

- Password/sign-on
- Access privileges

Version Control

- Level of control—granularity
- Version identification
- Maximum number of versions

Change Management

- Audit of changes
- Change impact analysis
- Change control level
- Automatic change propagation across versions and related objects
- Undo command

Auditing

- Ownership
- Date created
- Date last changed
- Status

Data access and validation

- Data manipulation
- Entry validation
- Consistency and completeness checking
- Rule Enforcement—policies and triggers
- Naming standards
- Requirements traceability

Queries and Reports

- Browsers
- IRDS command language support/access protocols

BOX 10.4 *(Continued)*

- Online query—SQL support
- Report writing

Multiuser/Multiple Platforms

- Concurrent access/update handling
- Check-out/check-in facility/realtime updating
- Realtime access/upload-download
- Distributed across multiple platforms

Open Architecture

- Public or proprietary interface
- Standards compliance
- Upload/Download information between repositories
- Batch import/export facility

Configuration Management

- Baseline management
- Automated build
- Backup and recovery

---

access to read only or full update as well as control of access, execute, and delete privileges.

Versioning, Change Control, and Configuration Management

Versioning allows multiple copies of repository information to exist. For example, different versions may exist for archive, production, baseline, and testing purposes. The repository version control function keeps track of multiple versions and allows some maximum number of versions to exist. The granularity of version control should go down to the individual entity or object level (e.g., the programs or modules that perform a task).

The **change management function** of the repository information management facility automatically keeps track of changes made to each repository component. The change control level should be down to the individual repository component. Because the repository not only stores the component but also the relationships between this component and others in the repository, the change management function can provide invaluable information about the impact of change. If one component is changed, it can help to identify all other components that may be affected by the change. For example, when a definition of a component has been changed, any user who accesses that component should be notified of the change.

In some cases, when a component is changed, automatic change propagation will occur across all versions and related components. This is done by defining a **trigger** that causes the signified related components to be changed when the component is changed. For example, when a screen is deleted, all related screen fields are also deleted because it makes no sense to have a screen field that is not related to a screen. The change management function usually has some sort of undo command that allows the user to put all components back to their state before the change was made. Change management helps keep all information up to date and in sync.

The repository allows for the capturing of **audit information** to record the change history of repository components. Whenever a component is changed, a trigger may prompt the user for change information, such as who made the change and when and why the change was made. Other audit information includes the owner, date of previous change, status information (e.g., test, production) and quality assurance metrics (e.g., error rates, complexity measures).

Configuration management (and in particular the system build facility) is the function of the repository information management facility that understands all the components of a software system and how to assemble the components into the current runtime version. Configuration management ensures that the latest version of each component is included. Also, configuration management includes backup and recovery procedures to protect against losing repository contents in the event of hardware and software failures.

Query and Reporting

To give the user the ability to view the contents of the repository, **query and reporting functions** are necessary. In some cases, SQL or the IRDS access language is used to form ad hoc queries concerning the repository information.

A navigator can be used to point to a repository object on the screen with a mouse and then give the user detailed information about that object or provide an editor for that object type. Users can search for objects by using keyword searches.

Browsers, such as Datatrieve from DEC and QMF from IBM, are forms-based languages for relational databases and can be used to view interactively the contents of the DEC repository CCD/Repository and IBM Repository/MVS, respectively.[8]

A set of standard reports is provided to view easily the contents of the repository. Both online and offline reports, either preformatted or customized, are provided. For example, information such as where each data element is used in the system, who created it, and when and how many times its definition has been revised are all available in cross-reference reports. Some basic types of repository reports include

- Contents/lists reports of entity and relationship types
- Cross-reference/where-used reports
- Analysis reports and security reports

Multiuser

Multiuser access allows multiple users to access concurrently the same repository information and controls the updating of information. Some repositories control the updating of repository information with a **checkout** facility. One user can check out repository components which that user intends to update. During the checkout period, other users can access those components but cannot update them. When the components are checked in, the changes must be approved by the repository validation function.

Other repositories allow components to be changed in realtime. Locking to manage concurrent access can be provided at the file, record, or component level.

Open Architecture

The repository should be **open architecture**. This means that one function of the repository information management facility is to provide interface information that enables tools to access its contents and share repository information management functions (e.g., CGI System's Pacbase Dynamic Call Interface, DEC's Standard Relational Interface, IBM'S Repository Common Programming Interface). Also, a **batch import/export** facility should be provided to transfer information into or out of the repository from or to other repositories, databases, or dictionaries.

Manipulation and Validation

The repository information facility must provide the ability to **manipulate and validate** its contents. Standard manipulation functions include creating, reading, updating, moving, and deleting repository components. Standard validation checking includes type and range checks, consistency and completeness checks, and naming standards enforcement. Repository analysis reports can be used to list checking problems and violations.

Some types of checking to be performed on a repository component are defined in the repository meta model along with other attribute information about that type. This kind of attribute information is called **rules or policies.** Rules define the constraints and requirements that are imposed on a repository component when it is entered into the repository or later on when it is changed. Checking is activated by a trigger.[9] For example, cardinality constraints and incomplete relationship information checks can be imposed on relationships.

The inclusion of the rules for checking repository information in the repository meta model eliminates the need to include this logic in the individual tools that use the repository. This simplifies the tools and standardizes the checking function. The rules can be changed without also changing the tools.

REPOSITORY ARCHITECTURES

Logically, the repository is thought of as a single store, but physically, it can be one or many. A single logical store enables easier management and control of repository contents. However, the underlying physical store can be either centralized or distributed, depending on the architecture chosen by the vendor and, in some cases, by the user.

There are several hardware platform combinations for a software tools environment. One possibility is a one-level platform consisting of a personal computer (PC) or a workstation. As shown in Fig. 10.7, this architecture includes one physical repository residing at the PC/workstation level.

The workstation/PC provides a highly interactive, responsive, and dedicated platform on which to carry out software tasks. In particular, its powerful graphics capabilities enable easy creation and manipulation of the structured diagrams used to specify and document software systems. Also, it supports rapid prototyping for creating system models to help discover and clarify user requirements. Workstations/PCs are the perfect platform for analysis and design tasks. They provide the maximum possible support for each individual involved in software development, maintenance, or project management work.

However, workstations must be connected to support communication and information sharing between developers. Connection of workstations is accomplished by linking them in a local area network. The physical repository store can be located on a remote workstation or a server on a local area network.

Software tool environments often are spread across multiple platforms creating a two- or three-tiered architecture (see Fig. 10.8). The two-tiered architec-

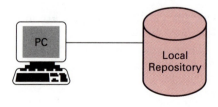

Figure 10.7 When the hardware platform for the tools environment consists solely of a workstation or personal computer, the physical repository also resides at this level.

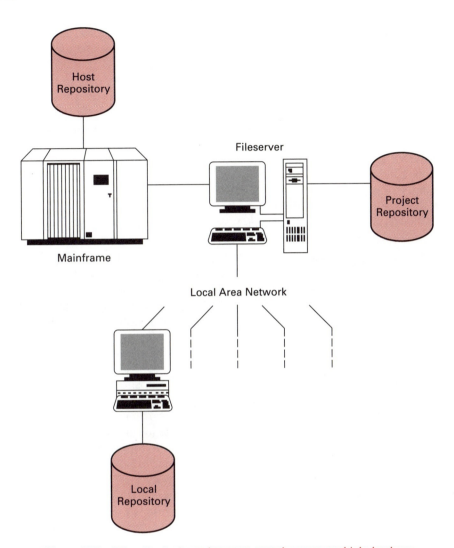

Figure 10.8 When the tools environment spreads across multiple hardware systems, the physical repository may reside at one or multiple levels of the hardware platform.

ture consists of a workstation/PC level connected to a host (either mini- or mainframe computer) level. The three-tiered architecture employs an intermediate hardware level between the host mainframe computer and the workstation level. Multiple-tiered platforms allow the distribution of software tasks among the tiers to reduce contention for expensive mainframe resources and to allow tasks to be executed on the hardware system that is most expedient. Also, because some tasks, such as code and database generation, system testing, and impact analysis, sometimes require the power and storage capacity of a mainframe (mini) computer, the multiple tiers are thought necessary.

In multiple-tiered platform architectures, the repository can be either physically centralized or distributed across the tiers. When physically centralized, the repository usually resides at the host (mainframe) level. All the repository contents physically reside at the host level and the tools may reside at any level.

Accessing, updating, and checking repository data can be done in either realtime or batch mode, depending on the vendor's repository design. When done in batch mode, the designated repository data are checked out from the repository to a user's local data store and then checked back into the repository after the user has completed the task on the data.

The IBM Repository Manager/MVS is an example of a host-based, centralized repository supporting a multitier tool environment.[10] DB2 is used as the data store and uploading/downloading is used to move data between the repository and a tool's local work space. For example, repository data can be selectively downloaded from the host-based IBM repository for use by PS/2 workstation-based tools and then later uploaded to the repository where a central administration function checks the data, collects changes from multiple users, and consolidates them.

A **centralized repository** based on the host allows the repository to take advantage of data integrity, recovery, security, and control facilities provided by a central data management system. A centralized repository essentially has one database and one repository manager that manages the contents of its database.

A **distributed repository** architecture allows for multiple physical databases. Although segments of the repository may reside in different physical devices in a network, logically it is still considered as one repository. A distributed repository can mean better performance, more efficient network use, and increased reliability. To improve project productivity and protect project security a separate physical project repository can be created. To reduce contention for information resources, separate physical repositories can be created to serve development activities, the production environment, separate departments, or geographic locations. DEC's CCD/Repository is an example of a distributed repository.[11]

EXAMPLES OF REPOSITORIES

Common Data Dictionary/Repository, from Digital Equipment Corporation, and Repository Manager/MVS, from IBM, are two examples of repositories. They implement many of the repository facilities and features that were discussed earlier in this chapter. They are important examples because both are likely to become de facto repository standards.

DEC's CDD/Repository

Common Data Dictionary/Repository (CDD/Repository) is the repository offering from Digital Equipment Corporation (DEC).[12] CCD/Repository is an active, distributed repository to be used to support development and maintenance for all types of systems, including technical, scientific, business, and embedded systems. As a distributed repository, separate physical repositories may reside in separate directories or on separate devices at one node or on different nodes connected by a local area or wide area network. Although CDD/Repository can be physically distributed across a network, logically it is considered a single repository serving as the collection point for system information and data. Its contents can be managed centrally or locally, depending on the user needs.

CDD/Repository is a shared store of information about software systems, data and projects, and procedures and rules for managing systems, data, and projects. Its purpose is to provide

- A means to centralize, standardize, and integrate information to aid system development, maintenance, management, and integration
- The establishment, maintenance, and consistent use of descriptions of systems and data

The CCD/Repository meta model form is an entity-attribute-relationship model in which entities are treated as objects. The model, called the repository information model, is commercially available and is extensible with respect to new object types, attributes, and relationship types. Box 10.5 lists examples of the types of information that can be stored in CDD/Repository. The CDD/Repository information model is organized into a set of categories, each containing a set of subject areas (see Fig. 10.9). It includes a model of the business, a model of software development, and a model of CDD/Repository itself.

CDD/Repository is based on a three-schema ANSI SPARC architecture. The physical level is implemented with VAX Rdb/VMS, DEC's distributed database management system. Rdb tables may be distributed on different devices across the network. CDD/Repository is available for the DEC VAX/VMS environment and RISC/ULTRIX environment.

The CDD/Repository information management facilities allow repository users to create and share repository objects in a controlled manner across life cycle phases, networks, and environments. Provided services include

- **Security:** Grant users and users groups access rights to read, write, delete, control access, execute, and create versions.
- **Versioning:** Provided at object or collection level.
- **Change management:** Locate all uses of a shared definition and support change propagation through notification.

BOX 10.5 DEC CDD/plus subject area definitions Examples

Category	Subject Areas
Mission	Business functions Business products Policies Enterprise plans Strategic systems plans Information architecture Business architecture Audit facilities
Personnel	People, skills, assignments Personnel resources and roles Security provisions Internal organizations External organizations
Requirements	Text documents Mail messages Notes conferences Mechanisms for associating requirements with structured system artifacts
Platform	Physical networks Network protocols Physical equipment Logical devices queues Operating systems
System Life Cycle	Industry standards Internationalization rules System life cycle deliverable definition System life cycle compliance advisories Methodology definition Methodology instruction Transformation algorithms Consistency/completeness rules Documentation format and composition instructions Review annotations/sign-offs Metrics and measurement tools Graphic representation facility Matrix representation facility Naming standards Class definitions

BOX 10.5 *(Continued)*

Project Management	Portability guidelines
	Data standards
	Online help facilities
	Change impact dependencies
	Project plan
	Test plan
	Software quality metrics
	Work breakdown structure, estimates, schedules
	Resource loading
	Problem reports
Category	**Subject Areas**
Portfolio	Libraries
	Archives
	DECwindows entry points
	Generators, simulators, prototyping tools
	Compilers, editors, testing tools
	System management resources
	Backup/recovery resources
	Network plans
	Physical inventory management
	Project history and metrics
	Menu structures
	Performance criteria and timing issues
	System build instructions
	Data object inventory
	Source code
	Object code
	Binary images
	Configuration dependencies
	Organization reference files
Data	Conceptual, logical, physical data and information representation
	Subject areas
	Form layout definition
	Reference sources
	Report layout definitions
	Input test data
	Test results
	Regression test scripts

(Continued)

BOX 10.5 *(Continued)*

Processes	System
	Program
	Module
	Callable routines
	Data flow models
	Data transforms
	Transaction
	Triggers
Distribution	Electronic data interchange standards and guidelines
	Messaging/RPC services
	Import/export
	File replication services
	Distribution planning
	Traffic analysis
	Distributed design methods

- **Configuration management:** Track versions, partition versions, and establish context that is a selection of a particular version of specific objects.
- **Viewing:** Provide a DECwindows/motif-based graphic callable interface; provide a hierarchical navigator to view contents in indented form and network navigator to show contents in ER form; provide online queries and reports of contents.
- **Checking:** Enforce standards and policies.

CCD/Repository is the cornerstone product of the DEC CASE environment called Cohesion, which is composed of DEC-supplied CASE tools (e.g., DECdesign, which is an analyst/design toolkit, VAX COBOL Code Generator, and VAX Rally) and third-party–supplied tools. More than 20 third-party CASE tools vendors have announced plans to provide tools that work within the DEC CASE environment (Excelerator from Intersolv Corporation, Foundation from Andersen Consulting, Corvision from Cortex, Powerhouse from Cognos). Also, DEC plans to offer a link between CDD Repository and the IBM Repository.

Cohesion is built on DEC's Network Application Support (NAS), which provides application access services, communication services, and information/resource sharing services to enable applications to work together in a heterogeneous, multivendor, networked environment. Cohesion can run under VMS, UNIX, MS-DOS, OS/2, and Macintosh and can create systems whose target en-

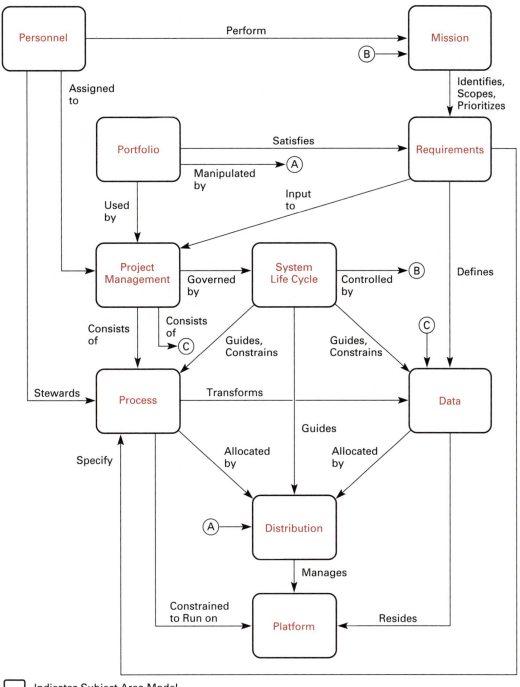

Figure 10.9 The major subject areas in the DEC CCD/Repository information model. DEC refines these subject areas into a more detailed set of information needed by Cohesion tools.

vironment is VMS, ULTRIX, UNIX, MS-DOS, OS/2 VAXELN, MVS, VM, DOS/VSE, CRAY, and a variety of embedded microprocessors. The repository services are part of the NAS information/resource sharing services.

The DEC CDD/Repository incorporates an object type hierarchy for defining a repository system called ATIS (A Tool Integration Standard).[13] ATIS is an object-oriented layer (sits on top of the ER layer) that makes it easier to extend the CDD/Repository meta model to support new object types and the integration of new tools. ATIS is being proposed by DEC as a tool interface standard to be incorporated into the ANSI and ISO IRDS repository standard. CDD/Repository plans to conform to the IRDS repository standard.

IBM REPOSITORY "A repository is an organized, shared collection of information supporting business and data processing related activities."[14] "The repository concept is to provide a foundation for an integrated toolset . . . control point for data and the enterprise information model," according to IBM.[15]

The initial IBM repository offering is called IBM Repository Manager/MVS. It provides a single point of control for defining and managing application information in the AD/Cycle, IBM's application development environment. The kinds of application information to be stored in the IBM repository include information about the corporation's organizational structure and goals, business processes, business data, life cycle process, application system components, and the relationships among all these. The goals for using the IBM repository focus on it as the means to eliminating redundant information, to improving application quality, and to increasing software productivity. The repository is "the primary vehicle for sharing application development information among (AD/Cycle) tools."[16]

The IBM repository is based on the ANSI SPARC three-schema architecture giving three independent views of data and function (see Box 10.6):

1. **Conceptual view:** Global repository view of information and function used to model entities, relationships, objects, and policies in ER form.
2. **Logical view:** Tool-specific view identifying functions that have access to information.
3. **Storage view:** View of physical representation of information for mapping from conceptual view to underlying relational database store.

The IBM repository is based on a central, host-based architecture. The physical level initially is implemented using DB2, an IBM SQL relational database; and data management facilities are provided by the DB2 database management system. Initially, the IBM repository is available for the IBM MVS/ESA and MVS/XA environments.

Besides providing an information store, the IBM Repository Manager/MVS provides host-based services for defining, accessing, sharing, and manip-

BOX 10.6 IBM repository Three-schema architecture

Data	Function
Conceptual	**Conceptual**
• Entities • Relationships • Entity aggregations • Objects • Integrity policies on attributes and relationships	• Policies on entity, attribute, and relationship 　—Security for authorized access rules 　—Trigger for rules on execution of process 　—Derivation for specific algorithms for creating entity attribute values
Logical	**Logical**
• Logical records, called templates, which are structures of fields • Templates combined into hierarchical structure • Integrity policies on fields	• Function policies 　—Security 　—Trigger 　—Derivation • Function procedural logic coded in COBOL or C
Physical	**Physical**
• Relational—tables and columns for storing instances of entities, attributes, and relationships	• Transactions, subsystems, and commands making up implementation of a tool

ulating information stored in the repository (i.e., services for populating and changing a repository).[17] Repository data can be described in an entity-relationship format or an object-oriented format. The repository provides facilities called ER services for defining, manipulating, and controlling data in the ER format. Through interactive dialogs or a program callable interface, repository services provide for

- Creating a model of information to be stored in the repository
- Defining a particular user's view of information in the repository

- Defining constraints and controls on use of repository information at a global or tool-specific level
- Reading, writing, updating, and deleting information

The repository provides tool services to enable tools to access and manipulate repository information directly in its ER format or through object services by requesting that a method be performed on an object.

Repository data access services are an element of an SAA Common Programming Interface (CPI). Tools using this callable interface may be written in COBOL, C, PL/1, or REXX.

The repository allows constraints or **policies** to be associated with its data. Policies are used to control the use of data. For example, policies can be used to specify data value range checks or actions to be taken when the value of data (either entities or relationships) changes. There are four types of policies:

- **Security:** to control access to repository data
- **Integrity:** to perform data value checks for entity and relationship types
- **Derivation:** to define calculation of data values for entity attributes
- **Triggers:** to define processes to be performed when repository data for entity and relationship types change state.

Policies can be applied organization-wide or tool-specific, depending on whether they are specified at the conceptual or logical level (see Box 10.6).[18]

The repository also allows its data to be described in an object format in which an object is a collection of data and operations that can be performed against that data. Facilities called object services are provided by the repository to define and access objects. Object data may be stored in the repository in ER format or in another data store in the AD/Cycle in another form. Object services allow tools to be built that control and invoke functions that manipulate repository objects through common methods (e.g., moving objects to and from the workstation).[19] Examples of objects are source code, panels, and text.

The IBM repository is the successor to former IBM information bases (dictionaries, directories, libraries). IBM supplies batch maintenance facilities to assist in migration from these types of data stores to the repository. For example, IBM Dictionary Model Transformer assists the batch migration from IBM OS/VS DB/DC Data Dictionary to IBM Repository Manager/MVS.

IBM Query Management Facility (QFM) is an interactive query and report writer for DB2 and SQL/DS relational databases. QMF is used to provide query and report writing facilities for ER data in the IBM repository for its end users. The user can specify either an entity type or aggregation type to query.

The IBM repository is an open architecture product whose tool interfaces and underlying meta model are public. IBM's business partners, Bachman, Intersolv, KnowledgeWare, Easel, Systematica, and Synon, as well as other third-party vendors, will be able to build tools that enable to the IBM repository.

Conceptual view dialogs and a batch loader facility are provided for exporting and importing repository information to and from tools.

The IBM repository complies with the de facto standard, IBM Systems Application Architecture (SAA). The IBM Repository is a foundation component of IBM AD/Cycle, which completely conforms to SAA. Also, IBM is an active member of the ANSI IRDS repository standards committee and supports the IRDS standard.

IBM AD Information Model

The meta model for the IBM AD/Cycle repository is called the **AD Information Model.** It is described by IBM as the "architected information interface between AD/Cycle tools and the application development information managed by the AD/Cycle repository."[20] It is a predefined meta model supplied by IBM along with the AD/Cycle repository to provide a consistent means of describing and accessing application development information for tools and users. The AD Information Model is a conceptual view of information that can be shared by tools and is the key to integration because it is the formal description of information to be managed by the Repository.

As shown in Fig. 10.10, the AD Information Model supports a model of the IBM repository at two levels: the object level and the entity-relationship level. The object level provides a high-level view of repository information and the ER level provides a detailed view.

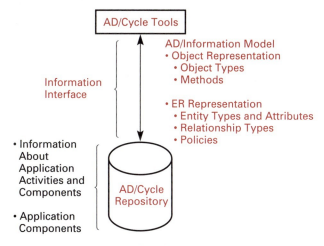

Figure 10.10 The IBM AD Information Model is the meta model for the AD/Cycle repository. It is the means for sharing information among tools and is the key to integration.

The IBM repository ER model provides for the definition of entity types, aggregation types, relationship types, and constraints (policies) to be enforced when ER data are manipulated. Examples of entity types are processes, agents, IMS DB description, and COBOL level 88 data items. Examples of relationship types are COBOL-Item-Has-Item-88, and Entity-Subarea-Consists-Of-Subarea.

The IBM ER model can be divided into four submodels:

- **Enterprise (ENT) submodel:** model of components of enterprise and their relationships represented in terms of entity type, process, attribute, information flow, relationship type, relationship link, business data type and information flow vector
- **IMS/VS (DLI) submodel:** model of IMS database descriptions (DBDs) and program specification blocks (PSB)
- **High-Level Language (HLL) submodel:** model of COBOL source program definitions
- **Global (GLO):** model of global constructs to store text, manage objects, and so on.

Each of these submodels is expected to evolve.

The AD Information Model is extensible by IBM software vendors and tool builders to support information needed by new tools and activities. New object types and their associated methods as well as new entity types and their attributes, new relationship types, and policies can be added.

REPOSITORY SERVICES SUMMARY

The repository is the data store for all information needed to create, maintain, and execute software systems, as well as information describing a corporation and its use of information. In addition to its role as a data store, the repository manages its contents. Like a database management system, the repository has information management facilities for providing security and access controls, for versioning, change management, and configuration management. Repository data manipulation services include the creation, updating, and deleting of repository data. The contents of the repository can be accessed by tools and by users (e.g., software developers, business analysts, end users). Program interfaces are provided to support tool access to the repository and an open architecture environment allowing many tools to access its contents. Query and report writing facilities are provided to give users access to the repository contents. A batch maintenance facility is available to populate the repository with data from outside data stores.

An important part of the repository is its meta model. The meta model describes the kinds and meanings of information that can be stored in the repository. Included within the meta model are rules used to check the validity of repository information and to govern access to and changes to repository informa-

BOX 10.7 Summary of repository services

- Supports application development and maintenance
- Represents data in ER form and is extensible
- Provides an object-oriented framework
- Provides data store and data manipulation services
- Stores data in relational form
- Provides security/access controls
- Manages versioning, change control, and configuration
- Supports multiusers
- Supports front-end CASE tools, generators, and re-engineering tools
- Provides programming interfaces for import/export of repository information to tools
- Has query and report writing facilities for users
- Features open architecture
- Provides batch maintenance facility for population
- Has repository information rules/policies to enforce control, consistency, and integrity

tion. The repository meta model is extensible so that it can be changed to accommodate new types of information and rules.

Box 10.7 summarizes the services offered by the repository.

REFERENCES

1. "Graphical User Interface," *CASE Outlook,* 89, no. 3 (May/June 1989), 33–36.
2. Peter Chen, "The Entity-Relationship Approach," *Byte,* (April 1989), 230–232.
3. *"Digital's Distributed Repository: A Technical Overview of Its Features and Functions,"* draft report, August 17, 1990, Digital Equipment Corporation.
4. "AD/Cycle Concepts," *IBM Report GC 26-4531-0,* September 1989.
5. "CCD/Plus Version 4.1 Fact Sheet," Digital Equipment Corporation, 1989.

6. Ali Hazzah, "Making Ends Meet: Repository Manager," *Software Magazine,* (December 1989), 59–71.
7. Amy Cortese, "DEC Challenges IBM CASE Strategy," *Computer World,* October 9, 1989, p. 120.
8. "Inside the CASE Repository," *CASE Outlook,* 89, no. 4 (December 1989), 14–19.
9. Hazzah, "Making Ends Meet."
10. "Repository Manager/MVS Version 1 Release 1 Programming Announcement," *IBM Report 289–457,* September 19, 1989.
11. Jerry Cashin, "Data Model Standards in Competitive Stage," *Software Magazine* (December 1989), 78–81.
12. *"Digital's Distributed Repository."*
13. Hugh Beyer, "Proposal for Extending Dictionary Standards to Support CASE," *Digital Equipment Corporation Report,* Nashua, NH, 1989.
14. "DEC's CASE Counterpunch," *CASE Outlook,* 89, no. 4 (December 1989), pp. 30–32.
15. "IBM on Repository, SAA, ADE and CASE—An Interview with James Archer," *Database Newsletter* (March/April 1989), 1, 15–19.
16. "AD/Cycle Concepts."
17. "Repository Manager/MVS Programming Announcement."
18. Hazzah, "Making Ends Meet."
19. "Repository Manager/MVS Programming Announcement."
20. "AD/Cycle Concepts."

11 REPOSITORY STANDARDS

ERA OF STANDARDIZATION

The 1990s will be an era of standardization as well as automation for the software industry. Automation and standardization go hand-in-hand. Computer technology standards of all types are proliferating. Standards are being proposed by official standards bodies and individual companies and professional societies, as well as through international efforts. It is estimated that more than 250 groups involving more than 7000 people are currently working to define hundreds of computer technology standards. Although it may take three to five years for these standards to impact the software industry, they may have a more immediate influence on CASE technology and repositories because many CASE tool vendors are active members of various standards committees.

Software tools standards are most urgently needed in the areas of user interface standards, data exchange standards, and repository standards. Box 11.1 lists some examples of emerging software technology standards.

Repository standards are important because they will enable software tool integration and the combining of tools from multiple vendors, as well as the exchange of information between repositories. The repository is the first database application to be standardized, and several repository standards are emerging.

In this chapter we will discuss the following repository standards.

- CASE Data Interchange Format (CDIF)
- Information Resource Dictionary System (IRDS)
- IBM SAA de facto Standard
- A Tools Integration Standard (ATIS)
- Portable Common Tool Environment (PCTE)

BOX 11.1 Examples of proposed software standards

Sponsor	Standard	
Electronic Industries Association	CDIF	CASE Data Interchange Format
ANSI/ISO/FIPS	IRDS	Information Resource Dictionary System—repository standard
IBM	SAA	Systems Application Architecture for portability across hardware platforms and cooperative processing
DEC & Atherton Technology	ATIS	IPSE (Integrated Project Support Environment) object-oriented interface
Open Software Foundation	OSF	Open Software Environment
IEEE	POSIX	Operating system interface standard
ECMA	PCTE	Interface specification for Ada and C tool standards

CASE DATA INTERCHANGE FORMAT (CDIF)

CDIF is a specification for a language whose purpose is to enable the sharing of information between CASE tools.[1] Although it is not precisely a repository standard, it is relevant to our discussion as most information shared between CASE tools will come out of or go into a repository. CDIF will be useful to load information into repositories if that information resides elsewhere, or to transport information from repositories to CASE tools. As such, this standard will play a practical role in determining the nature of the information that will initially populate repositories.

CDIF is an extension of the EDIF standard, which was developed to share information between CAD/CAM/CAE tools, and is sometimes referred to as EDIF/CASE. The means used by CDIF to share information between tools is typically an ASCII text file that is exported from one CASE tool and imported into another. The file itself contains system information as well as descriptors of that information and can accommodate graphics as well as text. For example, as we can see in Fig. 11.1, CASE tool A contains a data flow diagram (DFD) that the analyst wants to pass to CASE tool B. So, assuming that both tools have a

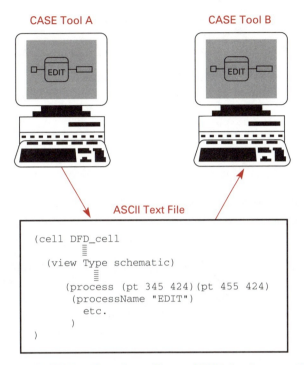

Figure 11.1 CASE Data Interchange Format (CDIF) is a language for sharing information between CASE tools.

CDIF facility, the analyst can create a CDIF export file in CASE tool A that contains information describing the DFD and then load that file into CASE tool B for CASE tool B to process.

If we look at the CDIF example in Fig. 11.1, we can better understand the CDIF language. First, it contains system information (e.g., the process name EDIT) as well as data about that information: it is a process, the process is a schematic (i.e., graphic), and the process is a part of a specific DFD. This follows a common paradigm: First we get system information and then we get data about that information. The data that describe the context and meaning of system information is usually called **meta data** or **schema** information (see Box 11.2). Second, CDIF uses nested structures to show objects containing other objects. Third, the graphics are described by points defining the location of the object.

Box 11.3 lists some of the objects described by the CDIF standard. Initial work has concentrated on exchanging graphic (diagramming) information used in the analysis and design phases, such as data flow diagrams and control flow diagrams. Currently, about 200 users, CASE tool vendors, computer vendors, government agencies, and academic institutions are on the CDIF committee,

> **BOX 11.2   Meta model**
>
> **Meta Data or Schema**
> Context and meaning of system information
>
> **Information**
> Actual system information

with approximately 30 of these being active members. EDIF has been officially approved and work is progressing on CDIF.

INFORMATION RESOURCE DICTIONARY SYSTEM (IRDS)

IRDS is a repository standard developed by the National Institute of Standards and Technology.[2] It defines the contents of the repository, the user interfaces, and the interfaces for moving information between repositories. The best way to understand IRDS

> **BOX 11.3   Objects covered by CDIF**
>
> Data flow diagrams
> Control flow diagrams
> Logical data dictionary definitions
> Process specification
> Module specification
> Entity-relationship diagrams
> State transition diagrams
> Warnier-Orr diagrams
> Decision tables
> Process activation tables
> State-event matrices
> Data elements (records)
> Fields (database and screen)
> Screens
> Panels
> Programs
> Modules

is to think of it as a business level design. It specifies all the repository contents, inputs, and outputs, but it does not specify a technical design or implementation plan.

It will be up to the individual vendors to actually develop the repository. The purpose of the IRDS standard is to ensure that each of these independently developed repositories will contain essentially the same information, will look the same to the user, and will be able to share information. If these things are all true, then the repository will be considered in compliance with the IRDS standard.

The IRDS standard includes six modules:

- Core Dictionary System
- Basic Functional Schema
- IRDS Security
- Extensible Life Cycle Phase Facility
- IRDS Procedure Facility
- Application Program Interface

Both the Core Dictionary System and the Basic Functional Schema are necessary for describing a typical information system in a repository. A data architecture underlies the modules and the IRDS itself.

IRDS Data Architecture

IRDS uses an entity-relationship model to organize the information in the repository. The IRDS entity-relationship model contains entities, relationships, and attributes. Here are some examples of **entities:**

- Payroll System KB500
- Payroll Master File
- Payroll Master Record
- Social Security Number

Here are some examples of **relationships,** which in IRDS are binary (i.e., one-to-one):

- FILE *CONTAINS* RECORD
- RECORD *CONTAINS* ELEMENT

Attributes represent properties of entities or relationships:

- **Entity attributes** are properties such as LENGTH; for example, the entity Social Security Number has a length attribute of 9.

- **Relationship attributes** are properties such as RELATIVE POSITION (e.g., the RECORD CONTAINS ELEMENT relationship could have a RELATIVE POSITION attribute of 3, meaning that the data element was the third element in the record).

Attributes also are collected into **attribute groups** (e.g., attributes LOW-OF-RANGE and HIGH-OF-RANGE together would make an attribute-group).

Entities, relationships, attributes, and attribute groups are each categorized into **types.** For example, Social Security Number, Last Name, and Date of Birth are all entities. They all also happen to be data elements, so they would be categorized into the entity type of ELEMENT. Likewise, Marketing Department and Finance Department would be categorized into the entity type of USER. Analysts can extend the repository by adding more entity, relationship, attribute, and attribute group types.

In IRDS, an **instance** is the data value of an entity or a relationship, so 3-9-49 is the data value of the entity Date of Birth.

Schema

The **IRD schema** is the way to organize as well as describe the system information in the repository. IRDS uses a four-level schema:

- IRD schema description layer
- IRD schema layer
- IRD data layer
- the data themselves

As we can see in Fig. 11.2, the IRD schema layer names and describes the entity types that the repository will contain, the relationships between them, and the attributes and attribute groups associated with those entities and relationships. For example, it is here that we would define ELEMENT as an entity type, and define the fact that LENGTH is an allowable attribute of ELEMENT. This is the meta model (information model) layer.

The IRD data layer contains the names of the specific entities and relationships within the type categories (e.g., Social Security Number, Last Name, Date of Birth), as well as the values of the attributes and attribute groups (e.g., LENGTH, RANGE).

The bottom layer contains the actual system information—the data values (instances) of the entities and relationships that may be stored in the repository or in some other data store (e.g., 345-44-1234 for Social Security Number).

The point of designing the repository in this "meta" fashion is to give the analyst the ability not only to add new system information to the repository but to change the nature of the information in the repository by defining new entity

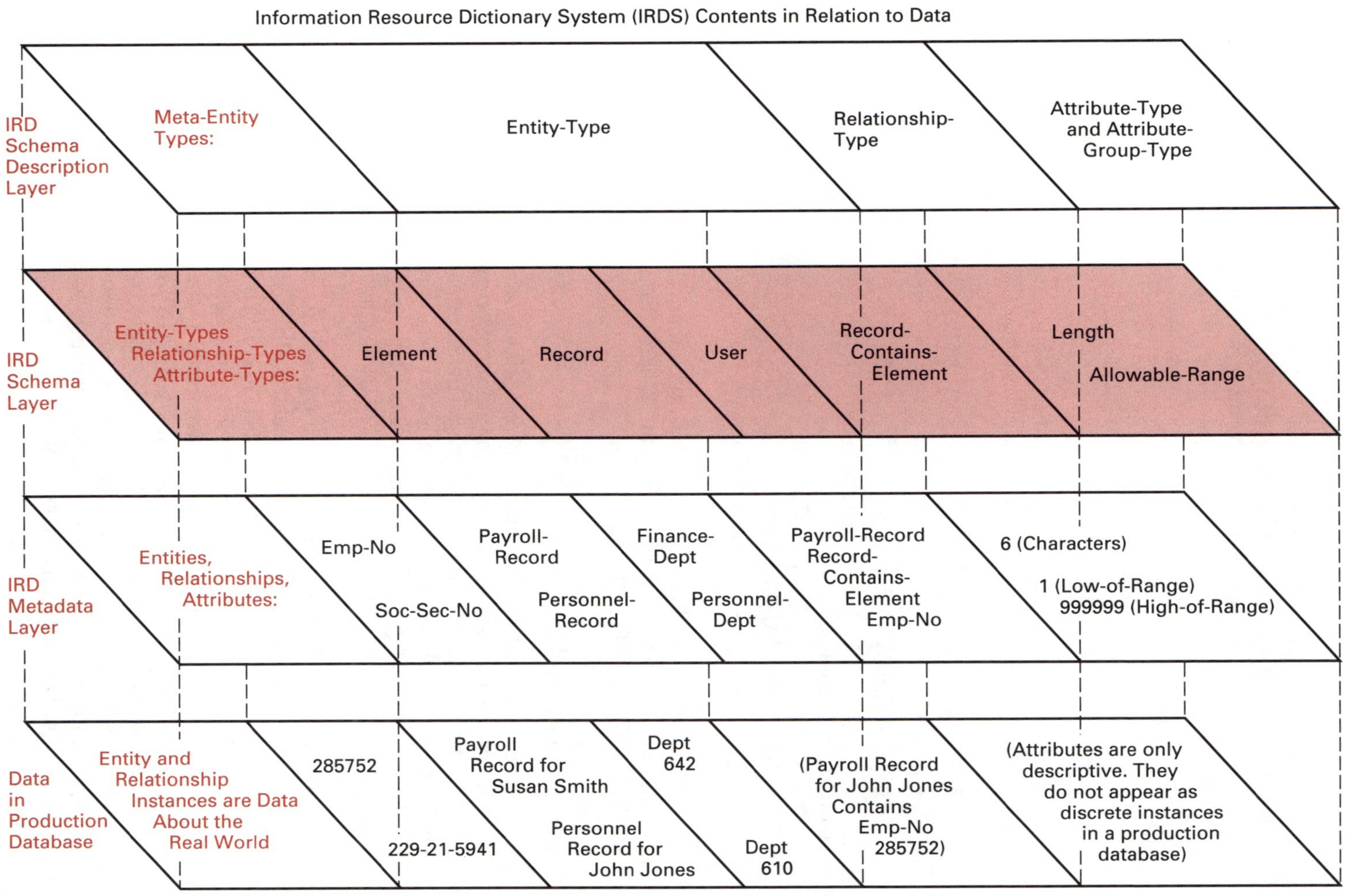

Information Resource Dictionary System (IRDS) Contents in Relation to Data

	Entity-Type		Relationship-Type	Attribute-Type and Attribute-Group-Type
IRD Schema Description Layer — Meta-Entity Types:	Element	Record	User	Length	Allowable-Range
IRD Schema Layer — Entity-Types Relationship-Types Attribute-Types:			Record-Contains-Element		
IRD Metadata Layer — Entities, Relationships, Attributes:	Emp-No	Payroll-Record	Finance-Dept	Payroll-Record-Contains-Element Emp-No	6 (Characters) 1 (Low-of-Range) 999999 (High-of-Range)
	Soc-Sec-No	Personnel-Record	Personnel-Dept		
Data in Production Database — Entity and Relationship Instances are Data About the Real World	285752	Payroll Record for Susan Smith	Dept 642	(Payroll Record for John Jones Contains Emp-No 285752)	(Attributes are only descriptive. They do not appear as discrete instances in a production database)
	229-21-5941	Personnel Record for John Jones	Dept 610		

Figure 11.2 IRDS uses a four-level schema to organize and describe repository information.

and relationship types (and their attributes) as needed. This "meta" design makes the repository inherently extensible.

Two schema are needed to describe most information systems: the minimal schema and the basic functional schema. The minimal schema is part of the IRDS core module, and the basic functional schema is the second IRDS module.

The Minimal Schema

The minimal schema includes those entities, relationships, and attributes necessary for control purposes. There are only three entities:

- IRD-USER
- IRD-VIEW
- IRD-SCHEMA-VIEW

and two relationships:

- IRD-USER-HAS-IRD-VIEW
- IRD-USER-HAS-IRD-SCHEMA-VIEW

The attributes and attribute groups of the minimal schema are used to control and audit access to the data and the schema (e.g., ADDED-BY, DATE-TIME-LAST-MODIFIED).

Basic Functional Schema

The basic functional schema makes up the starter set of dictionary data structures necessary to describe most existing information systems. Analysts are free to add schema (and the corresponding system information). Box 11.4 lists the entity types and relationship class types in the basic functional schema. A **class** is a higher-level categorization of relationship type (e.g., SYSTEM CONTAINS PROGRAM is a relationship type; CONTAINS is the relationship class type).

There is a list of specific attributes that each entity can have. Attributes are also associated with specific relationship types (e.g., relationships that process files have an ACCESS METHOD attribute; PROCESS relationships have a FREQUENCY attribute; RECORD CONTAINS ELEMENT has a RELATIVE POSITION attribute). In addition, there is a strict definition of what entities can take part in what relationships, and which entity is the first member and which is the second member (e.g., in SYSTEM CONTAINS PROGRAM, SYSTEM is the first member or source and PROGRAM is the second member or target).

Entities have two names: **access** names and **descriptive** names. The system knows the entity by the access name, which is typically short and must be unique across the entire repository. Entities can also have **synonyms**.

BOX 11.4 Basic functional schema

Entity Types

Date entity types
    DOCUMENT
    FILE
    RECORD
    ELEMENT

Process entity types
    SYSTEM
    PROGRAM
    MODULE

External entity types
    USER

Relationship Class Types

CONTAINS
PROCESSES
RESPONSIBLE FOR
RUNS
GOES TO
DERIVED FROM
CALLS

IRDS FUNCTIONS AND PROCESSES

The IRD core module contains four functions whose purposes are to maintain, report, and control the schema and data in the IRD schema layer and the IRD data layer:

- IRD: updating and reporting on data
- Schema: updating and reporting on the schema
- IRD-IRD interface
- Control facilities

These may be accessed via a **command language interface** or by a more user-friendly screen-driven **panel interface.** In order to conform to the IRDS standard, a repository must have one or both of these interfaces.

IRD: Updating and Reporting on Data

The update function handles the modification of system information in the repository. Users can create and delete entities and relationships and change them by changing their attributes. Output consists of reports and query facilities. Users are able to define the contents of the report or query (e.g., the entities, relationships, and attributes listed), the kinds of names to appear (access versus descriptive), the sequence of information, and the report destination.

Users can create entity lists of all entities, or subsets of entities based on entity names or character strings. The list can be further qualified via other entity characteristics, such as entity types, attributes, attribute character strings, and relationships. IRDS also provides for a change impact analysis report.

Schema: Updating and Reporting on the Schema

Just as the system information in the repository, the schema (meta data) describing that information can be updated and reported. To avoid confusion, the prefix "meta" is appended to the data in the schema layer. Meta entities, meta relationships, meta attributes, and meta attribute groups can be reported upon as well as added, modified, and deleted. Changing the schema changes the nature of the data that can be defined and managed by the repository.

IRD-IRD Interface

The IRD-IRD interface provides for moving data from one standard IRDS implementation to another. Because the IRDS standard is essentially a business level design, various repository implementations will have different internals. The IRD-to-IRD interface facility exists to transfer data between repositories that have different internals.

The interface has four functions:

- Creating an export file with a user-selected set of entities and relationships and a description of the underlying schema
- Creating an empty repository
- Checking compatibility of schema between two repositories
- Importing to the target repository

Control Facilities

There are four control facilities. All operate on the data in the repository; three operate on the schema.

For IRD:

- Versioning
- Life cycle phases
- Quality indicators
- IRD views

For the schema:

- Versioning
- Life cycle phases
- IRD views

Versioning

The versioning facility provides revision control for the data and schema, with the highest revision number reflecting the most recent update. Users are also allowed to keep two versions of the same data (e.g., 5-digit and 9-digit ZIP codes).

Life Cycle Phases

This facility allows the user to document for each entity in the repository the life cycle phase in which it is used. The life cycle phases are uncontrolled (i.e., development), controlled (i.e., production), and archived. Multiple uncontrolled life cycle phases can be defined and used.

Quality Indicators

A quality indicator identifies the level of standardization of ELEMENT entities (e.g., program, organization, national, international), or the degree to which the entity satisfies corporate quality assurance testing.

IRD Views

Within a life cycle phase, this is another way to categorize the information in the repository. For example, data and schema can be isolated into views based on project or organization.

Additional IRDS Modules

The core module and the basic functional schema are necessary to describe most information systems. The IRDS standard also contains specifications for the following additional modules.

IRDS Security

The security module defines access control. Global Security is based on function, type, and view and allows read-only access to the IRD or the schema. Access can also be controlled at the entity-type level. Entity level security lets the administrator set up read/write access on an individual entity basis.

Extensible Life Cycle Phase Facility

This module lets the user customize and control (via integrity rules) the movement of entities through the life cycle. Entities can be moved from uncontrolled to controlled to archived and from controlled to uncontrolled.

IRDS Procedure Facility

This module lets the user define, store, maintain, and execute sets of IRDS commands. This is useful for performing common, long, or repetitive IRDS tasks. Built-in functions are provided to extract system information and for character and numerical manipulations. This module requires the Command Language Interface.

Application Program Interface

This module provides an interface through which the IRDS commands and resulting input can be passed between the IRDS and programs with a call feature. In it, the IRDS is treated as a subroutine.

IRDS Services Interface

This module defines a specific protocol for an interface through which software external to the repository can directly access the IRD and IRD schema.

IBM SAA AND AD/CYCLE

AD/Cycle is the application development environment from IBM.[3] It is composed of software tools and services that assist each phase of the life cycle, including business modeling, analysis, design, implementation, testing, and maintenance. Both AD/Cycle tools and applications developed with them will conform to SAA guidelines.

SAA is a collection of objectives and standards covering communications (Common Communications Support, CCS), user access (Common User Interface, CUI), and application development (Common Programming Interface, CPI, and AD/Cycle). SAA systems include IBM mainframes with MVS, VM; AS/400 with OS/400; and PS/2 with OS/2. AD/Cycle is the basis for providing a comprehensive, integrated application development framework across SAA environments that offers

- Full-function life cycle support
- Common user interface
- Common repository
- Open architecture

AD/Cycle is an SAA strategy for improving application development and maintenance and is a repository-based environment.

As shown in Fig. 11.3, AD/Cycle has three basic parts: (1) a software life cycle process model, (2) a set of tools that provide automated support for the different life cycle phases, and (3) a set of services for integration of its tools.

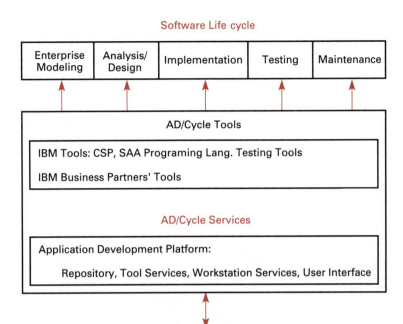

Figure 11.3   IBM AD/Cycle.

AD/Cycle Software Life Cycle Model

The AD/Cycle software life cycle process model is an iterative software development approach. The phases are depicted in Fig. 11.4. It is based on the model in the IBM product Application Development Project Support (ADPS). The AD/Cycle life cycle approach emphasizes the importance of a relationship between an enterprise's business requirements and its software systems. Building the right system for the user means understanding user requirements and building a system that meets those requirements. The AD/Cycle model begins with building an enterprise model that defines business processes and their data requirements and then uses it as the input requirements for the analysis and design phases. Thus, business requirements and systems are connected by basing system requirements on information in the enterprise model.

The first life cycle phase is **enterprise modeling.** A top-down approach is suggested for building the corporate organizational structure model, the business process model, and the business data model all of which compose the enterprise model. The enterprise model created in the first phase is validated by prototyping the business process to check that the requirements are correct and complete.

During the next life cycle phase, the requirements are **analyzed** and an application that meets those requirements is **designed.** The two major design ac-

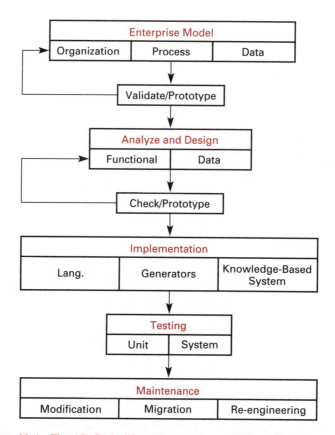

Figure 11.4 The AD/Cycle life cycle process model is an iterative process that consists of five basic phases.

tivities involve functional design to determine the application functions and applicable business rules and data design to create a logical data model for the data needed by the application functions. Prototyping the design is done to ensure that the design meets the requirements and is of high quality.

After the design phase, the application is **implemented** by using such third generation languages as COBOL, PL/1, FORTRAN, C, or RPG or generators, such as IBM Cross System Product. Application system unit testing and system testing follow implementation.

Maintenance is the final life cycle phase. The objective of AD/Cycle is to use the same tools to apply maintenance changes to the application as were used to develop the application. Application information stored in the repository will prove invaluable to simplifying maintenance work.

The AD/Cycle life cycle model defines the kinds of software activities to be supported by AD/Cycle tools. An optional part of AD/Cycle is the **application development process model,** which is stored in the AD/Cycle Repository.

It is used to guide developers through the phases, steps, and activities of the life cycle process. Also, it can identify which tools to use in which activities during the process. It can be customized to reflect an organization's methodology standards. It is methodology-independent.

AD/Cycle Tools

AD/Cycle tools will be provided by IBM and by its business partners (Intersolv, KnowledgeWare, Bachman, Systematica, Synon). Some tools will support primarily one phase of the life cycle (e.g., modeling tools, screen and report painters, code generators, test coverage analyzers), while other tools will be used across the life cycle. Examples of cross-life cycle tools include project and process management tools, impact analysis tools, and documentation tools.

AD/Cycle Platform

AD/Cycle includes an application development platform providing common services to support the integration of its tools:

- User interface services
- Workstation services
- Repository services
- Tool services

The **user interface services** provide a consistent way for users to access and use AD/Cycle tools. The IBM workstation PS/2 with OS/2 Extended Edition is the primary window into the AD/Cycle. The graphic interface is supported by OS/2 Presentation Manager and follows SAA CUA guidelines.

AD/Cycle is based on a cooperative processing approach that allows its tools to be distributed, with some tools operating on the PS/2 workstation and others on the host. In general, tools that support the early phases of the life cycle (i.e., enterprise modeling, analysis, and design) will run on the workstation where they can make use of the PS/2 graphics capabilities. Tools that support the latter phases of the life cycle (i.e., production, testing, and maintenance) and require the power and resources of a large computer will run on the host. **Programmable workstation services** include LAN connecting network support and configuration management.

One of the key components of the AD/Cycle application development platform is the repository and its associated meta model, called the **IBM Repository Manager** and the **AD Information Model,** respectively. The repository provides a single store and control point for all application-related information. The AD Information Model provides a common representation of application-related information for AD/Cycle tools and allows tools to share information across the life cycle phases.

Tool services include methods for accessing and manipulating repository information, library management, versioning, and configuration management and assistance in designing tools that can integrate to the AD/Cycle. This frees tool builders to concentrate on designing tool functions rather than common tool operations such as data manipulation.

AD/Cycle is an open architecture environment that allows customers and tool vendors to build and adopt tools to integrate with the AD/Cycle environment. The open framework of AD/Cycle provides publicly defined interfaces and common services that tools may use. In addition, the AD information model is commercially available and can be extended to accommodate new information needs of tools and users.

A TOOLS INTEGRATION STANDARD (ATIS)

ATIS is an object-oriented repository interface for an Integrated Project Support Environment (IPSE).[4] It is currently used by a product called Software BackPlane from Atherton Technologies. Digital Equipment Corporation has incorporated ATIS into its repository, CDD/Repository, and has proposed that ATIS be incorporated into the IRDS repository standard. IBM also has plans to incorporate ATIS into its AIX (UNIX) CASE strategy.

The ATIS standard defines a common, callable repository interface that allows independent CASE tools written to it to run against any repository using the interface.

ATIS is targeted for the science and engineering markets and, like SAA from IBM, provides an overall integration framework. Originally, the plan was built on the Software BackPlane for the framework, but since then the approach has changed to providing a variety of integration approaches. Some of the integration approaches that are under consideration include version control, configuration management, communications among tools, relationships among software objects, and dynamic extensibility for adding tools. For the BackPlane, a desktop, object-oriented approach is used, and functions supported include catalog support, control integration, work-flow control, data integration, user-model integration, and an incremental process for tool integration. The name of the committee pursuing this work on integration is CIS, or CASE Integration Services.

PORTABLE COMMON TOOL ENVIRONMENT (PCTE)

PCTE is an interface standard whose purpose is to allow portability of CASE tools across microcomputer/LAN environments.[5,6] The idea is to specify an interface for a set of functions to run between the operating system and the CASE tool and to have the CASE tool call the functions rather than making calls to the operating system.

For each operating system environment, the CASE tool can remain the same, and only the set of PCTE functions changes. As shown in Fig. 11.5, the CASE tool calls the PCTE interface, which in turn calls the operating system. If the same CASE tool were running on another operating system, it would still make the same PCTE calls, and the PCTE interface would translate them to the correct operating system instructions. In this way, portability across operating environments is accomplished.

Because PCTE is made for microcomputer LAN environments, and because it supports large-scale developments, it can facilitate the repository concept for support of team development. PCTE is installed on each workstation, along with the operating system, thus making possible the exchange of information. PCTE features include

- A multiple-window management facility that can contain both text and high resolution graphics
- Distributed processing so that execution of commands can be performed on any workstation connected
- Distributed storage and retrieval of information from any connected workstation, simulating a central database for the project

Thus, PCTE can function as a repository at the project level.

PCTE+ is an extension to support defense applications, and accordingly has access controls and other security facilities. PCTE+ is currently in the experimental stage. PCTE originated in Europe, as part of the ten-year ESPRIT project.

STANDARDS FOR AUTOMATION

Many standards are emerging in the CASE world, all driven by the need to automate in a common manner the means of defining and manipulating system de-

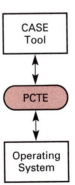

Figure 11.5 PCTE is an interface standard that promotes portability of CASE tools across microcomputer/LAN environments. The CASE tool calls the PCTE interface, which in turn calls the operating system.

velopment information. Repository standards are at the center of the action because they define the nature of the information in the tool, its input and its output means, and how it may be reused.

REFERENCES

1. Alan Hecht and Matt Harris, "A CASE Standard Interchange Format: Proposed Extension to EDIF 200," Cadre Technologies, Inc., White Paper.
2. David Ornstein, "Developing a CASE Interchange Format: EDIF/CASE," Sage Software White Paper.
3. Margaret Henderson Law, "Guide to Information Resource Dictionary Systems: General Concepts and Strategic Systems Planning," NBS Special Publication 500–152, April 1988.
4. *Repository Manager/MVS General Information*, GC26–4608–0, Version 1, Release 1, IBM Corporation, September 1989.
5. Hugh R. Beyer, "Proposal for Extending Dictionary Standards to Support CASE," Digital Equipment Corporation White Paper, Nashua, NH, 1989.
6. C. DeGroote, "PCTE—A Remarkable Platform," *Information and Software Technology*, 31, no. 3 (April 1989), 136–142.

12 PREPARING FOR REPOSITORIES

REPOSITORY ISSUES

The repository is a new technology that, for the most part, has been untried by most corporations. There are many questions concerning its ability to provide all the benefits and services users hope it will offer. Box 12.1 lists some of the frequently mentioned issues and problems.

Among the most important repository issues are concerns about the meta model (or information model). Because the repository meta model defines how and what information is represented, and this in turn determines which tools and which methodology(ies) can easily use the repository, an essential factor in selecting a repository is understanding its meta model. Although the meta model is extensible and therefore can be customized to suit a particular corporation's needs, extensibility can destroy tool integration if not properly done. How difficult is it to adapt existing tools to use the repository? How easily can the repository meta model be changed to accommodate new tools in the future? There are outstanding questions about how and if the meta model should be standardized (e.g., IRDS standard, IBM SAA Repository, AD/Information Model, ATIS standard).

Other concerns relate to repository cost and performance issues. Is the relational database management system an appropriate repository implementation vehicle, or is the object-oriented database management system more suitable to support the variety of information types and relationships to be stored in the repository? Is the repository capable of supporting large development teams and large software organizations?

Also, there are questions about whether a central or distributed repository architecture will provide better management and control of repository information. Box 12.2 lists some of the reasons for using a distributed repository.[1] Can the repository support a multivendor hardware environment?

A repository is not useful to a corporation unless it is populated with infor-

BOX 12.1 Repository issues

- Lack of approved standards to define meta model access methods
- Ability of ER model to represent complex, multipart relationships
- No existing enterprise models
- Multiple, incompatible existing dictionaries containing redundant, inconsistent data
- Difficulty of combining existing dictionaries used by different software tools
- Performance capabilities of large, complex repositories
- Central versus distributed architecture
- Adapting existing tools for use of the repository
- Changing repository meta model to support new tools and processes

mation about the corporation, its software systems, and its software life cycle process(es). Population of the repository is a major undertaking and therefore a major issue. Although the repository meta model, and perhaps the life cycle process model, will be supplied by the repository vendor, enterprise models as well as the information about the corporation's software systems must be supplied by the individual corporation. Most corporations have yet to build their enterprise models and do not have information about their software systems in a form that can be put directly into the repository.

PREPARING FOR A REPOSITORY

Although the repository technology is likely to evolve over the next five to ten years, the time for corporations to begin preparing for the repository is

BOX 12.2 Benefits of a distributed repository

- Reduces communication costs
- Increases reliability because failure at one location may not affect others
- Provides local control of data
- Enhances performance

BOX 12.3 Preparing for repositories

- **Develop a plan to move to repository usage in an evolutionary manner**
  - Analyze current application development and maintenance environment.
  - Investigate and establish a software life cycle methodology(ies).
  - Standardize process of application development and maintenance across organization.
  - Define target environment for application systems and tools.
  - Define organization's requirements for a repository.
- **Train in modeling techniques, life cycle methodologies and relational database technology, repository technology, and object-oriented methods**
- **Model the organization**
  - Build: Organization model
           Business data model
           Business process model
  - Consolidate, edit, and validate models.
  - Build from new and existing sources with support of modeling and re-engineering tools.
- **Establish a repository administration function**
  - Oversee population and maintenance of repository.
  - Establish naming conventions and standards for repository objects.
  - Management backup procedures.
  - Establish controls for versions and change management.
  - Plan for tool integration.
  - Help model the enterprise.
  - Assist in use of the repository.
- **Follow and adopt emerging repository standards**
  - Select tools that plan to adhere to standards as they emerge.
  - Select repository(ies) that adhere to standards.
- **Choose a repository, install it, populate it, and use it**
  - Inventory and consolidate current application system information.
  - Clean up and consolidate corporate data dictionaries.
  - Use tools to populate repository.
    - Database, dictionary conversion/migration tools
    - Batch interfaces to CASE tool repositories
    - Re-engineering tools: restructurers and reverse engineering tools
  - Use CASE tools and re-engineering tools that use and interface with the repository and share a common information model and support the enterprise methodologies.
  - If necessary, extend information model to include object types and methods required by tools and methodologies.
  - Implement use of repository based on organization's needs.

now. It will be a lengthy process (probably covering years) for most organizations to prepare for effective use of a repository. Using a repository will involve a substantial monetary investment and substantial organizational changes.

Box 12.3 is a list of the repository preparation activities. Many of these activities are the same as those needed to prepare for integrated CASE environments. Remember that effective use of CASE tools depends on first defining the software life cycle process, selecting methodologies that support that process, and then using an integrated set of CASE tools that provides automated support for that process. The repository is needed to support the methodology(ies) and CASE tools integration. The repository stores and manages the system deliverables required by the methodology(ies) and produced by CASE tools. Successful implementation of CASE fundamentally depends on successful implementation of the repository. In the first half of the 1990s, much of the work to advance the CASE technology will focus on addressing repository issues.

REPOSITORY IMPLEMENTATION PLAN

The place to begin to prepare for a repository is to develop a plan for migrating to the use of a repository. For most organizations, an evolutionary migration is best to enable the organization gradually to replace older technologies and methods with the repository technology and CASE and to spread out the associated costs. Because the repository is the cornerstone of an integrated CASE tools environment, the introduction of a repository should be planned along with the introduction of CASE tools. Any plan for CASE tool implementation must include a plan for repository implementation. Moving to a repository will require at least two to three years.

The first step in migrating to a repository is to analyze current hardware, software tools, methodologies, and life cycle processes used in the corporation and to standardize as much as possible to enable organization-wide sharing of the repository contents. This may involve choosing a new methodology that is more appropriate for use with the CASE technology. When making the methodology choice, the types of application systems to be supported and developed and the target operating environments must be considered.

TRAINING AND EXPERIENCE

Training is an important part of properly preparing for repositories. Inasmuch as proficiency in modeling techniques, methodologies, and the relational database technology is necessary, some staff training in each of these areas may be required. Models are used to represent the structure of an organization, to represent the design of software systems, and to represent the format of information stored in the repository. System developers, business analysts, and end users must learn the modeling techniques that support their job functions. Both entity-relationship modeling and object-oriented modeling expertise is needed.

Although most software developers have received some training in structured methodologies of one form or another, additional training will probably be required on how to use the standardized methodology along with the CASE tools that provide automated support for the methodology.

If a relational database is to be used as the repository store, the software staff responsible for providing repository support to the organization should have some familiarity with the relational database technology. If the repository employs an object-oriented layer above the relational store or if an object-oriented database is used as the repository data store, the staff also must learn about the object-oriented technology.

Gaining some experience early on will be valuable. If an organization does not have a corporate dictionary, it should begin using one as a way of resolving redundancies and conflicts in data names and definitions. Also, the organization should start using CASE tools that will interface with the repository even though the repository may not yet be available. Becoming proficient at using CASE tools is necessary because users will not interact directly with the repository, but rather with CASE tools that work with the repository. The CASE tools may have their own repository, which the organization can begin to populate and to learn about what types of objects are to be stored in the repository. Later this information can be migrated to another repository if necessary.

ENTERPRISE MODELS

A model of the enterprise must be stored in the repository. The enterprise model consists of three parts:[2]

- **Organizational model,** representing the organizational structure and its strategies
- **Business process model,** representing functions and activities
- **Business data model,** representing what information the business uses

Structured diagrams, data flow diagrams, ER diagrams, and matrices are used to represent various parts of the enterprise model. For example, the data model that shows what information entities an organization uses and how those entities relate to one another is represented using an ER model. A tree structured diagram is used to represent the organizational structure.

Each organization is responsible for building its own enterprise model. Enterprise modeling follows a top-down approach with the following basic steps:[3]

1. Define a high-level enterprise model.
2. Refine the model to a detailed level in steps.
3. Validate the model by prototyping processes.
4. Use the model to guide system analysis and design.

Information about the content of the enterprise models is obtained from users and from existing systems. Various users in the corporation are interviewed to discover the business activities to be performed and the information needed to support these activities. This is usually done following a top-down approach supported by CASE modeling tools, such as entity-relationship diagrammers. Also, re-engineering tools can be used to reveal the current data model that is used by existing systems. This is a bottom-up approach. Information from users and re-engineering tools should be consolidated and validated to create an accurate, complete enterprise model. Using both a top-down and bottom-up approach to build the enterprise model will not only speed up the modeling process but also help create the most accurate, complete enterprise model possible. Attempting to build an enterprise model without the assistance of powerful CASE modeling tools and re-engineering tools will be an enormous waste of valuable time.

Repository Administration Group

There is a need to establish a formal repository administration function to oversee the population and maintenance of the repository contents. One of the first tasks of the repository administration group is to help model the enterprise, ensuring that the form of the enterprise model is appropriate for easy inclusion into the repository. Other repository administration responsibilities include selecting the repository, establishing naming conventions and standards for repository components, and establishing controls for protecting, accessing, and changing repository components.

The repository administration group should follow and adopt emerging repository standards and advice in software tool selections to ensure that selected software tools (CASE and re-engineering) adhere to standards and can interface with the repository.

Ongoing repository administration functions involve advising users about what is in the repository and how to access it, as well as management of the repository contents.

Repository Population

Before the repository can be populated, it is important to take inventory of current software system information and resources, such as design models, data elements, files, databases, documentation libraries, and dictionaries. Use of such re-engineering tools as program code analyzers and restructuring and reverse engineering tools can be helpful in understanding what information is currently available, improving and updating this information, and migrating it into the repository. Data restructuring tools can be used to clean up (e.g., standardize names and definitions) and consolidate (e.g., identify aliases, homonyms, and synonyms) data. Also, with the aid of data restructuring and data reverse engineering tools, existing corporate data dictionaries can be consolidated to eliminate redundancies before they are used to populate the repository. Migration tools can be used to move from dictionaries to the repository. Conversion tools can be used to update and convert from one language to another or from one database (flat file) to another database.

A REPOSITORY FUTURE

The contents of the repository will grow over time as more corporate and system information is stored. As more information is stored, less new information will be needed to build new systems because much of the project management information, organization models, data models, data entities, and process models can be reused in other corporate application systems. This will lead to greater productivity and quality improvements in the future and help realize the promise of CASE.

REFERENCES

1. "Digital's Distributed Repository: A Technical Overview of Its Features and Functions," draft Report, August 17, 1990, Digital Equipment Corporation.

2. "AD/Cycle Concepts," *IBM Report GC 26-4531-0,* September 1989.

3. Ibid.

PART III **REUSABILITY**

13 SOFTWARE REUSE

A SOFTWARE REUSABILITY STORY

GTE Data Services, a wholly owned subsidiary of GTE, has 2700 employees.[1] Its charter is to create business application systems for GTE telephone companies. Its centralized development environment, consisting of 2000 people, is divided into customer sets, where each set has a development director and a life cycle director in charge of maintenance and enhancement. The staff is split almost equally between development and maintenance/enhancement. The principal language for building application systems is COBOL. Also, many systems are written in C. The majority of the applications run on an IBM mainframe; others run on a DEC, HP, Tandem, or a PC in a LAN.

Software reuse engineering at GTE began in 1986, when a vice president heard about software reuse at a conference and then started a small program. They began by collecting common program utilities that were called **assets**. Assets are object modules, not source code. The asset is not modified by the user for individual program use, but rather used in read-only mode. Within a year, there were 300 assets in the GTE catalog. However, acceptance for the reuse program grew slowly because of the "not-invented-here" syndrome. Although the program was originally utility-oriented (e.g., general asset routines such as read and write), it is now becoming business model–oriented (e.g., data functions in business models, such as customer billing record, that are used by many systems).

The GTE asset catalog now has been pruned based on use to approximately 220 assets totaling 960,000 lines of code written in COBOL, C, Assembler, and even Lotus. Assets range in size from 6 lines to 120,000 lines of code (e.g., Table Control System).

To date, the asset that has provided the greatest productivity benefits is the Table Control System. The developer defines the application-specific tables and the Table Control System generates millions of lines of code—a gigantic savings to GTE. Also, because programs built with reusable assets adhere to GTE naming standards and other requirements, the quality assurance function is satisfied.

The PACBASE repository from CGI Systems, Inc., houses the reusable assets. GTE claims that software reuse got a "shot in the arm" with CASE technology and in particular the repository. The repository makes it easier to make assets known, to modify assets and understand the impact of change, to keep statistics about reuse levels and quality, and to browse through the asset catalog. Also, it is possible to keep higher-level assets, such as design models, in the repository.

Linking the reuse and CASE strategies has greatly increased the value and acceptance of both technologies at GTE.

The Information Asset Engineering (IAE) Group was created to support the reuse program. It now consists of 35 people and is part of the Software Productivity Group, which in turn is part of the CASE Group. The IAE Group provides support for productivity tools (including reusable assets) used at GTE Data Services and the Software Productivity Group is charged with introducing CASE.

Reuse specialists in the IAE Group are responsible for creating and managing GTE's reuse catalog, for promoting its use through the publication of success stories, and for guiding developers in the use of assets. The ratio is one reuse specialist per 100 to 150 developers/maintainers. Reuse specialists work with system developers and maintainers to explain what assets are available and how to reuse them. Their involvement in system development has changed the process.

The reuse specialist is a member of the development team from the beginning of the development process. During the requirements stage, the percentage of the system to be composed of assets is decided. A company reuse target is the percentage of delivered code to be provided by assets and is set on an annual basis at the vice-president and director level. The reuse target has been raised each year. The current target is 20 to 25 percent for development projects and 10 percent for maintenance/enhancement projects. The reuse level of current GTE production code is approximately 15 percent.

The use of assets is bringing both productivity and quality improvements to GTE. To measure productivity, GTE uses Putman's SLIM estimates for project time, number of people, and software defects. GTE reports on average a 20 to 30 percent increase in productivity when a new development or major enhancement project uses software reuse. Quality improvements are measured in terms of projected versus actual software defects found during development. GTE reports almost zero defects found in reusable components and that 95 percent of system defects found were discovered by system developers during development and only 5 percent by customers during production. GTE noted that the use of CASE tools has enabled the company to find defects earlier in the development process when they are cheaper to correct.

The experiences of GTE have shown that the software reusability strategy works best when it is applied at the beginning of a software development or enhancement project. Reuse specialists must get involved during the first project phases and must stay involved throughout the project as a part of the development team. Support must start from the top at the vice-president level, where company reuse targets are set, and managers must continue to sell the value of reuse throughout the project.

A GROWING TREND

GTE's software reuse story is rare, as only a very small percentage of corporations actively practice software reuse as a normal part of the software development process. Yet it marks a growing trend and change that may be more important in advancing software than software automation.

A NEW PARADIGM

Software reuse has the potential to bring about a revolutionary change in the way we build software. It represents a new, but very fundamental software paradigm in which the exception, not the rule, is to build software systems from scratch. The norm in software development based on reuse is to go to an automated library of reusable components, select appropriate components and perhaps modify them, and use them to create a new system. Only as a last resort is software developed from scratch.

Software reuse is a significantly different paradigm because it emphasizes the product first and the process second.[2] Thus far, we have measured software advancements in terms of process improvements. Structured methodologies and CASE technologies are two examples of approaches to systematize and streamline the software life cycle process. With reusability as the software paradigm, software advancement depends on the creation of repositories populated with standardized, interchangeable, reliable components and development methods that explicitly incorporate reuse techniques.

Software reuse requires a change in our view of software development. Software development can no longer be seen as a craft that is adapted to each new application and to each individual developer's personal preference. One experienced programmer commented: "Reusing other people's code would prove that I don't care about my work. I would no more reuse code than Ernest Hemingway would have reused other author's paragraphs."[3] This sort of view of programming is blocking software progress and must give way to a new view in which software is produced (or manufactured) from reusable components. Software reuse offers us an untapped potential for improving software productivity and software quality by an order of magnitude.

Software reuse includes not only the reuse and sharing of source code but also the reuse of project plans, prototypes, test data, data models, designs, and requirements specifications. By reusing software components and other software work products, as well as software development experience, to the greatest extent possible, software reuse can significantly

1. Streamline and simplify software development
2. Improve software quality
3. Reduce software costs

But a word of caution is needed here. Revolution is an overused term in the software field. Most software managers and developers are anything but excited at the suggestion of another promised software revolution. No software revolution thus far has significantly changed or speeded up the software development process. So why should software reuse lead to a software revolution?

Primarily because software reuse is a software paradigm that multiplies the impact of software automation. Basically there are two ways in which to speed up software development:

1. Use of automated techniques to eliminate and speed up software process tasks
2. Use of reusable software components and software experience to reduce the size of the development effort

It seems obvious that both are necessary to increase software productivity substantially and revolutionize software development. Software automation combined with the software reuse has revolutionary potential.

AN OLD SOFTWARE IDEA

The concept of software reuse certainly is not new. Software libraries have existed for years in most organizations. They are filled with routines that are commonly found in many kinds of software systems (e.g., date conversion routines, mathematical functions, statistics libraries, linear programming packages, I/O processing routines). For example, the subroutine was the first labor-saving technique invented by programmers. A subroutine for the sin (x) was written in 1944 for the Mark I calculator.[4]

Many experienced programmers have their own personal library of reusable software components. It has been observed that some of the most productive software developers have productivity rates five times as great as the average. Much of their productivity can be attributed to an extensive use of reusable software components, standard program forms, and standard implementation methods.

Software reuse has been recognized as an important software productivity strategy for more than two decades. At the first NATO Conference on Software Engineering, which marked the beginning of the software engineering discipline, reusability was the subject of one of the two invited conference addresses. McIlroy presented the concept in his address, "Mass Produced Software Components."[5]

BENEFITS OF REUSE

The benefits of software reuse are clear. As shown in Box 13.1, reuse can reduce the risk of project failure, shorten development time, and greatly increase the productivity of the individual software developer. According to Jones:

> Depending on the quantity of reused code, productivity rates of more than 25,000 lines of code per person-year are not uncommon, with peaks of more than 100,000 lines of code. It is now technically possible to develop some new applications that consist entirely of reused code, with no unique hand-coded modules being developed at all.[6]

And according to Boehm:

> Toshiba's system of reusable components for industrial process control has resulted in typical productivity rates of over 2000 source instructions per man month for high-quality industrial software products.[7]

BOX 13.1 Benefits of software reuse

- Reduce development time and cost
- Improve software quality
- Increase productivity
- Share knowledge about system and how to build systems
- Facilitate learning about system architecture and how to build good systems
- Share system specification, design, code, and other project documents produced by other teams

In addition, software reuse is viewed as an important way to improve software quality by reducing errors when highly reliable reusable components are used to create software systems. However, the most significant potential benefit of software reuse may not occur until the software maintenance phase. Software systems created from reusable components are likely to be much easier and cheaper to maintain because the reusable components are more reliable and more familiar to the software staff.

MANY FORMS OF SOFTWARE REUSE

The application of the concept of software reuse can take on many different forms, such as

- Reusable prototypes
- Reusable data
- Reusable system and program architectural frameworks
- Reusable program architecture and data structure designs
- Reusable data models
- Reusable program code fragments
- Reusable software packages
- Reusable software life cycle processes

OPPORTUNITIES FOR REUSE

There are many opportunities for practicing software reuse because of so much redundancy across software systems:[8]

- 40 to 60 percent of all code is reusable from one application to another.
- 60 percent of the design of all business applications is reusable.
- 75 percent of program functions are common to multiple programs.
- 15 percent of program code is unique to a specific application.

It was estimated in 1983 that only 15 percent of all the software code written was unique, and that 85 percent of the code was common across applications and could have been created from reusable software components.[9]

Flow graphs (discussed in Chapter 4) have been used to reveal redundant process logic.[10] In one FORTRAN system, 25 percent redundancy was discovered when system flow graphs were studied. In another case, it was discovered that several hundred COBOL normalization routines that reference a central database could be replaced by one standard normalization routine.

Reusability Studies and Projects

Studies of existing software programs reveal that most of the functions performed by one program are common to many different programs (see Fig. 13.1). For example, in a study of commercial COBOL application programs at the Raytheon Company, many functions common at a company level, plant level, and application level were found to be reusable.[11] Based on an examination of 5000 production COBOL programs, Raytheon developed a library containing 3200 reusable modules.

By using the Raytheon library, software developers have been producing programs that on average contain 60 percent reusable code. Raytheon found that software reuse can deliver a 50 percent increase in software development productivity. In addition, software developers at Raytheon feel that software reuse introduces a new level of program standardization that makes programs easier to understand and to maintain. This can mean a 60 percent reduction in maintenance effort.

The Programming Environment Project at the University of California, Irvine, reported that a 62 percent software reuse level in building prototypes helped increase productivity by 20 percent.[12] In Japanese software factories, an 85 percent software reuse level helped increase software productivity eightfold.[12] Finally, Hartford Insurance Group has reached a 30 to 40 percent reuse level for application system development, which provides a savings of 250 person-days per month.[13] The ongoing cost to support the Wang-based reusable components li-

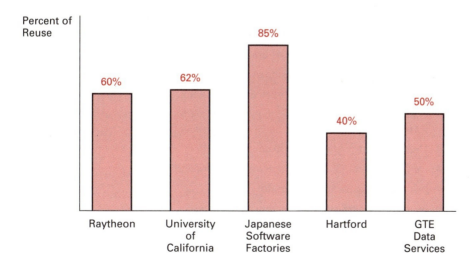

Figure 13.1 Many organizations have found that they can develop a major portion of new software systems by reusing software components from previous systems.

brary, which is used by more than 1000 software developers, is 25 person-days per month.

PROBLEMS WITH SOFTWARE REUSE AND SOLUTIONS   Although recognized as a great productivity idea, software reuse has had only limited success. The state of the practice of software reuse in the United States is "embarrassing," according to Freeman.[14] Most software developers and managers do not show the slightest interest in explicitly incorporating reusability into their software development strategy. Why?

One reason is that software reuse requires planning for reusability when a software component is originally defined and implemented. Another reason is that it is difficult to determine what exactly is a reusable component and how to represent it in a way that it can easily be classified, described, recognized, and reused. Box 13.2 lists the major obstacles to practicing software reuse.

Perhaps the best way to learn how to make software reuse a practical software strategy is to look at two well-known reuse success stories: the Japanese software factories and the Raytheon Company.

BOX 13.2 Problems of implementing in practice what sounds like a good idea

- Question of what is reusable
- Difficult to discover components that are common across systems
- Lack of standardization in programs
- Programming language dependence
- Deciding what goes into library and then finding it
- Understanding the interface requirements as well as internals of a software component
- Understanding side effects from change
- Describing and classifying software components
- Not part of software methodologies
- No management support for reusability
- A reusable software component may cost 25 percent more to develop than component not designed for reusability
- Biggest benefits of reusability are long term
- Not practical to retrofit reusability into existing software components

Japanese Software Factories

The Japanese are the world masters of software reuse because they apply reuse to a greater extent than anywhere else in the world. Japanese management strategies rather than technology is mainly responsible for their success.

The Japanese are also the world masters of software standardization, which is the basis for their success with reusability. They have standardized both the software process and the software product to the extent that they describe software development as "software production." And, as for any production process, improved productivity and quality follow from standardization. The Japanese claim an order of magnitude increase in software productivity due to software reuse.[15] Management supports and enforces this standardization through standards and procedures and training programs.

The Japanese have developed libraries of reusable software components and taught their software developers how to use them in building software systems, as well as created an integrated set of software tools that support reuse. Reusing software components is an explicit part of their development strategy. Management rewards those who build software with reusable components.

Raytheon's Discovery

Raytheon began its search for common software components in 1976 when the company realized that many software functions were common across its COBOL application systems.[16] Raytheon began by examining and classifying more than 5000 production COBOL programs according to the following categories:

- Edit or validation programs
- Update programs
- Report programs

Next 50 representative programs were selected from the three categories for further study to discover any common program functions. It was found that 40 to 60 percent of code was common across the programs, and three common logic structures were created: select, update, and report. The programming staff experimented with the structures when building new COBOL programs and provided practical feedback on how to refine the reusable functions (or abstractions). In all, Raytheon software staff discovered several common abstractions in its business application systems:

- Six major functions
- Several functional module types
- Seven logic structures

Once refined, management made the abstractions a standard to be incorporated into all new COBOL systems. With this reusability standard, Raytheon achieved a level of software reuse ranging from 15 to 85 percent in its COBOL systems. Much of Raytheon's success can be directly attributed to the role management played in supporting the project to first discover the reusable components that would be useful in their organization and then to enforce the use of these reusable components in software development projects.

ORGANIZATION LEVEL REUSE

Both the Japanese and the Raytheon experiences point out that for reuse to be successful it must be practiced at the organization level, not simply at the individual level. The cost of discovering reusable components and creating and maintaining a library of reusable components cannot be recovered unless the components are used many times; usually, a minimum of three times is required to reach a payback point.[17] Practicing reuse at the organization level requires the development and acceptance of organization standards.

As is often true for technology, the people issues outweigh the technical issues in determining the successful use of a technology. Neither the Japanese nor Raytheon had special or particularly sophisticated software tools to support software reuse. What they did have was a commitment from management and an acceptance of software reuse by their software staff. To obtain that acceptance they included their staff in the process of discovering/defining reusable components, they conducted software reuse training programs, and they recognized and rewarded those who practiced software reuse.

MAKING REUSE PRACTICAL

From the Japanese software factories and the Raytheon Company examples, we can see that the solution to the software reuse practicality problem is multifold. Five things are absolutely necessary to make reuse a practical as well as powerful technology:

- Choosing an appropriate formalism for representing a reusable software component
- Providing tools to support a development approach based on reuse
- Providing a library of reusable parts
- Using a software development methodology that fosters reuse
- Enlisting management support and enforcement for reuse

REFERENCES

1. From an interview with Ed Riedy, GTE Data Services, Tempo Terrace, FL, November 1990.

2. Brad J. Cox, "Planning the Software Industrial Revolution," *IEEE Software* November 1990, 25–33.

3. Ibid.

4. Donald Knuth, *The Art of Computer Programming*, vol. 1 (Reading, MA: Addison-Wesley, 1973), pp. 182–188.

5. M. D. McIlroy, "Mass Produced Software Components," in *Proceedings of NATO Conference on Software Engineering*, ed. Naur and Randell (Brussels: Scientific Affairs Division, NATO, 1969), pp. 88–98.

6. T. Capers Jones, "Reusability in Programming," *IEEE Transactions on Software Engineering*, SE-10, no. 5 (September 1984), 488–493.

7. B. W. Boehm, "Improving Software Productivity," *Computer*, 20, no. 9 (September 1987), 43–57.

8. Will Tracz, "Software Reuse: Motivators and Inhibitors," in *Software Reuse: Emerging Technology Tutorial*, (Washington, DC: IEEE Computer Society Press, 1988), pp. 62–67.

9. Edward J. Joyce, "Reusable Software: Passage to Productivity," *Datamation*, September 15, 1988, pp. 97–98, 102.

10. Thomas McCabe, "Reverse Engineering, Reusability, Redundancy," *American Programmer*, 3, no. 10 (October 1990), 8–13.

11. R. G. Lanergan and C. A. Grasso, "Software Engineering with Reusable Design and Code," *IEEE Transactions on Software Engineering*, SE-10, no. 5 (September 1984), 498–501.

12. T. A. Standish, "An Essay on Software Reuse," *IEEE Transactions on Software Engineering*, SE-10, no. 5 (September 1984), 494–497.

13. Joyce, "Reusable Software."

14. Peter Freeman, "A Perspective on Reusability," in *Software Reusability Tutorial*, (Washington, DC: IEEE Computer Society Press, 1987), pp. 2–8.

15. Tracz, "Software Reuse."

16. Lanergan and Grasso, "Software Engineering with Reusable Design and Code."

17. Will Tracz, "Where Does Reuse Start?" in *Reuse in Practice Workshop*, Software Engineering Institute, Pittsburgh, July 11–13, 1989.

14 REUSABLE SOFTWARE COMPONENTS

WHAT IS A REUSABLE SOFTWARE COMPONENT

Building software from reusable components gives developers a big lead on development, but of course, it also assumes that a set of standard, reusable components is available. What types of software components are candidates for reuse? Box 14.1 suggests some possibilities.

Packages

Most often when we think of software reusability we think of reusing program code, either a complete program or some of its parts. Software packages are one example of program level reuse. In the case of packages, the user takes the complete program in an as-is generic form, adjusts the program through parameters, or more extensively changes some of the program code to customize the package. Packages are particularly popular in such application areas as payroll, banking, insurance, accounting, networking, inventory control, and system software.

Perhaps the biggest unforeseen danger with application packages is the difficulty of customization and ongoing maintenance. Many packages must be customized to suit a particular organization's requirements. The costs and time for customization can be much larger than one might expect. For example, one organization purchased a $600,000 payroll system and then spent 30 staff-years to make the necessary modifications to install it.[1] This was only the beginning of costly expenditures for the package because it is likely that future modifications will be needed to support changing organization requirements. If the modifications have to be made in a language such as COBOL, PL/1, or FORTRAN, the maintenance for the package will require many additional staff-years of effort. To facilitate maintenance, excellent documentation and clean design of the

BOX 14.1 What is a reusable software component?

- Program code (whole programs, code fragments)
- Design specifications (logical data models, process structures, application models)
- Plans (project management plans, test plans)
- Documentation (help screens, user documentation)
- Expertise and experience (life cycle model reuse, quality assurance, application area knowledge)
- Any information used to create software and software documentation

package are needed. These characteristics need to be examined when the package is purchased. Also, tools that provide change impact analysis and change control are needed.

Box 14.2 lists the major pitfalls of packages. To avoid these pitfalls, a careful analysis of the application is required before a decision is made as to whether to develop a program or buy a package:

- Consider the functional characteristics of the application itself. How complex is it? What is the priority of implementation? What is the time scale for development? (A large development backlog may be a good enough reason to consider a package. In-house projects may take several years to develop and may go seriously over budget at the end of it. An application software package should be implemented in a matter of months at a fixed price.)
- Do the application data have close links to other applications, for example, in a database environment? Can the database administrator accommodate the package with some form of bridge between it and the database systems?
- Will senior management resist the whole idea of purchasing applications from outside sources? (One way around this problem is to present the clear economic advantages and point out that the programming staff will be free to concentrate on more important areas of application development.)
- Is the documentation of the package complete and of high quality? (Documentation, which is so often neglected with in-house development, can be a necessary prerequisite for the purchase of a software package. It is also a good indication of the quality of the product itself. Metrics tools can be used to measure the quality of the package.)

Selecting an application package should be approached systematically using a formal, logical procedure. Box 14.3 lists suggested steps in acquiring a package.

BOX 14.2 Pitfalls of application packages

- The package is insufficiently parametrized and does not fully adapt to changes in requirements.
- DP modifies the package when it is installed and subsequent maintenance becomes almost as expensive as for in-house application programs.
- Expensive maintenance becomes necessary later on when the hardware, operating system, terminals, or network are changed or when user requirements change.
- The package is difficult to maintain due to poor documentation, lack of hooks for user-created code, ill-structured design, absence of source code, excessive complexity, low-level languages, or poor-quality coding.
- The package has been made difficult to maintain because it has been tinkered with, and modifications that are ill-documented and difficult to understand have been made to the package.
- The package does not fit with corporate database implementation and strategy.
- The software house that owns the package ceases operations.
- The package is incompatible with existing systems to which it must interface.

The advent of CASE technology is changing the application package market. In the past, package vendors delivered their product in the form of source and/or object code and associated documentation. Customization of the package was done at the code level. Today, vendors are delivering the package design model and associated documentation with or without the source code, all of which are stored in a repository. Customization is done at the design level with the use of CASE tools and then the code is generated with CASE tools.

Parts

Reusing parts of a program (i.e., fragment reuse) involves taking code from one program and reusing it in another program. Usually, the parts to be reused are taken from a program that performs a similar function in the same application domain, and reuse is at the discretion of the individual programmer. Most programmers tend to reuse code from programs that they or their teammates have previously written because they know of its existence and intimately understand the inner workings of the code. Thus, parts reuse is often practiced at the individual level.

BOX 14.3 Steps in the acquisition of an application package

- List the present and future requirements of the application in detail.
- Survey all available packages for that application.
- Examine their documentation. Quantitatively measure the quality of the package using metrics tools and program code analyzers.
- Check whether they are sufficiently parametrized.
- Can CASE and re-engineering tools be used to evaluate, customize, and maintain the package?
- Draw up a short list of suitable packages.
- Examine the vendor. Will it provide adequate service?
- Talk to users of these packages.
- Check the ability of the package to link into the corporate database plans and interface with other systems where necessary.
- Conduct benchmarks if performance is critical.
- Allow end users to use packages on a temporary basis if the end-user interface is critical.
- Write an appropriate contract.

A form of parts reuse that is practiced at the organization level is shared libraries of reusable code modules. These library modules perform application-specific functions and common program functions, such as HELP, I/O, sorting and invoking, controlling, and terminating program calls. As a matter of fact, organizations employing software reuse (see Chapter 13) have created libraries of reusable source code (see Box 14.4).

A higher degree of reusability is more likely to be achievable when the parts are originally designed with reusability in mind. Box 14.5 lists properties of a reusable software component. For example, in a reusable procedural component, all data descriptions, literals, constants, and input/output control should be external to the component; further, there is explicit parameter passing, information hiding, and good documentation, and the code is well structured. In an object-oriented approach, the concept of encapsulation makes an object more amendable to reuse because the implementation details are hidden from users of the object. The implementation details of the object data and methods can be defined and changed without affecting their higher-level descriptions.

BOX 14.4 Example of reusable components libraries

- Raytheon Company — 3200 COBOL source code modules
- Hartford Insurance — 35 COBOL source code modules consisting of 15 programs and 20 subroutines stored in a library maintained on a Wang minicomputer available online to 1200 developers
- AT&T Pacific Bell — Thousand of C language components written for UNIX, giving 250 developers on-line access to the library
- GTE Data Services — 220 reusable components consisting of 960,000 lines of COBOL, C, and Assembler available to 2000 developers

BOX 14.5 Properties for a reusable component

- **Additivity:** Able to combine components with minimal side effects and without destructive interaction
- **Formal mathematical basis:** Allow correctness conditions to be stated and component combination to preserve key properties of components
- **Self-contained:** Each component embodies only a single idea
- **Easily describable:** Easy to understand
- **Programming language–independent:** Not unnecessarily specific about superficial language details
- **Verifiable:** Easy to test
- **Simple interface:** Minimal number of parameters passed and parameters passed explicitly
- **Easily changed:** Easy to modify with minimal and obvious side effects
- **Reusable:** Has high reuse potential; likely to be usable in many systems

Limitations of Code Reuse

At the code level, software reuse is very limited. Code reuse is language-, operating-system-, and application-dependent and is most often practiced at the individual level. Also, there are the difficulties of finding code to be reused and of retrofitting reusability into the code (because most code was not written with reuse in mind). However, the major problem with code reuse is that the code usually must be changed before it can be reused. With change comes the risk of introducing errors and other unforeseen and unwanted side effects. The danger of changing code has been a major deterrent to considering software reuse as a viable software development technique.

Libraries of reusable source code components are unlikely to revolutionize software development or to provide an order of magnitude improvement in software productivity.

HIGHER-LEVEL REUSABLE COMPONENTS

A higher form of software reuse is needed to overcome the inherent limitations of code reuse. The closer we get to code level, the less feasible and less grand-scale software reuse becomes. Higher-level reuse enables both the reuse of components *and* the frameworks connecting the components. Therefore, we must think in terms of reusing higher-level software abstractions, such as program designs and architectures, instead of source code. At higher levels of abstractions, the problems arising from programming language dependencies, implementation-specific details, and code inefficiencies disappear. State of the practice of software reusability is code reuse, but state of the art is higher-level reusable components.

Higher-level reusable components are more valuable to an organization because they represent application-problem solutions rather than implementation solutions, which lower-level components provide. Although not as general in nature as lower-level reusable components, higher-level components do represent a family of solutions within a particular application domain that can be modified to build many application variations. Also, because higher-level reusable components are likely to be of higher quality than components created for one-time use, and because requirements and design errors are more expensive than programming errors, higher-level components use can result in much lower software costs. Finally, reusing higher-level components can lead to reusing or automatic generating of lower-level components, which can further reduce software costs. For example, from reusable designs, we can produce code, test cases, and documentation by employing CASE tools.

Several higher-level reusable components are in use today. We next discuss three examples of such components.

Frames

Figure 14.1 shows an example of a program composed of a hierarchy of reusable components called **Bassett frames.**[2] At first glance, it looks like a traditional, well-structured program in which the modules are arranged such that the most general functions appear at the top of the hierarchy and the most detailed at the leaves. However, a second look shows that the frames are actually arranged in the opposite order; the most detailed frame is placed at the root and the most general frames are the leaves. The root frame serves as the master blueprint for the program structure. It isolates all the unique aspects of the program into this top-level frame, called the specification frame. The rest of the program (approximately 90 percent of the code) is composed of reusable frames.

Higher-level frames assemble and modify lower-level frames to construct the desired program. The frames, a form of macros, are a generic solution to a class of related programming problems. They can be tailored for use in a specific program by modifying the frame at predefined change points (see Fig. 14.2).

Reusable frames are the basis for producing COBOL application programs with the CASE COBOL code generator NETRON/CAP, from Netron, Inc. NETRON/CAP uses three types of reusable frames:

1. Standard frames (see Fig. 14.3)

2. User-written corporate standard frames (e.g., screen and report designs, edit validations, security routines)

3. Frames generated by NETRON/CAP from user application-specific instructions.

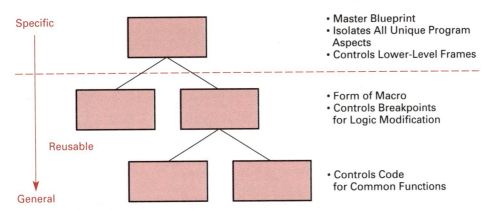

Figure 14.1 An example of a program composed of a hierarchy of reusable frames, called Bassett frames.

```
000273%INSERT  ;MAINT-ADD
000274%INSERT  ;MAINT-ADD-PREPARE
000275%INSERT  ;MAINT-ADD-PROCESS
000276. INSERT  ;MAINT-ADD-NULL-TEST
000277        IF   SAMPLE-SOCINS = ZERO
000278             MOVE "Y" TO ;MAINT-ADD-NULL.
000279%    Use only if ADD is enabled.
000280%    Test for a null record and set ;MAINT-ADD-NULL.
000281%    Null records will not be added to the file. Default is:
000282% [ If ;MAINTFILE-FDREC = SPACES
000283%        MOVE "Y" TO ;MAINT-ADD-NULL.
000284%
000285%INSERT  ;MAINT-DELETE
000286%INSERT  ;MAINT-DEL-PREPARE
000287%INSERT  ;MAINT-DEL-PROCESS
000288%
000289%INSERT  ;MAINT-MODIFY
000290%INSERT  ;MAINT-MOD-PREPARE
000291%INSERT  ;MAINT-MOD-PROCESS
000292%INSERT  ;MAINT-MOD-HOLD-SCREEN
000293%    Section to "hold" records on screen prior to full screen
000294%    modify.  Must insert some logic (or nothing) at this point if
000295%    you specify MODMODE = S.  If you dummy this out, then records
000296%    won't be locked while user makes on-screen modifications,
000297%    which might cause problems when modifications are actually
000298%    processed.
000299%
000300%INSERT  ;MAINT-RESET-RECORD
000301%
000302%INSERT  ;MAINT-LOCKMODE-TOGGLE
000303%
000304%INSERT  ;MAINT-DFLT
000305%    If "Set default" function enabled, default record
000306%    can be changed here.
000307%
000308%INSERT  ;MAINT-DFLT-PREPARE
000309%INSERT  ;MAINT-DFLT-SETUP
000310%INSERT  ;MAINT-DFLT-PROCESS
000311%
000312%INSERT  ;MAINT-LINK
000313%INSERT-BEFORE  ;MAINT-LINK-PREPARE
000314%INSERT-AFTER   ;MAINT-LINK-RETURN
000315%INSERT  ;MAINT-GET-LINKPROG
000316%
000317%INSERT  ;MAINT-INV-UNUSED-REC
000318%    Clears fields of unused record locations on screen.
```

Figure 14.2 Bassett frames contain predefined engineering change points where the frame can be modified, such as with the insertion of new logic.

The tool automatically chooses the appropriate reusable frames, modifies them according to the specification frame directions, and assembles them to create the program. As the corporation uses the tool, it adds to its own corporate standard frames library, and this simplifies the building process for future corporate applications. Because in most cases, only the specification frame is

General Use Frames

BROWS.F	• provides code to display the contents of a datafile
STANDARD.F	• provides COBOL standard divisions
SCROLL.F	• performs record scrolling
LINK.F	• provides program linking
CONCAT.F	• concatenates two strings of any size
MATCH.F	• compares two strings
FILE.F	• provides code for opening and closing a file and reading and writing a record
FILE.FA	• used by FILE.F to support alternate keys
PARMS.F	• performs parameter passing
SDATE.F	• provides output format for date and/or time
PATH.F	• determines if a file exists in any one of a number of given paths
EXISTFIL.F	• determines the path of a file
STACK.F	• controls the definition and operation of stacks
STACK.F1	• performs push and pop operations for STACK.F
BITOP.F	• toggles bits on or off by comparing them with a mask

Figure 14.3 Standard Bassett frames included in the NETRON/CAP reusable components library, from Netron, Inc.

changed when the program is modified, the software maintenance effort is greatly reduced.

DesignWare

The design specification for a software system is another form of a higher-level reusable software component. By its very nature, it is a specific, rather than generic, type of component because it is used to build a particular type of application, such as a payroll or inventory control system. In some cases, not only is it application-specific, but it is also industry-specific. As an example consider Customer/1 from Arthur Andersen and Company.

Customer/1 is a reusable design specification for a DB2 customer information system for the utilities industry. The design specification includes the various functions expected in a company's customer information and marketing system, such as billing, service orders, meter reading, nonmetered services and charges, maintenance accounts received, credit and collection, and customer contact. Note that some of these functions (e.g., meter reading) are peculiar to the utilities industry.

Customer/1 is a complete blueprint for building a customer information system. The design components include screen layouts, information flow diagrams, a relational database design, data element descriptions, DB2 tables, and conversation prototypes. Along with the design components, Customer/1 includes a set of tools to modify the design to suit each user's unique requirements and to generate the software code and documentation from the design. Later, the tools can be used during the maintenance phase to modify the system at the design specification level and to regenerate the affected portions of the system.

Andersen calls this package of reusable system design components and supporting tools **DesignWare**. Another DesignWare product offered by Andersen is Invest/1, an investment management and accounting system for insurance companies, banks, and investment houses.

Andersen's approach recognizes the need to build custom applications for an organization and to be able to easily alter the application to meet changing organization needs. It marks the trend not only of reusing software designs but also of creating reusable components that are application- or domain-specific.

Templates

Texas Instruments offers a line of reusable **templates** that can be used with the CASE tool Information Engineering Facility (IEF) to produce applications. The template is a complete application design model that is ready for code generation. The IEF CASE tools are used to modify the design and to generate code.

One template offered by Texas Instruments is the General Ledger Template. The package contains

- Customizable IEF design model consisting of 30 entity types, 42 online transactions, and 15 batch procedures that generate 600,000 lines of COBOL code
- Modifiable user's guide
- Tape containing data to initially populate a database with currency and country codes defined by the International Standards Organization

The template can be immediately generated as a generalized solution for a general ledger application or for a prototype to experiment with user requirements, or the template can be modified and then the code can be generated. A broad range of standard general ledger system procedures are included in the template package:

- General transactions
- Ledger parameter maintenance
- Journal entry maintenance
- Online reporting
- Batch processing

- Country and currency maintenance
- Chart of accounts maintenance
- Organization structure maintenance

Cliches

Figure 14.4 shows another example of a program created from reusable components. In this case, the reusable component is called a **cliche.**[3] The first five lines in Fig. 14.4 are commands for instantiating the cliche "simple report" to create the Ada program shown below the commands.

A cliche is defined as a commonly used combination of elements, such as implementation, design, and specification concepts. The cliche consists of roles and constraints. Roles are filled in by the user with instance-specific data. Constraints provide the fixed elements of the cliche, check the roles that are filled in, and fill in any roles left unfilled. Simple report has seven roles: file name, title, enumerator, print item, line limit, column heading and summary; and four constraints: file and title name default, line limit of 65, default formats for printing items in report, and column headings.

Cliches are programming language–independent. They can be represented as plans that are formal, hierarchical flowcharts in which both data flow and control flow are represented. Plans abstract away inessential features of a program. In this more general form, they are more reusable.

Cliches are part of the artificial intelligence system called the **Programmer's Apprentice,** which is currently under development at the MIT Artificial Intelligence Laboratory. Programmer's Apprentice (PA) is a program development system whose ultimate purpose is to automate the programming process. On the way to this goal, the PA will serve as an automated member of a programming team, learning more about the software process with each software project experience. The PA programming team model is based on the chief programmer team concept where the human team member is the chief programmer and the PA is the team. The PA and the chief programmer share programming knowledge through a library of cliches.

PA uses a knowledge-based editor **KBEmacs** to combine cliches to create programs. KBEmacs is capable of performing many intelligent programming tasks, such as determining what data type should be used, reusing variable names in logically related contexts, analyzing the effects of changes to the program, and helping the human programmer understand the program. KBEmacs automatically generate program documentation along with the code.

One application of the PA is to support rapid prototyping. An Ada or Lisp program without such details as error checking could be built very quickly using cliches.

Another application of the PA is creating better system designs. Cliches can be used to represent design concepts. Because there are probably only a few hundred different design concepts, building a comprehensive library of reusable

```
Define a simple_report procedure UNIT_REPAIR_REPORT.
Fill the enumerator with a chain_enumeration of UNITS and REPAIRS.
Fill the main_file_key with a query_user_for_key of UNITS.
Fill the title with ("Report of Repairs on Unit" & UNIT_KEY).
Remove the summary.
```

↓

```ada
with CALENDAR, FUNCTIONS, MAINTENANCE_FILES, TEXT_IO;
use CALENDAR, FUNCTIONS, MAINTENANCE_FILES, TEXT_IO;
procedure UNIT_REPAIR_REPORT is
   use DEFECT_IO, REPAIR_IO, UNIT_IO, INT_IO;
   CURRENT_DATE: constant STRING:=FORMAT_DATE(CLOCK);
   DEFECT:DEFECT_TYPE;
   REPAIR:REPAIR_TYPE;
   REPAIR_INDEX:REPAIR_INDEX_TYPE;
   REPORT:TEXT_IO.FILE_TYPE;
   TITLE:STRING(1..33);
   UNIT:UNIT_TYPE;
   UNIT_KEY:UNIT_KEY_TYPE;
   procedure CLEAN_UP is
      begin
         SET_OUTPUT(STANDARD_OUTPUT);
         CLOSE(DEFECTS); CLOSE(REPAIRS); CLOSE(UNITS); CLOSE(REPORT);
      exception
         when STATUS_ERROR => return;
      end CLEAN_UP
begin
   OPEN(DEFECTS, IN_FILE, DEFECTS_NAME); OPEN(REPAIRS, IN_FILE, REPAIRS_NAME);
   OPEN(UNITS, IN_FILE, UNITS_NAME); CREATE(REPORT, OUT_FILE, "report.txt");
   loop
      begin
         NEW_LINE; PUT("Enter UNIT Key:"); GET(UNIT_KEY);
         READ(UNITS, UNIT, UNIT_KEY);
         exit;
      exception
         when END_ERROR => PUT("Invalid UNIT Key"); NEW_LINE;
      end;
   end loop;
   TITLE:="Report of Repairs on Unit" & UNIT_KEY;
   SET_OUTPUT(REPORT);
   NEW_LINE(4); SET_COL(20); PUT(CURRENT_DATE);
   NEW_LINE(2); SET_COL(13); PUT(TITLE); NEW_LINE(60);
   READ(UNITS, UNIT, UNIT_KEY); REPAIR_INDEX:=UNIT.REPAIR;
   while not NULL_INDEX(REPAIR_INDEX) loop
      READ(REPAIRS, REPAIR, REPAIR_INDEX);
      if LINE > 64 then
         NEW_PAGE; NEW_LINE; PUT("Page:"); PUT(INTEGER(PAGE-1), 3);
         SET_COL(13); PUT(TITLE); SET_COL(61); PUT(CURRENT_DATE); NEW_LINE(2);
         PUT("  Date    Defect   Description/Comment"); NEW_LINE(2);
      end if;
      READ(DEFECTS, DEFECT, REPAIR.DEFECT);
      PUT(FORMAT_DATE(REPAIR.DATE)); SET_COL(13); PUT(REPAIR.DEFECT);
      SET_COL(20); PUT(DEFECT.NAME); NEW_LINE;
      SET_COL(22); PUT(REPAIR.COMMENT); NEW_LINE;
      REPAIR_INDEX:=REPAIR.NEXT;
   end loop;
   CLEAN_UP;
exception
   when DEVICE_ERROR |END_ERROR|NAME_ERROR|STATUS_ERROR =>
      CLEAN_UP; PUT("Data Base Inconsistent");
   when others => CLEAN_UP; raise; end UNIT_REPAIR_REPORT;
```

Figure 14.4 Given the five commands at the top, the Programmer's Apprentice, from the MIT AI Laboratory, can automatically generate this 54-line Ada program.

design components is certainly in the realm of possibility. However, the PA is not yet fast enough or complete enough to be used as a practical tool. Although it is unlikely that libraries of cliches will be available for industrial use in the near future, the PA is likely to contribute greatly to advancements in integrated tools environments that provide process guidance. The PA is an important research project bringing together software automation, software reuse, and artificial intelligence.

REFERENCES

1. Edward J. Joyce, "Reusable Software: Passage to Productivity," *Datamation,* September 15, 1988, pp. 92–97, 102.

2. Paul G. Bassett, "Frame-based Software Engineering," *IEEE Software* (July 1987), 9–16.

3. Charles Rich and Richard C. Waters, "A Research Overview," *IEEE Computer* (November 1988), 11–24.

15 TOOLS AND METHODS FOR REUSABILITY

REUSABLE COMPONENTS LIBRARY

An absolute prerequisite for software reusability is a library of relevant reusable components and an automated library management system. Components stored in the library should have a standard representation form and should be well documented. The library management system should organize, protect, and manage the reusable software components. Search mechanisms are needed to locate components of interest, and analysis mechanisms are needed to understand the components and to measure their quality. Cross-referencing capabilities are needed to identify relationships among components. Box 15.1 lists the properties needed for a reusable components library.

Probably, most reusable component libraries will be domain- or industry-specific (e.g., an insurance business reusable software components library). Higher-level components (e.g., requirements specifications) tend to be more application-specific. A high degree of reusability can be achieved when building such applications as banking, insurance, order entry, inventory control, and reservations. For these types of applications, customized versions of the system can be built mainly from a library of reusable components including reusable architecture frameworks.

Repository: Cornerstone Tool of Reuse

The **repository** is the perfect mechanism for providing a reusable components library and a library management system. It can store a variety of different types of software system components, ranging from the description of a single data element to a complete software system design, as well as the relationships among components. Directories of repository contents and the repository query facility can help locate candidate components for reuse. The contents of the repository can be viewed at varying levels of detail in a graphic or narrative form,

BOX 15.1 Properties of a reusable components library

- Comprehensive DBMS for storing and retrieving components to facilitate access, search, version, control, and security
- Operations that allow user to create, edit, view, and combine components
- Organization scheme to act as navigational aid through library
- Standardized component representation formalism
- Easy to grow

making it easy to understand a component in terms of its function and its sub-components. Cross-reference reports identify relationships among components.

The information management system of the repository provides security, access privileges, versioning, change control, and configuration management functions. Repository manipulation facilities allow authorized users to create, move, update, and report on components. Validation facilities allow users to perform checks, such as type and range checks, and complexity analysis when creating or modifying repository components.

Meta Model: Representation Formalism for Reuse

The **repository meta model** provides a standard formalism for representing reusable components. Most repositories use an entity-relationship model to define the kinds of components that can be stored in the repository. This powerful model can carry semantic information in the form of associated attributes about a component. In addition, it can define the rules controlling the use and modification of the component. With the common frame of understanding that the meta model provides, the components can be easily reused across software tools, applications, and developers.

Also, the meta model makes higher forms of reusability possible. Because design level and specification level software information can be defined by the meta model, the repository meta model provides a representation formalism that fosters implementation level, design level, and requirements level reuse.

The meta model is an important reason for requiring the tools that support reusability to be integrated. Because integrated tools share the same repository and meta model, they represent information in the same way. This enables the production of information that can be reused by other tools and the reuse of information produced by other tools within the environment.

The repository, along with its meta model, forms the cornerstone of software tools needed to support reusability. Success of software reuse hinges on a practical representation formalism capable of representing different levels of software abstraction. The repository meta model provides such representation formalism.

TOOLS FOR REUSABILITY

Although the Japanese software factories and Raytheon Company examples did not use any special or advanced software tools to support their reusability approach, realistically software reusability cannot be practiced at the organization level without adequate tools. One of the reasons why software reusability is a technology whose time has come is that the tools needed to support it are now available. A repository-based, integrated software tools environment provides the basis for an organization level environment supporting software reuse.

What types of tools should be included in this environment? There are two aspects of software reusability to consider:

1. **Building reusable components**
2. **Using reusable components**

Tools are needed to support both of these aspects.

Building Reusable Components

To build a library of reusable components we need tools that aid in

- Identifying components that can be widely reused
- Defining components and adapting them for reuse
- Classifying and storing the reusable components in a library
- Representing reusable components in a standard form

Tools for Identifying Components for Reuse

The best and fastest way to create reusable components is to mine them from existing software systems. Although the components may need to be modified or generalized for reuse, this process is still better than developing new components. A component that already exists can provide an example of a working algorithm that can save a great deal of development time.

Domain analysis is the process of discovering objects and operations common across systems within the same domain.[1] It is an important technique used to discover a relevant and comprehensive set of reusable components for an organization. Although much of domain analysis is still a manual activity that needs human assistance to make inferences about concepts not explicitly in the code, it can be aided by various automated tools. Re-engineering tools, CASE tools, knowledge-extraction tools, entity-relationship diagrammers, and parsing tools support domain analysis.

Re-engineering tools are at the top of the list of tools to aid in discovering common software components that can be reused. In particular, reverse engineering tools can be used to find higher-level software abstractions by reverse engineering them from the existing software physical level descriptions, such as source code and data description languages (DDL). For example, an organization-wide logical data model represented as an ER diagram can be created by reverse engineering and consolidating the current DDL's across a corporation's production application systems.

Whereas data reverse engineering tools can be used to find reusable data models, logic reverse engineering tools can be used to find common, reusable program architectures embedded in a corporation's existing application source code.

Tools for Storing and Classifying Reusable Components

The repository serves as the data store and classification mechanism for reusable components. One possibility for classifying reusable components is a hierarchical organization scheme in which components are organized by application type and by function within the application. Object-oriented techniques such as inheritance and classes also offer a means for organizing reusable components.

Tools for Representing and Describing Reusable Components

The repository meta model provides the standard formalism for representing reusable components and a graphic format for describing the components. When a reusable component is presented in graphic form, its subcomponents and interrelationships are easier to understand.

Software templates and frame-based knowledge representation systems describe a reusable component in a way in which common abstractions are separated from details that must be appropriately filled in for each use of the reusable component. Specification languages offer an implementation-independent description for reusable components.

In a **hypertext system**, different kinds of pieces of information are linked through associations that resemble the way the human mind works.[2] As shown in Fig. 15.1, hypertext systems can be used to provide a connected set of information, including diagrams, code, and test plans, that describe the component at different levels of abstraction (design level, implementation level) and for different purposes (design phase, testing phase).

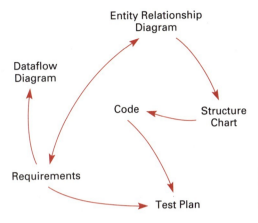

Figure 15.1 Hypertext systems are a connected set of different kinds of information that can be used to describe a software system.

Tools for Producing and Refining Reusable Components

Object-oriented programming languages such as Smalltalk, C++, and Ada support the creation of reusable objects through such techniques as encapsulation, inheritance, abstract data types, and object classes. Because the quality of reusable components must be as high as possible, testing tools, metrics tools, and standards checkers are important for ensuring the creation of high-quality reusable components.

CARE System

The Computer Science Center at the University of Maryland has developed a system called CARE (Computer-Aided Reuse Engineering) to extract and measure reusable components from ANSI C and Ada programs.[3] The approach is to create components for code reuse by taking and packaging components from existing systems. The components are measured in terms of properties, such as functional usefulness, reuse cost, and quality, that indicate their potential for reuse. Each component is packaged along with its functional specification, test cases, and a reuse guide, which are all stored in a repository.

An important part of CARE is its reusability attributes model, which attempts to measure automatically reuse properties. For example, McCabe Cyclomatic complexity and Halstead's Software Science metrics are used to predict a component's correctness, testability, structuredness, and understandability. (Recall the discussion of these metrics in Chapter 4.) A component's functional usefulness is measured in terms of reuse frequency, which is calculated as the ratio between the number of calls to a component and the average number of calls to a standard class of reusable components.

Besides measuring reuse properties, the CARE model also attempts to determine acceptable ranges for the measures. Based on case studies in which reusable component candidates were extracted from 187,000 lines of existing ANSI C code in nine systems, initial ranges have been set. For example, a component whose reuse frequency is greater than 0.5 and whose complexity lies in the range of 5 to 15 is considered highly reusable.

These studies indicate that 5 to 10 percent of the existing code accounts for the majority of a system's functionality and should be analyzed for reuse potential. This greatly reduces the amount of code that must be examined. The studies also point out that the metrics used to support software re-engineering also can be used to support software reuse engineering.

USING REUSABLE COMPONENTS

To use reusable components effectively in building application systems, we need tools to

- Find the reusable components
- Understand the reusable components
- Modify the reusable components
- Combine and incorporate the reusable components

Tools for Finding Reusable Components

The substantial investment in creating a reusable components library will not pay off unless the components are used multiple times by multiple developers. The first requirement for ensuring their use is that the components are easy to find in the library. Because the library will probably be domain-specific, it is likely that it will not contain more than a few hundred reusable components. Therefore, simple search methods, such as keyword in context (KWIC), function index, hierarchy of function categories, plus keyword index, structured queries, and pattern matching, are effective techniques for finding components in the library.

Tools for Understanding Reusable Components

Another requirement for ensuring the use of reusable components is that the components are easy to understand. Re-engineering tools that help software maintainers understand existing systems also can help developers understand reusable components. Re-engineering tools that aid understandability include program analyzers, logic and data tracers, logic and data restructurers, and logic and data reverse engineering tools.

Hypertext systems that link reusable components to documentation also facilitate understanding.

Tools for Modifying Reusable Components

Software reusability is not practical unless the reusable component can be easily and safely modified because only rarely can the component be reused without first modifying it. Tools for automatically analyzing the impact of change and for implementing the change are needed.

Re-engineering tools and the repository information management facilities give where-used and how-used information to help determine the impact from change. Program code analyzers can identify exactly what is affected by each design change, and repository trigger functions can automatically propagate the change through all related components. Re-engineering tools such as metrics tools and standards checkers and repository validation functions can check the completeness, consistency, compliance to standards, and quality of the modified components.

With program code analysis tools, we can automatically find the answers to such questions as these:

- Where are all the places in the system in which a particular variable is modified or referenced?
- What modules call this module?
- What parameters are passed to a module?
- Is there any unreachable code or unused data elements?
- What test cases will give the greatest coverage of changed code?
- Which code implements this requirement?

While some re-engineering analysis tools provide static views of the program procedural and data structures, others provide dynamic views of the program execution, giving an accurate picture of the program execution-time behavior to evaluate run-time efficiency and to detect efficiency problems.

Tools for Combining and Incorporating Reusable Components

Finally, software reusability is not practical without tools to support the assembly of reusable software components. CASE tools, such as syntax-directed program editors, generators, verification systems, and performance experts guide the system developer to combine efficiently and correctly the components to create the new system.

For example, the intelligent editor in the Programmer Apprentice System has knowledge about the programming language syntax and a side effects checker. It has a special set of commands (DEFINE, FILL, SHARE, REPLACE, REMOVE, COMMENT) designed to facilitate software components reusability and program modification.[4] Before executing a command, the PA editor automatically checks the side effects of change on the program and reports them to the developer.

Enabling Technologies for Reuse

Boxes 15.2 and 15.3 summarize the tools that assist each aspect of reusability. Note that there is an overlap between the tools used to support software maintenance and software reuse because software reuse and software maintenance are similar activities. Also, note that the tools range from simple, familiar, third generation tools such as compilers and editors, to CASE tools such as diagramming tools and code generators, to experimental, advanced technology fifth generation tools such as semantic clustering and automatic classification tools and natural-language processors.

BOX 15.2 Tools for producing reusable software components

Identify/Domain Analysis

- Re-engineering tools
  - reverse engineering tools
- Object-oriented tools
- Parsers
- Frame-based knowledge representation systems
- Knowledge-extraction expert systems
- Semantic clustering and automation classification tools

Describe/Represent

- Structured diagrammers
- Software templates
- Frame-based knowledge representation systems
- Specification languages
- Hypertext systems

Classify/Store

- Repository
- Object-oriented tools
- Boolean information retrieval
- Thesaurus constructor
- Rule-based expert system shell

Produce/Refine

- Object-oriented languages
- Re-engineering tools
  - Error, metrics, and standards checkers
  - Program logic analyzers
  - Configuration managers
- Testing tools

BOX 15.3 Tools for using reusable software components

Find

- Repository
  - Query and browsing facility
- Hypertext systems
- Pattern matchers
- Natural-language processors

Modify

- Re-engineering tools
  - Change impact analyzers
  - Program code analyzers
  - Metrics tools
  - Testing tools
  - Configuration managers
- CASE Tools
  - Code generators
- Repository
  - Policies and triggers
  - Cross-reference reports

Understand

- Re-engineering tools
  - Reverse engineering tools
  - Cross references
  - Program logic analyzers
  - Restructurers
- Hypertext systems

Compose/Incorporate

- Repository
- CASE Tools
  - Prototyping tools
  - Diagramming tools
  - Analysis/design toolkits
  - Code generators
- Object-oriented languages
- Transformation systems
- Specification languages
- Compilers/editors
- Macro expanders
- Configuration managers
- Testing tools

However, advanced technology and artificial intelligence tools are not really needed to practice software reusability. At a minimum all that is needed is a repository to act as the reusable components library and re-engineering tools to help discover, understand, and modify components for reuse. The repository and re-engineering tools are the enabling technologies for software reusability.

METHODS FOR REUSABILITY

Reusability considerations should permeate the entire software life cycle to reap the full benefits. Because software reuse as a development approach requires a library of reusable components and tools that support reusability, it cannot be an afterthought. For example, the software development plan should include reusability considerations in terms of software component standards, management support, training needs, software tools and methodologies, and goals for achieving certain levels of reuse. At NTT, the project plan for all new systems must include a minimum software reuse level of 20 percent; that is, at least 20 percent of the system must be constructed from reusable components.[5]

Like software automation, software reuse requires a systemization of the software life cycle process. Standardizing on the use of a structured methodology can provide a repeatable process base on which to incorporate a software reuse approach for development and maintenance. Standardizing the software product means that software systems can be more easily created from reusable parts and architectural frameworks.

However, most structured methodologies today do not directly support reusability because software reuse techniques are not explicitly incorporated into the methodology steps, rules, or examples. One exception is information engineering in which an enterprise-wide data model is created and reused in the development of individual application systems. Another exception is object-oriented methods in which object reuse is a fundamental development strategy. Object-oriented development approaches include such reuse-supporting techniques as encapsulation, inheritance, and classes.

A major software technology trend for the 1990s is to extend widely used structured methodologies and programming languages (C, COBOL) to included object-oriented methods and techniques. This will make software reuse more feasible in the future.

OBJECT-ORIENTED DEVELOPMENT

The object is the central concept in object-oriented development. An **object** is a package of data and operations that manipulate these data. According to Booch, most importantly, "an object is something that exists in time and space (has state) and may be affected by the activity of other objects."[6] Viewed from the outside, the object is an indivisible unit. In an object-oriented development approach, a software system is viewed as a collection of related objects that interact with each other. The benefits of an object-oriented development approach are the following:

- System design is easier because objects can be defined directly in terms of the real-world problem domain, rather than in terms of abstract program functions.
- Systems are easier to change because interdependencies between objects are minimized by localized use of data and procedures.
- System construction is simplified because new systems can be created by **reusing** and extending existing objects.

An object-oriented approach is supported by the following concepts:

- Encapsulation
- Object class
- Inheritance
- Data abstraction

Encapsulation

Encapsulation enables an object to "hide" its implementation of its data and operations on its data from other objects in order to make the object independent. Implementation of the object's operations is called **methods** and data are called **instance variables**. The user of an object knows only what the object does (i.e., its behavior), but not how it is implemented. Manipulation of an object is allowed only through an external interface. Users invoke operations on object data by sending a message to the object. The message specifies the receiver object, the selector indicating the methods to be performed, and any arguments to be passed.[7]

Encapsulation allows the representation or implementation of an object to be changed without affecting any other objects. This simplifies software maintenance.

Object Class

Objects are grouped into classes or types that share the same methods. Individual objects are called **instances** of the class. When a new class of objects is needed, it is created by **reusing** an existing class that is similar to the needed new class. The existing class thus becomes the starting point for creating the new class. The new class is created by modifying the old class in the following manner:[8]

- Extension: Adding instance variables and methods
- Variation: Redefining or overriding some of the features of the existing class
- Specialization: Combination of extension and variation

Inheritance

Inheritance is the technique of creating new classes of objects by choosing an existing class and describing how the new class differs. Classes of objects are hierarchically arranged. The existing class is called the **superclass**, and the new class derived from it is called the **subclass**. Subclasses inherit the methods of their superclasses with the exception of the modifications noted above. Therefore, subclasses are more specialized than their superclasses.

Inheritance is the method for **software reuse** and maintenance in an object-oriented approach. It speeds up the software development and maintenance process by avoiding building software components from scratch and benefiting from reusing already tested components.

Data Abstraction

Abstraction allows an object to be described without any reference to how it is represented and how operations performed on it are implemented.

Object-Oriented Programming Languages

Some languages are better suited to the application of object-oriented development than others. Smalltalk is probably the best; Ada, C++, LISP, and LOOPS are also appropriate. COBOL and FORTRAN, though, are poorly suited for object-oriented development. For example, COBOL does not support information hiding because all data are global (i.e., there are no local variables). However, COBOL is being extended to add features that support an object-oriented approach.

SOFTWARE REUSABILITY: A DEVELOPMENT SCENARIO

The following is a scenario for reuse-based software development. To begin, the system developer selects from the repository a design specification for a system that is similar to the system to be built. The developer locates candidate designs by searching the repository directory for systems that perform the same or similar function as the system being currently designed. The design specification is in the form of a family of related structured diagrams that represent the program architectural structure, procedural components, data structures, and data entities and attributes. The repository automatically links all related system diagrams and associated documentation. Code generation tools are used to generate automatically documented program code and database/file definitions from the design specification.

The existing system can serve as an executable prototype model for the new system. By using the prototype, the developer can see more clearly how the design must be modified to meet the requirements of the new system. Also, end users can try out the prototype to help clarify their needs.

Probably, the design cannot be used as is; it may be too general or address only a subset of the functions required. Therefore, the existing design must be modified to meet all the requirements for the new system. It is important to note that the changes will be made at the design specification level, not at the code level. Because the repository stores various types of reusable system components, as well as the relationship between system components, and automatically tracks and controls all changes, it is practical and safe to modify design components. With the use of change impact analysis tools and change control, the developer can adjust the design to meet the requirements of the new system.

Adjusting an existing design rather than designing from scratch should substantially reduce analysis and design effort. Generating code from the adjusted design rather than manually coding the system should substantially reduce implementation time.

PARTS APPROACH VERSUS WHOLE APPROACH

As shown in Box 15.4, there are two basic approaches for building software from reusable software components: the parts approach and the whole approach.

The **parts approach** is a **composition method** that starts with reusable atomic parts and assembles them to create the new program. Either a top-down or bottom-up stepwise refinement strategy is followed to construct the program. This is problem solving by abstraction (i.e., use of a simplified view of the problem to guide the problem-solving process). Construction methods for the parts approach are mainly concerned with organizing and combining parts to

---

BOX 15.4 Software development approaches

Top-down Structured

- Problem solving by abstraction
- Synthesis
  - Define new architectural framework and new parts and reuse existing parts
- Stepwise refinement, functional decomposition
- Check interfaces

Reusability

- Problem solving by recognizing
- Analysis
  - Find matching parts by pattern matching or examples
- Incremental modification
  - Fill in template
  - Extend
  - Combine
  - Slice
- Check side effects from change

form new programs according to well-defined composition rules. One example of composition rules is the UNIX pipeline, a method of constructing programs from simpler programs by connecting one program's output to another program's input.[9]

The parts are designed to be self-contained and represent one simple data or procedural component. The correctness of each part is checked before it is used as a building block. The program grows one part at a time. Much of the development effort focuses on building the framework to integrate the reusable parts. Checking the interfaces and interdependencies between parts is critical because this represents the newly created portion of the system and this is where development errors are most likely to occur.

On the other hand, the **whole approach** is an **analysis method** that starts with a reusable program design architecture and modifies it in steps to meet the requirements of the new program. An incremental modification strategy is followed in which an existing program is adjusted to evolve into the new program.[10] Some possible adjustments include

- Filling in parameters or stubs in templates or roles in cliches
- Enhancing an existing component with new features (e.g., inheritance)
- Slicing an existing component to eliminate unwanted functionality
- Changing data types
- Creating new low-level components

The program evolves one adjustment at a time. This is problem solving by recognizing and editing (i.e., find an almost satisfactory solution and then incrementally modify it until it becomes a satisfactory solution). Each time the pro-

---

BOX 15.5 Development concepts

Parts Approach Concepts	Reusable Whole Approach Concepts
Abstraction	Generalization
Synthesis	Analysis
Creating	Recognizing
Assembling	Editing
Refining	Pasting
Building block	Template

gram is modified, unwanted side effects from change may occur. Therefore, much of the development effort focuses on checking for possible side effects and creating new low-level components.

Box 15.5 summarizes the different development concepts associated with the parts approach versus the whole approach. They represent two different theories in engineering problem solving. Of the two, the whole approach is the simpler. It is easier for the human mind to recognize than to create from scratch, to edit than to assemble, and to fill in details than to create the overall framework.

The repository, CASE tools, and re-engineering tools help the developer find an appropriate reusable program design, analyze the impact of design changes, perform program design consistency, correctness, and completeness checks, and generate program code from the program design.

And of the two, the whole approach has the greater potential for increasing productivity. We can get higher leverage from reusing larger, higher-level reusable components. The whole approach enables the developer to reuse whole programs and program design specifications, whereas the parts approach focuses on the reuse of software components such as functional modules, macros, and object classes. The whole approach greatly reduces the size of the development effort because it keeps the overall structure invariant and allows developers to focus on smaller problem requirements.[11]

ROSE: Design Reuse System

MCC has built an experimental design reuse system called ROSE-2 that supports the whole approach.[12] ROSE-2 contains high-level design abstractions called **design schemas** that present the design in the form of constant and variable parts. The user does not have to be concerned with the constant portion because it remains the same for each application. Therefore, the user can focus on modifying the variable portion to customize the design to meet the requirements of the new system.

ROSE-2 allows the user (system analyst) to specify customization in terms of software requirements rather than design features. ROSE-2 can automatically generate the customized version of the design. ROSE-2 presents the design to the user in the form of data flow diagrams that can be edited by the user.

ROSE-2 stores in related libraries lower-level reusable components that can be automatically selected and assembled to create an executable prototype. ROSE-2 also has access to a code generator that can generate C, Ada, or Pascal from the completed design. Because ROSE-2 provides traceability between the system requirements and the design, the user can experiment with different system requirements and use ROSE-2 to quickly build the design and generate an executable prototype. This helps guarantee that the "right" system is built.

A major difficulty with this approach is building a library of design schemas. Domain analysis, which is primarily a manual technique, is currently used.

REUSABILITY: A DEVELOPMENT AND MAINTENANCE STRATEGY

Software reusability not only dramatically changes software development but also reaches into the maintenance phase of the life cycle. When software reusability is used as a development strategy, the techniques needed for developing a program become much more similar to techniques needed for maintaining a program, because both the software development process and maintenance process focus on making changes and controlling the impact from change. The line that has always existed between software development and software maintenance disappears. Software reusability is both a software development and software maintenance strategy.

The development scenario based on software reusability presented earlier in this chapter is equally appropriate as a maintenance scenario. This is one reason why reusability has the potential to improve substantially overall software productivity. It is also the reason why reusability revolutionizes the software development process. Reusability reduces software development and maintenance to the same process—one based on modifying an existing system to meet current requirements. Reuse-based development and maintenance both focus on how to change software effectively.

SUMMARY

Software reuse is one important answer to software productivity problems. Software reuse is much broader than simply reusable code. Possibilities for software reuse include reusable code, designs, requirements specifications, software packages, prototypes, application generators, and transformation systems. Higher levels of reuse (i.e., above the code level) offer greater promise because they avoid problems of implementation specifics and the subtleties of side effects from modifying existing code and offer greater cost savings.

At the higher level (i.e., reusable designs), reusable components will for the most part be domain- or application- specific and represent a family of software designs. It is likely that libraries of reusable components will be created for different domains (applications). Industries such as insurance and banking and systems such as defense and communications will lend themselves particularly well to reusability.

With reusability, we must reconsider the fundamental ways in which software is developed. Reusability represents a major software paradigm shift. When reusability is the principal development approach, incremental modification replaces stepwise refinement as the program construction strategy. The application system is created by modifying an existing system that performs a similar function to fit the requirements of the new system. The developer focuses on how the existing system differs from the new system.

Software tools play an important role in making software reuse a practical system-building strategy. The repository (and its information management system) form the cornerstone of the tools needed for software reuse. Other tools that support reuse are integrated tools environments containing CASE tools and re-engineering tools.

REFERENCES

1. William Agresti and Frank McGarry, "The Management Workshop on Software Reuse: A Summary Report," in *Software Reuse: Emerging Technology Tutorial*, pp. 88-93.

2. Stephen Davis, "A Word About Hypertext," *Datamation*, July 1, 1989, pp. 41–42.

3. Gianluigi Caldiera and Victor R. Basili, "Identifying and Qualifying Reusable Software Components," *Computer* (February 1991), 61–70.

4. Richard Waters, "Programmer's Apprentice: A Session with KBEmacs," *IEEE Transactions on Software Engineering*, SE-11, no. 11 (November 1985), 1296–1320.

5. Will Tracz, "Where Does Reuse Start?" in *Reuse in Practice Workshop*, Software Engineering Workshop, Pittsburgh, July 11–13, 1989.

6. G. Booch, "Object-Oriented Development," *IEEE Transactions on Software Engineering*, SE-11, no. 2 (February 1986), 211–221.

7. J. Jacky and I. Kalet, "Object-Oriented Discipline for Pascal," *CACM*, 30, no. 9 (September 1987), 772–776.

8. J. Micallif, "Encapsulation, Reusability and Extensibility in Object-Oriented Programming Languages," *JOOP* (April/May 1988), 12–35.

9. T. J. Biggerstaff and A. J. Perlis, "Foreward: Special Issue on Software Reusability," *IEEE Transactions on Software Engineering*, SE-11, no. 11, (November 1985), 474.

10. Waters, "Programmer's Apprentice."

11. Bruce H. Barnes and Terry B. Bollinger, "Making Reuse Cost-Effective," *IEEE Software* (January 1991), 13–24.

12. Ted J. Biggerstaff and Mitchell D. Lubars, "Recovering and Reusing Software Designs," *American Programmer*, 4, no. 3 (March 1991), 2–11.

PART **IV** **EPILOGUE**

16 THE THREE Rs

ENABLING TECHNOLOGIES OF SOFTWARE AUTOMATION

In the 1990s most of us are looking forward to enjoying higher levels of software automation. We have decided that it is strategically important to embrace software automation. We know where we are going.

The direction is toward repository-based, integrated CASE environments. This direction defines the state of the art of software development and maintenance. However, for most organizations this is not yet state of the practice.

State of the practice is being bogged down by outdated systems and outmoded technologies. There is a big gap between state of the art and state of the practice that must be bridged for our organizations to reap the benefits of software automation (see Fig. 16.1). Those organizations that cross this gap the most quickly are likely to be the most competitive and the most successful.

So the question now is not where are we going, but how do we get there. How can we most quickly and safely move our organizations beyond old technologies and systems? The answer is that we must start with the basics, with the three Rs: **re-engineering, repository,** and **reusability**.

Re-engineering is the positioning technology. Re-engineering can upgrade existing systems to the latest technologies and position them to take advantage of integrated CASE environments. Also, re-engineering can help populate repositories with enterprise and software system information.

Repository is the enabling technology of CASE. The repository is the cornerstone for building an integrated CASE tools environment that can serve the entire enterprise. It is the control point for the description of the enterprise, its data, and its software system.

Reusability is the leveraging technology. Reusability allows organizations

Figure 16.1 There is a gap between state of the practice and state of the art of software development and maintenance that must be crossed to move organizations through the 1990s and beyond.

to ensure that their investment in CASE will pay off. In the long term, reusability is the most important of the three Rs because it can bring organizations an order of magnitude increase in software quality and productivity.

Re-engineering, repositories, and reusability are the bridge to the powerful software technologies of the 1990s. They are the enabling technologies of the 1990s, and the way to reach the higher levels of software automation.

INDEX

A

Abstraction, 258
Access names, 200
Activity reports, 139
Ada, 47, 125, 243, 244, 251, 258
Adaptive maintenance, 14, 15, 16
AD/Cycle, 12, 186, 188, 189, 204
   platform, 207-8
   software life cycle model, 205-7
      analysis/design, 205
      application development process model, 206
      enterprise modeling, 205
      implementation, 206
      maintenance, 206
      tool services, 208
   tools, 207
AD Information Model, 189-90, 207
Adpac Corporation, 92
AEGIS Naval Weapon System, 47
Aggregation type, 167
Analysis, 25
Analysis of Complexity Tool (ACT), 41, 43
APL, 52
Application Browser, 112
Application Development Workbench, 114
Application packages, 233-35, 236
ARRAE, 123

Arthur Andersen and Company, 241-42
Assembler, 47, 52, 221
Assets, 221, 222
ASTEC, 121
Atherton Technologies, 208
ATIS, 173, 186, 208
Attribute groups, 198
Attributes, 197
Auditec, 37
Audit information, 176

B

Bachman Information Systems, Inc., 103, 104, 105, 106, 107, 108, 147
Bachman reverse engineering, 102, 103-8
   diagram manipulation, 109
   expert advisor, 107, 109
   forward engineering, 103, 104, 105-8, 110
   reverse engineering, 102, 104
Basic, 47
Bassett frames, 239-41
Batch data tracers, 36, 38
Batch import/export, 177
Battlemap, 49
Benchmark Technologies, 138
Blackhawk, 147
Branch, 133
Business Software Technology, 137

C

Cardinality, 167
CARE system, 251-52
CASE, 7, 8, 28, 44, 49, 63, 96, 99, 114, 127, 129, 130, 149, 157, 158, 162, 163, 164, 165, 169, 170, 171, 208
CASE Data Interchange Format (CDIF), 194-96
CCC, 139, 140
CDSI, 147
Centralized repository, 180
CGI Systems, 110-11, 222
Change activity reports, 140
Change control, 130, 141, 142, 176
  check-out/check-in, 135-36
  reporting, 139-41
  security, 134-35
  system building, 136-39
Change history reports, 140, 141
Change-Man, 135
Change management, 26, 129
CIS (CASE Integration Services), 208
C language, 44, 47, 49, 75, 77, 125, 168, 188, 221, 251
Class, 200
Cliches, 243-45
Cobalt Blue, 77
COBOL, 7, 39, 44, 46, 47, 49, 52, 54, 62, 63, 64, 67, 71, 72, 73, 74, 75, 83, 111, 112, 114, 147, 168, 188, 221, 226, 229, 258
Code analyzers, *See* Program code analyzers
Cohesion, 184, 185
Command language interface, 201
Common Data Dictionary/Repository, 168, 173, 180, 181-86, 208
Common data interface, 165
Common Programming Interface (CPI), 188
Common user interface, 165
Complete program, 36
Complexity metric. *See* Metric tools
Computer Data Systems, Inc., 38, 74
Conceptual integrity, 35
Concise program, 35
Configuration management, 26, 129, 176
  change control, 130, 134-41, 142
  functions of, 130
  library management, 130-34, 141, 142
Consistent program, 35
Corrective maintenance, 14, 15, 16, 17
Counts, 53-55
Customer/1, 241-42
Cyclomatic complexity. *See* McCabe Cyclomatic Complexity

D

Data dictionaries, 85, 89, 91
Data restructuring:
  benefits of, 84
  candidates for, 84-85
  definition of, 84
  tools for, 85-86
    checklist of features, 93
    data dictionary load, 89, 91
    data element trace and updating, 89, 90, 91
    data record analysis and updating, 86-89
    operations environment analysis, 91-94
  understandability and, 83
Data reverse engineering, 101-2
  Bachman reverse engineering, 102-10
  CGI systems reverse engineering, 110-11
  logic reverse engineering versus, 127-28
DataTec, 87, 88, 90, 91, 147, 152
Data tracers:
  batch, 36, 38
  interactive, 37, 39
Datatrieve, 176
DEC, 165, 176, 180, 181-86, 208
Delta method of storage, 132
Descriptive names, 200
Design Recovery, 113, 114, 115, 116
Design schemas, 261
DesignWare, 241-42
DiNardo software maintenance study, 16
Distributed repository, 180
Domain analysis, 249-50, 261

E

Eden Systems Corporation, 48
Endevor, 137
Enterprise models, 215-16
   repository administration group, 216
   repository population, 216-17
Enterprise repository:
   dictionary integrator, 163
   process integrator, 164
   system integrator, 163-64
   tool integrator, 163
Entities, 197
Entity attributes, 197
Entity-relationship diagram, 104, 105, 106, 109, 166-67, 248
Environmental changes, 14
EPOS/RE-SPEC, 122, 124, 125, 126
Excelerator, 113, 114, 115, 116
Export function, 110
Extended Cyclomatic Complexity, 45
Extensible meta model, 172

F

Failures, 14
Fjeldstad and Hamlen software maintainers study, 19, 20
Flow graphs, 37, 39, 40, 70, 72, 226
   mathematically rigorous, 40
   as testing aid, 40-41, 43
For__STRUCT, 77
FORTRAN, 44, 46, 47, 52, 64, 69, 72, 75, 76, 77, 226, 258
Forward engineering, 99, 103, 104, 105-8, 110
Fragile software systems, 19-20, 28, 29, 67
   recognizing, 30-31

G

General Ledger Template, 242
General Motors Research Laboratories, 51
GO TOs, 70, 71, 73, 74

Graph theory, 40, 70, 71
GTE Data Services, 221-23

H

Halstead Software Science, 50-53, 251
   effort, 52-53
   length, 51
   purity ratio, 51
   volume, 52
Hartford Insurance Group, 63, 227
Histogram analysis, 54, 57, 59
Hypersoft Corporation, 112
Hypertext system, 250, 251, 252

I

IBM, 176
IBM Repository Manager/MVS, 180, 186-90, 207
Information Engineering Facility (IEF), 242
Information Engineering Workbench, 114
Information Resource Dictionary System (IRDS), 196-97
   basic functional schema, 200-201
   data architecture, 197-98
   functions and processes:
      additional IRDS modules, 203-4
      control facilities, 202-3
      IRD-IRD interface, 202
      IRD: updating and reporting on data, 201-2
      schema: updating and reporting on the schema, 202
   minimal schema, 200
   schema, 198-200
Inheritance, 257-58
Inspector, 54, 56, 147, 152
Instances, 198, 257
Instance variables, 257
Integral, reverse engineering at, 145, 148-49
   business point of view, 151
   CASE for existing systems, 149
   re-engineering experiences at, 150-51
   re-engineering mistakes at, 149-50

Integrated Project Support Environment (IPSE), 208
Interactive data tracers, 37, 39
Interdependency report, 140
Intersolv Corporation, 113, 114, 115, 116
Invest/1, 242
ISPW, 138

J,K

Japanese software factories, 229, 249
KBEmacs, 243
Knot Count metric, 49-50
KnowledgeWare, 114

L

Language Technology, 54, 56, 147, 152
Library management, 130-31, 141, 142
   component identification, 131
   logical representation, 131
   parallel development, 133-34
   revision control, 131-32
   version control, 132-33
Lientz/Swanson software maintenance study, 16, 17
LISP, 258
Lists, 53-55
Logic analyzers, 36
Logic reverse engineering, 101, 111-14, 115, 116
   code generation, 125
   comparison with program code analysis, 111
   data reverse engineering versus, 127-28
   design language, 118-20
   design modification, 120
   documentation, 123-26
   error checking, 120, 123
   export, 127
   logical design repository, 117
   physical design repository, 114, 117-18, 119
   source code repository, 126
LOOPS, 258
Lotus, 221

M

McCabe and Associates, 41, 43, 49
McCabe complexity metrics:
   automatic complexity measurement, 46, 47-48
   complexity threshold, 45-47
   cyclomatic complexity, 44-45, 46, 251
   essential complexity, 45, 46
   extended cyclomatic complexity, 45, 46
Maintainability, 33
Maintec, Inc., 37
Meta data, 195, 196
Methods, 167, 257
Metrics tools, 26, 27, 30
   automatic complexity measurement, 46, 47-48
   automating software metrics, 34
   checklist, 58
   counts produced by, 53-55
   Halstead Software Science, 50-53, 251
   Knot Count metric, 49-50
   lists, 53-55
   maintainability and, 33
   McCabe Cyclomatic Complexity, 44-49, 251
   program complexity and, 42, 44
   program summary analysis, 54-59
   software maintenance and, 59
   understandability and, 34-36, 42
Migration, 25
Motif, 165

N

NETRON/CAP, 239
Netron, Inc., 239
Normalization function, 110

O

Object-based language, 118, 120, 121
Object data, 167
Object-oriented development, 256-57
   data abstraction, 258
   encapsulation, 257

inheritance, 258
object class, 257
Object-oriented programming languages, 258
Open architecture, 177
Optima software, 135
OSI, 165

P

PACBASE, 110-11, 222
PacBell, 28, 145
   restructuring at, 151-52
      creation of the System Renewal Group, 152
      gaining a competitive advantage, 153
      quality measures, 152
Pacific Bell. *See* PacBell
Panel interface, 201
Parallel development, 133
Parts approach, 259-61
PASCAL, 44, 125
Pathvu, 57, 147, 148, 152
PC-Metric, 46, 47
Perfective maintenance, 14, 15, 16, 17
PL/1, 44, 47, 48, 51, 52, 168, 188
PM/SS, 92
Portable Common Tool Environment (PCTE), 208-9
Portfolio summary analysis, 54
   histogram analysis, 54, 57, 59
   quadrant report, 54, 55, 56
   system structure report, 49, 54
Presentation Manager, 165
Pretty Printer, 147
Price Waterhouse, 123
Program code analyzers, 26, 27, 31, 33, 36-37, 38, 253
   automatic complexity measurement, 46, 47-48
   checklist, 58
   comparison with logic reverse engineering, 111
   counts produced by, 53-55
   lists, 53-55
   software maintenance and, 59
   understandability and, 34-36
Program complexity, 42, 44

Program logic restructuring, 67-68
   advantage of, 68
   analysis and documentation, 78, 81
   benefits and side effects of, 64, 68-70
   definition of, 63
   method of, 70-71
   tools for, 71-73
      checklist of features of, 79-80
      formatting options, 75-78
      structuring options, 73-75
Programmable workstation services, 207
Programmer's Apprentice, 243, 244, 253
Programming Environment Project (University of California-Irvine), 227
Pseudocode-based languages, 120, 122, 123
Purity ratio, 51

Q

Q/Auditor, 48
Quadrant report, 54, 55, 56
Query and reporting functions, 176
Query Management Facility (QMF), 176, 188

R

Raytheon Company, 227, 229-30, 249
Recoder, 147, 152
Redocumentation tools, 26
Re-engineering, 8, 23-24, 267
   as bridge to new technologies, 27-28
   case studies:
      at Integral, 148-51
      at Shearson Lehman Brothers, 145-48
   objectives of, 24
   reasons for, 29
   replacement versus, 29-30
   types of, 25
   types of tools used for, 25-27
Re-Engineering Product Set, 103, 104, 105, 106, 107, 108, 147
Relationship attributes, 198
Relationships, 197
Replacement, re-engineering versus, 29-30

Repository, 100, 157-58, 247, 267
  architectures, 178-80
  benefits of, 158-59
  contents of, 159-60
  definition of, 158
  enterprise, 163-64
  enterprise models, 215-17
  examples of, 180
    CDD/Repository, 181-86
    IBM Repository Manager/MVS, 186-90
  future of, 217
  implementation, 172-73, 214
    repository engine, 173
  information management:
    manipulation and validation, 177-78
    multiuser access, 177
    open architecture, 177
    query and reporting, 176-77
    security, 173, 175
    versioning, change control, and configuration management, 175-76
  issues related to, 211-12
  as more than a CASE repository, 162
  as more than a dictionary, 161-62
  preparing for a, 212-14
  summary of services, 190-91
  tool integration and, 164-65
  training and experience, 214-15
Repository information model, 168, 181
Repository meta model, 165-66, 248-49
  entity-relationship model, 166-67
  extensibility, 168-72
  object-oriented model, 167-68
Repository standards, 193-94
  A Tools Integration Standard (ATIS), 208
  CASE Data Interchange Format (CDIF), 194-96
  IBM SAA and AD/Cycle, 204-8
  Information Resource Dictionary System (IRDS), 196-204
  Portable Common Tool Environment (PCTE), 208-9
  standards for automation, 209-10
Restructurers, 26

Restructuring, 25. *See also* Data restructuring; Program logic restructuring
  candidate programs for, 66-67
  definition of, 61
  fragile software systems and, 67
  objectives of, 62
  at PacBell, 151-53
  productivity through, 61-62
  reducing the maintenance burden with, 62-63
  structured programming and, 64-66
  structured retrofit and, 64
  style and structure and, 62
Retool, 74
Retrofit, 152
Reusable components library:
  meta model, 248-49
  repository, 247-48
Reusable software components:
  building, 249
  CARE system, 251-52
  definition of, 234
  development and maintenance strategy, 262
  example of, 237
  higher-level, 238
    cliches, 243-45
    DesignWare, 241-42
    frames, 239-41
    templates, 242-43
  limitations of code reuse, 238
  methods for, 255-56
  object-oriented development, 256-58
  packages as, 233-35, 236
  parts approach versus whole approach, 259-61
  ROSE-2, 261
  program parts as, 235-37
  properties for, 237
  tools:
    for combining and incorporating, 253-54
    for finding, 252
    for identifying components for reuse, 249-50
    for modifying, 253

for producing and refining, 251, 254
for representing and describing, 250
for storing and classifying, 250
for understanding, 252
for using, 255
REVENGG, 121
Reverse engineering, 25, 26. *See also* Data reverse engineering; Logic reverse engineering
   benefits of, 96-97
   definition of, 95
   forward engineering and, 99
   future software maintenance automation and, 100
   at Integral, 148-51
   into a repository, 100-101
   source code and, 97-99
REXX, 188
ROSE-2, 261

S

Scan/COBOL, 38, 147
Schema information, 195, 196
Shearson Lehman Brothers, re-engineering at, 145-46
   future of, 148-49
   maintenance automation focus, 146
   maintenance workbench, 146-47
Smalltalk, 251, 258
SmartEdit, 147, 148
Softool Corporation, 139, 140
Software automation, 8
Software Back-Plane, 208
Software maintainers:
   responsibilities of, 17-18, 19, 20
   users and, 14
Software maintenance:
   adaptive, 14, 15, 16
   causes of, 14
   corrective, 14, 15, 16, 17
   definitions of, 11-13
   existing systems and, 28-31
   factors affecting maintenance effort, 16-17
   managing, 23-24

   metrics tools and, 59
   nature of maintenance work, 15-16
   perfective, 14, 15, 16, 17
   program code analyzers and, 59
   reducing, 5-6
   size of, 3-5
   software development technologies to reduce, 6-7
   statistics related to, 31
   support for, 20-21
   understanding, 11
Software Products and Services, Inc., 122, 124, 125, 126
Software reusability, 267
   benefits of, 225-26
   concept of, 224-25
      as a development and maintenance strategy, 262
   development scenario for, 258-59
   forms of, 226
   growing trend of, 223
   by GTE Data Services, 221-23
   opportunities for, 226
   organization level, 230
   potential of, 223-24
   practicality of, 230
   problems and solutions, 228
      Japanese software factories, 229
      Raytheon Company, 229-30
   studies and projects related to, 227-28
Source code, 97-99
Structured programming, 64-66
   definition of, 65
   properties of, 66
Structuring engines, 64
System structure report, 49, 54
Swanson/Beath software maintenance study, 16, 17, 21
Synonyms, 200
Systems Application Architecture (SAA), 165, 189, 204

T

Templates, 242-43
Testing tools, 26, 27

Texas Instruments, 242
Translators/converters, 26
Trigger, 176

U

Understandability:
    data restructuring and, 83
    definition of, 34
    factors of, 35-36
    metrics tools as predictors of, 42
    tools of, 36
User(s), and software maintainers, 14
User interface services, 207

V

Versioning, 132, 175-76
Version report, 140
Via/Insight, 38, 39, 147, 152
Via/Renaissance, 152
ViaSoft, 38, 147, 152

W,X

Whole approach, 260
Windows, 165
XA Systems, 57, 87, 88, 90, 91, 147, 152
X-11, 165